GROWTH AND RURAL TRANSFORMATION

About the Author

R. M. Mohan Rao, an M.A. (in Rural Development) and Ph.D., has retired recently from Andhra University, Visakhapatnam after serving about three and half decades in various capacities in the Department of Co-operation and Applied Economics. He was Founder Director of the SAARC Centre and has been the Director of the NABARD Chair Unit since 1998. He also worked as an FAOTCDC consultant to the Government of Zambia on Agricultural Finance in the year 2000.

Prof. Rao has conducted many field-based research studies for various organisations such as All India Rural Credit Review Committee (1969). The NABARD (1985), Indo-Dutch project on Alternatives in Development (1984-86) and Department of Rural Development, Ministry of Agriculture (1992). He has many books and research papers to his credit.

GROWTH AND RURAL TRANSFORMATION

A Comparative Study of the Republic of Korea and India

by

R.M. MOHAN RAO

Prof. NABARD Chair Unit
School of Economics
Andhra University
Visakhapatnam

CONCEPT PUBLISHING COMPANY, NEW DELHI-110059

ISBN : 81-8069-034-2

First Published 2004

Published and Printed by
Ashok Kumar Mittal
Concept Publishing Company
A/15-16, Commercial Block, Mohan Garden,
New Delhi-110059 (India).

Phones : 25351460, 25351794
Fax : 091-11-25357103
Email : publishing@conceptpub.com

FOREWORD

Prof. R.M. Mohan Rao's study is part of a series under Indo-Dutch Project sponsored and supported by ICSSR. The objective of the Project is to illuminate rural transformation in developing countries through comparative and historical analysis of select countries. Prof. Rao has chosen India and Korea for this purpose.

Both the countries were at the same level of development in 1950s. But Korea has achieved phenomenal growth rate during the period 1961-1985. Per capita G.D.P. is more or less the same in both the countries in 1950s. There is a five fold increase in Korea between 1961 and 1985, while in the case of India there was only a doubling of the GDP per capita. This difference in growth rate resulted in differences in the structure of the economy. The primary sector in Korea which absorbed 72 per cent of work force in 1960 recorded a rapid decline to 34 per cent by 1980. In India during 1961 and 1981 there was only a small percentage decline from 72 per cent in 1961 to 69 per cent in 1981.

Remarkable growth in Korea's per capita GDP resulted in the improvement of quality of life of people. Other indicators such as per capita calorie intake per day, life expectancy, infant mortality and adult literacy rate reflect such differences.

The determinants of growth and structural transformation in Korea and India were studied under both economic and non-economic factors. The role of State, religion and education is found to have significance in explaining growth and differential transformation. Under economic factors structural changes in agriculture, role of agriculture in economic growth, terms of trade and growth of non-agricultural sector are considered. Agrarian reform was successful in Korea. As a result of this Korean society became more equitable, more democratic and egalitarian.

The role of agriculture in Korean economic growth is controversial. Agriculture's contribution to capital formation has been minor. But in two ways agriculture's contribution to growth is significant. Firstly, agriculture released labour for use in non-agriculture. Secondly, agriculture supplied cheap food for wage earners in non-agriculture. In Korea, the agriculture sector was pulled along by a dynamic industrial sector. In India agricultural growth has not resulted in linkages and capital intensive industrialisation has not achieved the labour absorption. In recent years much reliance is placed on rural non-farm activities for promoting growth and for poverty alleviation. The Korean experience shows that rural non-farm employment is not a feasibility. Instead, non-farm employment tends to be concentrated in urban areas because of better infrastructure. Low incomes are augmented by remittances from urban people. Prof. Rao argues that policy stress should be on favouring dispersal of industries to small towns and linking subsidies and concessions to such industries with employment potential rather than mere location in a backward area.

There has been a considerable debate on terms of trade to agriculture in India. Indian price policy is accused of lowering the terms of trade to agriculture and consequentially adverse development. The Korean case illustrated that non-price factors are more important than price factors in promoting growth. In fact the State has procured foodgrains from the farmers through cooperatives. This facilitated development of cooperative societies.

Part-II of the Study focuses on micro aspects. It is based on field surveys by the Author in two Korean villages and two Andhra villages. This part also brings in historical analysis of structural changes at the micro-level. For this purpose 1970 to 1985 is studied. The role of rural institutions in rural transformation is studied by focusing on Korean PACS. Establishment of the single National Federation of Cooperatives to support the primaries and integration of diversified functions in a single organisation at the primary level is found to be major factor for the success of primary cooperatives. In India functional cooperatives with accent on marketing and processing with their own structure are at the Taluk, District, State and National level. There are hardly any known linkages among functional cooperatives of different types. The share of institutional borrowings in the total borrowings of sample borrowers during 1985-86 showed Korea to be far advanced. Around 93 per cert of Korean rural households borrowed from institutional source whereas in Andhra only 54 per cent borrowed from rural financial institutions. The difference between the two countries with respect to marginal farmers is much greater.

The case studies of the copperatives in the sample villages of Korea and Andhra and the census and sample study also testify the relatively dismal picture of coöperatives in Andhra compared to Korea.

Access to domestic power supply, water supply and cooking gas, possession of consumer durables are studied in Korea and Andhra villages. The study is conducted for the period 1970 to 1986. Even by 1970 Korea was in advance over Andhra villages in respect of water supply and cooking gas.

Small farm rice economy of Korea and Andhra forms the theme of Chapter Six. Despite the relatively unfavourable cool climate, the yields of paddy per single crop per hectare are much higher right from mid 1950s in Korea. Japanese colonial policy of importing paddy from Korea as distinguished from British colonial policy of importing industrial raw material accounts for this difference.

Rice economies of the two countries are compared by using paddy as a measure. Fertiliser price in kg. of paddy is much higher in Andhra compared to Korean villages.

The conclusion of the Study is while the differences in the Gross Value of Produce (GVP) are not very significant between Korea and Andhra, the paid out costs in Andhra are more at the aggregate level. The very low share of farm business income in the G.V.P. in many size groups is attributable to the losses/low returns for other crops and unremunerative prices of cotton in the year under Study. The significant conclusion of the Study is that the performance of the non-agricultural progress resulting in higher remittances and reduced costs contributed to the rural prosperity in Korea.

The final Chapter draws the major inferences and lessons drawn from the Study.

Korea had the advantage of massive American aid even in the 1950s. This aid was used for developing the infrastructure and export-oriented labour-intensive industries. India on the other hand was starved of foreign aid in the initial period. Capital intensive-industries were promoted thus depriving investment in small industries. 'The Korean miracle' may be attributed to American support in the initial period. But human resource development in Korea was given much emphasis even from the initial period. By 1971 literacy in Korea was more than 70 per cent and vocational education was given prominence. India lagged behind in literacy as well as in vocational education.

Rural infrastructure development in Korea has helped the process of training an educated work-force for the industrialisation of the Country. Above all, the institutional development in rural areas is facilitated by the successive stages in the agricultural sector.

Prof. Rao through his painstaking analysis of the differential transformation has brought the reasons for the Korean miracle. He is probably the first Asian to conduct a field survey in Korean villages. His meticulous enquiry and analysis has thrown light on the puzzle of differences in the quality of life of two farming communities despite marginal difference in gross value of output per acre. He concludes that quality of life of farmers in Korea is not so much due to agricultural growth but non-agricultural growth which absorbed the surplus agricultural population. This has lessons for India. Though agricultural growth is important, the development of non-agriculture for absorbing the growing rural population is important. One lesson India can draw from Korea is that urban metropolitan centres are required to be developed as labour intensive industrial centres.

The role of non-economic factors in the development process is strikingly brought out by Prof. Rao. Of those factors, the value system which could be traced to Confucian ethic is important. This led to good governance. For India the lack of value systems to promote development process is noted to be a factor in the stagnation of Indian growth rate.

Prof. Rao needs to be congratulated for bringing out his useful survey of Korean and Indian situation—in rural transformation. This book will be of use to a wide circle of readers who are interested in the growth process and in understanding the Korean miracle.

G. Parthasarathy
Former Consultant
UNFAO, Rome

PREFACE

Rural development and transformation continue to figure prominently in the development strategies of Third World Countries which have yet to complete transition from an agrarian to an industrial society. Out of scepticism with past strategies (based on Western experience) drawing lessons from the more successful ones within the region is gaining ground. The shared commonalities in the initial conditions of many Asian countries with few success stories provide a strong case for exploring experiences in Asian rural transformation.

Of the three Asian success stories *i.e.*, Japan, Taiwan and Korea, the last is preferred for a comparative study with India, as its achievements are considered a 'miracle'.

Even though no two cultures like Korea and India can be identical, a comparative study in between the two would be of contemporary relevance in drawing conclusions about the fundamental strategies adopted in tackling such a basic process as rural transformation; this too against a backdrop of similar social issues and dissimilar community approaches.

Between Korea and India, there are basic similarities in the initial conditions, *viz.* , colonial legacy, late entry into development phase, common problems (demographic pressure, predominance of non-viable small farm economy), and shared concerns for development and for meeting the 'revolution of rising expectations'. However, there are also sharp differences in achievements both in relation to growth and equity.

Korean experience in achieving a peaceful agrarian transition is remarkable. It showed the opportunities for rapid rural transformation through appropriate strategies of development. These experiences in themselves are of immense interest to Third

World Countries of South Asia struggling hard to achieve a breakthrough in the development arena.

This comparative study of South Korea and India (Andhra) has been made possible by Prof. Jan Breman, Institute for Social Studies, the Hague and late Prof. S. Chakravarthy of the Indian Council of Social Science Research. I am grateful to both of them for giving me a rare opportunity for conducting this study.

This study is the brain child of Prof. G. Parthasarathy. In undertaking and completing it, I enjoyed his unstinted support and guidance. I am beholden to him for this.

I would like to put on record that this study has become possible with the generous financial assistance of the Indo-Dutch Project and the timely and constant assistance provided by the ICSSR. I take this opportunity to express my gratitude to Dr. (Mrs.) R. Barman Chandra, Executive Director, of the ICSSR for the utmost cooperation and support she extended for completing this study. I am thankful to Dr. Peter Van Stuijvenberg, Dr. H.A.J. Coppens of the IDPAD and Mr. R.R. Prasad, Deputy Director and his staff in the ICSSR for their timely help.

I also had the benefit of support and assistance from many institutions and individuals in Korea. In particular, I am indebted to Kon-Kuk University, Seoul for giving access to its facilities and for permitting Prof. Young Chul Kim to associate with this project. I am grateful to Dr. Yung Chan Kwan, President, Kon-Kuk University for welcoming me to the campus, to Prof. Hyo Jik Yoon, for generously sparing his personal library and for many acts of kindness and to Prof. Suck Hyun Han, for his affection and support in my pursuit. I am much obliged to all of them.

The National Agricultural Cooperation Federation (NACF), Seoul provided a rare opportunity to me to meet and exchange views with scholars from South-East and East Asian Countries by extending invitation to all the international workshops and seminars hosted by it. In this connection, I am grateful to M/s. Chul Hi Lee, Ki Won Suh and Nai-Soo Lee, of the NACF.

The access to Korean institutions and academics has become possible through the good offices of my friend Prof. Young Chul Kim. But for his support and generous assistance this study would have become impossible. He took the trouble of visiting the sample villages both in Korea and Andhra, spent considerable time in preparing, pre-testing and editing the questionnaires. I am indebted to him and to his family members for making my stay in Korea pleasant and rewarding.

There are many other scholars, particularly Prof. K. Venkateswarlu, Prof. D.L. Prasada Rao and Prof. P.V. Sarma of Andhra University, who have kindly spared their time to go through parts of the manuscripts. I also benefited from my discussions with many Korean scholars and officials, Prof. Jin Hwan Park, Prof. In Keun Wang, Mr. Kyu Song Bae, Dr. Shin Haeng Huh, Mr. Joong Il Sub, Mr. Sam Suck Song. The International Workshop on Comparative Studies on Rural Transformation in Asia sponsored by the IDPAD in 1986 was of great help. Discussions with the participants particularly with Professors, Jan Breman, S. Chakravarthy, John Harris, P. C. Joshi, C.H. Hanumantha Rao, K. Subba Rao and Sudipto Mundle enriched my understanding of the theme. I am grateful to all of them.

I am indebted to many academics from whose works I have liberally drawn and to the chiefs and staff of the NACF branches and the PACS in Korea and to the District and Mandal Officers and to the staff of the PACS in Andhra.

I must also express my grateful thanks to Andhra University authorities, Prof. K.V. Ramana, Dr. M. Gopalakrishna Reddy, Vice-Chancellors, and Prof. B. Prasada Rao, former Head of the Department of Cooperation and Applied Economics, for enabling me to undertake this study.

Equally significant is the help and assistance I received from my colleague Dr. P. Krishna Mohan in the initial stages. I am deeply indebted to my colleague Prof. D. S. Prasad presently Head of the Department of Cooperations and Applied Economics who stood by me for long hours for bringing out the final Report. Sri Satyanarayana of the Computer Centre, Andhra University, who processed the census data. I acknowledge the assistance of my research students, Dr. Ch. Subrahmanyam, Dr. R. Rama Krishna, Ms. M. Anuradha, and Mrs. B. Padma Narayan in the initial stages. Dr. B. Piraburam, my research student and Dr. N. Subba Rao, my nephew, are of immense help in the final stages of this Report.

In Korea M/s. Ham and Jeong Kang Soo took the responsibility for the field work. I have also benefited from my interaction with Mr. Choi Dong Uk who has collected Korean literature and translated parts of it for my use. I am thankful to all these young friends of mine for their help.

I thank all the respondents in the four selected villages for sparing their invaluable time. I acknowledge the hospitality extended to me by the Korean households.

This is a revised version of the earlier report based on the advice of the anonymous referees. I am grateful to them for their valuable comments. I am thankful to Shri M.R.B. Narasinga Rao for going through the revised draft and making it more readable.

M/s. K. Durga Prasad and P. Matchi Raju have taken pains in typing the revised draft and Ms. S. Visakha completed the final version. I appreciate their valuable assistance.

I am grateful to Prof. G. Parthasarathy for writing the 'foreword' and to Prof. R. Radhakrishna, former Vice-Chancellor and currently Director, Indira Gandhi Institute of Development Research, Mumbai for encouraging me to bring out this Study in this form. I am also grateful to the UGC for financing this publication.

Finally, my wife Prof. M. Indira Devi and my children have cheerfully extended all possible cooperation. I am obliged to all of them. I am also thankful to my daughter R. Bhamaramba, apart from my wife for going through the manuscript.

August 2002 R.M. MOHAN RAO
Visakhapatnam

CONTENTS

LIST OF TABLES

LIST OF MAPS

LIST OF ANNEXURES

1

INTRODUCTION

The Third World countries are at crossroads in their march towards development on account of the growing scepticism in the adaptation of Western models of development and ideological limitations to embrace the socialistic path. Most of these countries are likely to remain predominantly rural even by the turn of this century. Yet understanding the process and trends in rural transformation continues to be mostly at a surface and phenomenal level (Joshi, 1983, p.1).

Comparative studies help identify the commonalities in the process of rural transformation. Common themes of development based on international comparisons will help countries evolve appropriate strategies and in determining policies and processes that are beneficial to the existence of rural life (Volgyes, 1980, p. 13). Further, such studies provide opportunities for evaluating theoretical and policy debates of the past.

Rationale behind Comparative Study of Korea and India

With 'farms of the size of postage stamps' and peasant ownership, Korea became a synonym of development since 1970s. Korean success in attaining record yields and ensuring better standards of living despite farms smaller than in India even in 1980s will be of great interest not only to India, but also to most of the South-Asian countries, which are finding it difficult to make small farms viable.

Small farms predominate in most of the Asian developing countries, cultivating only 10 to 12 per cent of the total cultivated area (FAO, 1970, Vol. II, p. 407; Vyas, 1983, p. 41) and there are worsening trends in size-distribution of holdings with intensification of population pressure in South and South-East Asian countries (Booth and Sundrum, 1984. p. 142).

In India, the viability of small and marginal farms continues to be a serious problem (Vyas, 1978, pp. 24-32; Raj Krishna,1979; Parthasarathy, 1988, p. 85). Known approaches to alleviate problems of the small farmers have not yielded the desired results as is evident from the growing 'immiserisation' (improvement of farmers) (Rudra Ashok, 1978, p.1002), and increasing trend in the marginal holdings. To sustain growth without improving the incomes of the small and marginal producers is anomalous (Vyas, 1983, p. 42). There are serious limitations for extending institutional support to small farmers in India (Parthasarathy, 1973, and 1976; Rao, V.M., 1983, pp. 1177-90). In this context Korean experience in rural transformation is considered relevant.

Korean success in attaining higher yields on small farms, effective implementation of land-reforms in early 1950s and its positive impact in facilitating creation of participatory institutions at the village level will be of great interest to countries like India, where institutional structures like cooperatives and extension agencies are considered to be not so responsive in serving the interests of marginal and small farmers.

The shared commonalities in problems and differential transformation experienced in the two countries are important considerations in undertaking this study.

Problems in Comparative Studies

Perlin's observation that comparison is a road strewn with mines and pitfalls (Perlin, 1986, p. 18) appears to be more true in case of comparative studies in rural transformation, which are devoid of any established norms or guide-lines relating to choice of units of comparison, time frame, interpretation of facts, critical areas of enquiry and of lessons to be drawn (Lonsdale and Avery, 1980, p. 325).

Some of the crucial issues involved in comparative studies relate to appropriateness of units of comparison (Perlin, 1986, p. 5), relationship in time and commonality in problems between the entities under comparison (Black, 1966, p. 392 and Myrdal 1982,

p. 40), critical evaluation of evidence (Perlin, 1986, p. 17; Halliday, 1987, p. 38; Black, 1966, p. 43 and Lerner, 1958, p. 85) and greater effort at objectivity. The need for a holistic approach was also emphasised (see Hunter, 1969, and Hoffman, 1980).

Limiting generalizations for comparable stages of development in each of the dimensions under study (Hunter, 1969, pp. 295-8; Myrdal, 1982, p. 673) and juxtaposing uniformities and variables within a limited frame of reference, drawing distinctions between functions, structures and institutions wherever possible and careful identification of entities compared at various stages are advocated to draw meaningful inferences (Black, 1966, pp. 43-6).

Critical Variables in Studying Rural Transformation

Comparative studies in rural transformation and modernization in Asia, Africa, Latin America, Middle East and Eastern Europe looked at structural transformation of the economy as crucial. But, the indicators used to judge this varied, *viz*., (i) shift of population from rural to urban areas; (ii) share of agricultural output (Volgyes, 1980, p.112); (iii) percentage of population engaged in agriculture (Hoffman, 1980, p. 30) and (iv) share of agriculture in national income (Halliday, 1987).

In addition to looking at structural transformation, almost all studies in the area stressed the crucial role of institutions in the rural transformation. The two major institutions emphasized relate to State (Volgyes, 1980, and Halliday, 1987) and land tenure (Thiesenhusen, 1989, pp. 136-7; Landsberger, 1980, p. 273 and Volgyes, (1980, p. 112) Other variables considered are agricultural development (Hoffman, 1980, p. 23; Volgyes, 1980, p. 112 and Hunter,1969, p. 295), living standards and equity between rural and urban areas, between sexes and classes (Halliday, 1987).

Framework for the Study of Rural Transformation

The Concept

The concept of rural transformation involves examination of

changes in all aspects of rural life (Kurien, 1982, p. 58), that follow modernisation (Volgyes, 1980, p. 4) and development (Hoffman, 1980, p. 23) in rural communities. Further, elements highlighted in the case of modernisation by Hunter (1969, p. 295) development by Mosher (1976, pp.10-11) and of transformation by Volgyes (1980, p. 89) explicitly differ. While the emphasis in development is on goals, on means in modernisation and on the end-products in transformation, basic to all these concepts is efficient use of factors of production, greater use of science and technology, appropriate changes in organisation, values and institutions.

Even as modernisation is falsely identified with Westernisation, implying thereby adoption of Western technology, materialistic value system and modes of life, it has in the past not always contributed to real development. Irrelevant change of traditional institutions, traditional technology and traditional modes of life could have a negative role. Change need not always be associated with modernisation as it is understood (Myrdal, 1982, pp. 57 and 698).

Although development in a conventional sense means 'to grow', it is distinct from growth in terms of material goods, as it is more than mere growth of material goods or rise in incomes. Moreover, it is a multi-dimensional process (Todaro, 1981, p. 56) implying thereby the movement of the whole system upwards (Myrdal, 1982, p. 1868).

Change as a process involves only modification of certain elements and as such is not based on 'predetermined intention' and is viewed in terms of cause and effect relationship, devoid of the value premise embedded in the concept of development. However, concepts like 'planned change' or 'induced change' are not free from value premise and they are synonymous with development.

Even though transformation could be considered as a process similar to modernisation and development, it has a unique characteristic feature in the sense that it refers mostly to the final form rather than an ongoing process.

Rural transformation, thus may be defined as a period in the rural society, with a higher degree of functional specialisation, greater use of modern techniques and cultural practices. It also consists in the emergence of an institutional infrastructure that facilitates the maximum exploitation of resources with the available knowledge to its best advantage. Further, structural changes are associated with the transition of Agrarian Economy to Urban Industrial Economy, migration of rural people and their absorption in the industrial sector. These result in an increase in physical assets of rural people, greater degree of integration with urban economy and improvement in the quality of life.

The Approach

While capital accumulation, industrialisation and markets are ba: to the western capitalistic mode of transformation, according to Marxian approach, development is a unilinear, ongoing process of growth in a sequential transformation from one stage to the other, *viz*., Feudalism, Capitalism and Socialism.

However, institutional approach calls for a multidisciplinary perspective to understand transformation not necessarily limited to Marxian analytical categories and to Marxian stages of development. Central to this is the role of non-economic and economic institutions *viz*., State, Religion, Education and Agrarian Structure. The institutional approach is preferred to the Western and Marxian models to study Asiatic rural transformation particularly Republic of Korea (RoK) and India, as they have adopted a gradualistic process to usher in change through State policy to subserve interests of growth and equity.

Objectives of the Study

The objectives of the study are:

1. To examine growth and structural transformation in Korea and India since 1950s;
2. To analyse the factors accounting for differential growth and transformation in the two countries;
3. To assess the role of rural institutions in rural transformation;

4. To examine the changes in the economy and life of rural households in Korea and Coastal Andhra; and
5. To study the small Farm Rice Economy in Korea and Coastal Andhra.

Methodology

Socio-economic levels in the 1950s are compared to demonstrate the striking similarities in the levels of development between the two countries. The difference in the growth processes between the two countries are examined to show differential transformation even with similar socio-economic levels in the 1950s. A holistic approach was chosen as non-economic aspects having a bearing on the transformation process are also considered.

In assessing the impact of rural institutions, stress is laid on agrarian structure and Rural Delivery System. In addition to their study at the macro level, attention was also paid to village and household levels. To examine the changes in the lives of rural households and farm economy, Coastal Andhra region was considered ideal in view of the predominance of paddy cultivation under canal irrigation as in Korea. For this, 1970 was considered as a benchmark, as Green Revolution was ushered in both Korea and India in late 1960s.

Areas of Field Work

In Korea, Keum-pan village located in North Cholla Province with developed canal irrigation and predominance of paddy cultivation and Jook-jeon (Juk-jeon) village located in North Chung Chong Province were chosen based on the classification of villages by the National Agricultural Cooperative Federation (NACF), Korea.

In Coastal Andhra, Eletipadu, located in Iragavaram Mandal (Tanuku taluk), West Godavari District, a predominantly rice growing area of Andhra Pradesh (earlier covered under Intensive Agricultural District Programme – IADP) served by canal irrigation since the colonial times and Gollapadu located in Muppalla Mandal (Sathenapalli taluk) Guntur District with wider access to irrigation since 1970s under the Nagarjuna Sagar Project were selected. Predominance of areas under irrigated paddy and less susceptibility to flood and drainage problems weighed in the selection of the Mandal/taluks. The villages in the Mandals were short-listed based on the percentage of rural population engaged in household industry in view of reportedly higher levels of off-farm employment in Korea. The sample village in West Godavari District was finalised after joint visits to the shortlisted villages with the Korean counterpart, Prof. Young Chul Kim of Kon-Kuk University, Seoul who had stayed at Andhra University for about five years (1973-78) and who had fairly good acquaintance with the agro-economic situation of Andhra.

Selection of Sample Households

Ri-Jangs (village heads) maintain fairly comprehensive statistics of the village economy in Korea. The list of farm-households by size of operated area made available by the Ri-Jangs in Korea and a comprehensive census schedule canvassed in Coastal Andhra formed the basis for random selection of farm households for the intensive study. The sample households selected are in proportion to the distribution of households in each size-group in the respective sample villages. In all, 120 farm-households at the rate of 30 from each of the four sample villages were selected for the study.

The farm-household schedule (FHS) designed and administered to farm-households in Korea, after pretesting, was carefully modified to suit the farm economic conditions of Coastal Andhra. The FHS was designed to get details on the farm family, assets, consumer durables, input-use, yields, non-farm incomes, membership in formal and informal organizations and the services availed from institutions like cooperatives and extension agencies.

Census

Though not a part of the original project design, a detailed census of all households in the sample villages was made so as to capture the transformation process. Towards this end, a five-page census schedule was designed, pretested and administered to all the 393 households in Eletipadu and 476 households in Gollapadu, while owing to time and resource constraints, only 50 to 60 per cent of the households in Korean sample villages could be covered. However, due care was taken to ensure proportionate coverage of non-farm as well as different strata of farm-households. As many as 116 out of 192 and 103 out of 192 households respectively were covered through census in Keum-pan and Juk-jeon Ri (villages) of Korea.

Study at the Institutional Level

The institutional survey focussed on the objectives of the institution, the nature of services rendered, the structure of the institution, nature of assistance, support provided and the nature and means of control and coordination exercised by higher level structures, nature of incentives offered, if any, for better performance by staff and means for promoting horizontal and vertical coordination among related institutions. Interviews were held with the functionaries of the institutions using a structured schedule.

As Korea is a unitary State with limited autonomy for provincial bodies, the study of institutional aspects covers National, Gun (District), Myon (Sub-division) and Ri (Village) level institutions involved in agriculture and rural development activities. From all these institutions, particularly those at the National level, annual reports and other published information available in English was obtained to supplement the information elicited through interviews.*

The information elicited from most of these institutions was qualitative in nature, except in the case of cooperatives. As cooperatives are the focal points in delivering inputs and related services to rural population in Korea, quantitative details on the working of these institutions were obtained to judge their efficiency in providing the services.

* The response to the interviews was not always free and frank in Korea because of the political situation in general, and the prevalence of ethnocentric values of not to talk ill of their own country and its administration to an alien in particular.

The same questionnaire with a few modifications was administered to Mandal/Block, and District level institutions in Andhra Pradesh. The nature of linkages between the institutions at the State and Central levels are perceived through the information elicited at the lower level agencies and wherever possible, supplemented with information available in the annual reports of the National bodies and earlier studies.

The Field Work Per Se

The survey in South Korea was conducted during October-November 1985, with the help of an English/Korean household schedule with the assistance of an interpreter. Administering a questionnaire, to a time-conscious Korean farm-household necessitated employing Korean investigators to save time. Graduate students of Kon-Kuk University were trained for the purpose by Young Chul Kim and Lee, Deputy Director, Research Department of the NACF. The filled-in schedules were edited and the responses were translated into English under the supervision of Young Chul Kim.

The same investigators along with some others trained for the purpose were employed to canvass the bilingual census schedules written in Korean and English languages. Institutional level interviews were conducted with the help of an interpreter.

Field work in Andhra was carried out in May-June 1986 with the help of the faculty members and Post-doctoral scholars of the Department of Cooperation and Applied Economics.

Presentation of the Study

The study is divided into two parts, Part-I, consisting of two Chapters (2 and 3), traces the growth and structural transformation and the factors contributing for differential growth and transformation in Korea and India. Part-II is based on field work at the institutional and household level in Korea and Coastal Andhra, which consists of Chapter 4, presenting the results of field studies on people's participation in rural institutions and the significance of rural institutions in the economy of farm-households in Korea against the backdrop of evaluation of institutions at the macro level. Chapter 5 shows the changes in the socio-economic profiles of the rural households in the sample villages, along with their relative status in factor markets and access to institutions during 1970-86. The small farm rice economy of Korea and Andhra as seen through the study of sample farm-households is discussed in Chapter 6. The concluding Chapter presents findings emerging from the study.

PART-I

RURAL TRANSFORMATION IN KOREA AND INDIA— A MACRO PERSPECTIVE

This Part consists of Chapter 2 and Chapter 3. Chapter 2 traces the growth and transformation in Korea and India based mainly on secondary data. This is followed by an analysis of the factors accounting for the differential growth and transformation. In Chapter 3, in understanding the process of transformation, the role of the State, religion and education in facilitating the transformation process were examined.

2

GROWTH WITH DIFFERENTIAL TRANSFORMATION

An Overview

All developing countries, irrespective of ideologies and commitments to planning for economic development, strive towards growth with justice. The Repubiic of Korea is perhaps the only country among market economies which has transformed itself from a poor agricultural economy with a dual structure to a so-called 'Newly Industrialised' country in a remarkably short span of 20 to 25 years. Though Korea and India differ in physical size, resource endowments, political structure and external factors influencing the development process; yet they have taken the development path almost at the same period, and thus provide a case for comparison.

Differences between Korea and India

Differences of ethos between Korea and India are manifold:

1. With respect to physical size and population, India is 33 times larger than RoK in terms of physical area (0.99 lakh sq. km. for Korea, 32.80 lakh sq. km. for India and Indian population is 16.5 times more than of Korea (21.8 million in 1954 in Korea and 361 million in 1951 in India).
2. Korea was a nation from the ashes (Keon, 1978) and as a colony of Japan, was devastated during World War II. The Korean War of 1950-53 further ruined the Korean economy. The post-war reconstruction was done with massive inflow of foreign assistance, particularly from U.S. (Kim and Park,

1985, p. 5). Though India was an erstwhile colony of the British it was not ravaged like Korea at the time of World War II. It ushered in development as an independent country since 1947. The economies of both Korea and India were geared to markets of the imperial powers. But in Korea, modern industrial sector took its firm roots even as it was dominated by the Japanese (Blumenthal and Lee, 1985, p. 225), while in India it was not so. The effects of partition on the resources of the country are also different. India did not to suffer much from the loss of industrial and natural resources as compared to Korea which lost most of the basic industries as well as 92 per cent of the total electric power generation capacity because of the North-South Division.

3. The per capita foreign aid (both military and economic) of South Korea during the period 1946-75 amounted to U.S. $ 600; U.S. aid to Korea during 1946-75 was 3½ times higher than for the whole of Latin America (U.S. $ 8,871 million to Korea, 2,562 million to Latin America) and 8½ times for the whole of Africa (U.S. $ 1,030,400). Owing to massive U.S. aid, Korea had virtually no debt obligations in the early period of its industrialisation. Nonetheless, the estimated foreign debt of Korea was about U.S. $ 47 billion as of mid-1986, was the largest in Asia and the fourth biggest in the world after the Latin America's "Big Three", Brazil, Mexico and Argentina. As against South Korea's heavy pumping of foreign aid and reliance on foreign debt, the external assistance apportioned to India from 1947 to the end of March 1986 totalled to a meagre Rs. 46,565 crores, which comes to around U.S. $ 52 per capita.
4. In the development arena, Korea pursued an outward looking strategy welcoming multi-nationals to set up their firms, while India took recourse to self-reliance which did not land her in such a foreign dependent plight.
5. As about changes in agrarian structure, Korea has successfully implemented radical land reforms by 1950s

while India could only attempt at altering the agrarian structure, initiated in 1950s and kept it as an unfinished task.

6. There are regional variations and disparities of development in India because of her vast geographical area, while there was relative homogeneity in Korea because of its limited area.
7. As about relevant social systems, Korean society facilitated occupational mobility, while Indian caste system became a hindrance for mobility. On the social front, the Korean society is highly homogeneous as against the heterogeneity of the Indian society. Though Korea's 'Kolpum' system,[1] a product of the Shilla state that ruled Korea during eleventh century A.D. is compared often to the caste system in India because of its tribal and hereditary nature and its strictness, it was not that relevant to the twentieth century Korea. Even the unique class system of Korea[2] which differentiated between the classes is not so rigid as the Indian caste system.
8. As regards the literacy levels of people, the measures taken for the spread of education among the Korean masses during the Yi dynasty period as well as the role played by youth in spreading literacy during the summer vacations as part of their struggle against Japanese colonialism had a positive impact in promoting literacy in Korea. In India, such literacy movements did not take place. In Korea, even in the nineteenth century, most individuals could read writings in Hangul (Ban *et al.*, 1980, p. 311). Because of colonial legacy, only 16.6 per cent were literate in India in 1951.
9. Coming to the nature of the State, the Korean State emerged from several authoritarian traditions like Confucianism, Japanese colonialism and U.S. patronage, the Republic of Korea is nicknamed 'Korea Inc.' (Halliday, 1987, p. 44). As against this, the Indian State is influenced by liberalism, to be called a 'soft State', whereas the Korean activation of social energy is on a scale rarely seen in history, which made it a strong State (Yoo and Wade, 1981, p.128).

Finally, Korea in her early history had solved certain problems which inhibit modernisation in many other societies today. Important among these are : development of national consciousness, tremendous capacity of the Government, to influence people's behaviour throughout the country, non-existence of policy thrust for equity because of previous social levelling during Japanese rule and the war, reforms of land tenures, educational development and adherence to the labour-intensive pattern of development. In the case of India, colonial rule and its policies kept on aggravating inequalities and Indian efforts to bridge these could not so far succeed.

Notwithstanding the differences in ethos, similarities abound between Korea and India.

Similarities between Korea and India

1. Korea and India have a colonial legacy and in both cases, imperialism penetrated through trade treaties, the Kangwha treaty[3] between Korea and Japan in 1876 (Kim, An-Jae, 1981, p. 228) and according permission to East-India Company at Surat in 1608 by Jahangir, the Mughal Emperor. Both the economies were subjected to colonial exploitation policies and reforms aimed at gearing the colonies to subserve the interests of the imperial economies, exporting primary products and importing manufactured goods. Between 1910-39, most of Korea's exports to Japan were raw materials such as minerals and agricultural products, while more than one-half of imports from Japan were manufactured goods (Kim, An-Jae, 1981, pp. 228-9). The distinguishing characteristic of Indian foreign trade in 1870, which continued for several decades, is the importance given to raw materials in exports and of manufactured goods in imports, the Britishers being prime traders both ways (Chopra, 1975, p. 831).
2. Both have become independent after a continuous colonial rule. Independence was bestowed on Korea in 1945 but not seized (Yoo and Wade, 1981, p. 145) and India won

freedom in 1947, strange coincidence that both celebrate Independence Day on 15th of August every Year.

3. Both were confronted with demographic problems of high rates of growth of population of more than two per cent. However, in Korea since 1971, it was below two per cent (Kim and Park, 1985, p.15), while it continued to be high in the case of India. A related feature is similarity in the concept of family in both the countries which stress on, what sociologists call, 'familism'. Even in mid-1970s the average Korean sees himself as a member of his family rather than as an individual (Kim, Jongbin, 1980, p. 49). The Indian rural family, as described by Desai, is similar to the Korean family (Desai, A.R. 1978, p. 36).
4. Another common feature of the two countries is that both are small-farm economies to which reference has been made. Marginal holdings with less than one hectare account for more than 50 per cent of the operational holdings in both the countries. But 68 per cent of Korean farm-households cultivate less than 0.5 hectare. More than one-half of the farm-households in India operate less than one hectare. Marginal (less than one hectare) and small (one to two hectares) holdings account for nearly two-thirds of the total operational holdings in India (Dantwala, 1986, p. 62).
5. In both the countries, Government plays a crucial role in the transformation process and through greater intervention in the economy than in most of the Western Countries. Korea's economic growth is 'Government-Oriented' (Kim, Jongbin, 1980, p. 47). while the India, the directive principles enunciated in Article 39(b) and (e) of the Constitution provide greater say for the State in managing the economy.
6. Both accept the basic premise of market economy and yet accord a significant role for the public sector. Because of the greater share of the public sector in Korea, the plans had a greater direct effect on the economy than in Japan (Blumenthal and Lee, 1985, p. 227). Public sector plays a dominant role in the industrialisation of India.

7. Both Korea and India have adopted planning mechanism to usher in growth. The Planning Commission in India and the Economic Planning Board (EPB) in Korea issue plans that spell out the nature of the priorities of the Government and the direction towards which the economy should move. Both governments use direct and indirect subsidies to promote industrial growth as well as to step up agricultural productivity. Both developed institutional infrastructures to promote industry and agriculture.

The basic similarities in the initial conditions like colonial legacy, late entry into the development arena, common problems like demographic pressure, non-viable small farm economy, shared concern to bring about development to meet the 'revolution of rising expectations' which happen to be a common feature of all newly liberated countries with a colonial past; the commonality itself, despite differences, could provide a strong case for a comparative study of India and South Korea. Further, comparison of societies with reasonably similar problems provides useful insights (Black, 1966, p. 39).

Comparative Perspective on Growth and Transformation

Coming to the appropriate time-frame for comparison between Korea and India, though they became independent in 1945 and 1947 respectively, planned efforts at transformation of the economy varied. While India ushered in planning in 1950 itself, Korea was under military rule of the U.S.A. for more than two years and the Republic of Korea was founded only in 1948. The Korean War (1950-53) and the post-war reconstruction of the economy as well as internal disorders delayed the planned development of Korea till 1962, when the First Five-Year Economic Development Plan was launched. Many Korean experts picked up 1962 as the starting point of its growth (Kim Jongbin, 1980, p. 47; Kim An-Jae, 1981, p. 231). Comparative performance and outcome of development in both Korea and India are examined with reference to growth, structural transformation and their impact on the living standards as well as in promoting equity-oriented development.

Growth

Both Korea and India are poor and populous countries with a dominant primary sector when they have initiated planned development. In terms of per capita GDP, there are no observable differences in the initial period . In 1950, (at 1970 prices) it was U.S.$65 in Korea and 60 in India. However, Korea witnessed remarkable growth, under various Five-Year Plans, which are considered to fall somewhere in between indicative and commanding nature, effectively implemented by a strong State under the military leadership of Presidents Park Chung Hee (1962-79) and Chun Doo Hwan (1980-88), during which periods "the Korean economy has consistently achieved and often surpassed the ambitious targets set by planners for economic growth and development" (Hasan and Rao, 1979, p. 3).

Of Indian economy the performance in terms of rate of growth fell short of the targeted growth rates and assumed a constancy to be labelled as 'Hindu Rate of Growth' by the late Raj Krishna. With NDP growing at 3.57 per cent per annum and population growing at 2.24 per cent, as it happened over a period of 34 years from 1950-51 to 1984-85, it necessarily takes 52 years to double the per capita NDP and not 27 years as envisaged in the perspective of the First Five Year Plan. India in this way enters the twenty-first century with problems of inadequate growth (Dandekar, 1988, pp. 49-50). It means that India is unable to attain the growth targets fixed. Apart from economic reasons, the inefficient implementation of plans is considered to be responsible for this state of affairs. On the economic planning in Nehru era, it is alleged that plans were excellent but were not properly implemented as bureaucracy sabotaged the process (Bhambhri, 1988, p. 48).

The rates of growth of gross domestic product (GDP) in Korea for the non-plan period 1953-61 are not available. The rates of growth of GDP in India is worked out to synchronise with the Korean plan periods for the purpose of comparison (*see* Table 2.1).

Korean economy grew at the rate of 4.4 per cent per annum during the post-liberation and pre-consolidation period, *i.e.*, 1953-1961. In India during the pre-Plan period of 1948-51, the

Table 2.1: Relative growth rates of gross domestic product in Korea and India

(per cent per annum)

Period	*Korea*	*India*
1951-56	—	3.87
1956-61	—	3.78
1962-63-1966-67	4.4	2.06
1967-68-1971-72	7.8	4.13
1967-71	9.6	3.86
1972-76	9.7	3.32
1977-81	5.8	3.82
1962-82	8.2	3.82

Source : Korea : 1. Ahn Choong-Yong, 1985, p. 2.
2. Kim Young Chul, 1986, p. 1.
India : Computed from CSO, 1979, 1984.

economy grew at the compound rate of only 1.2 per cent per annum (Chopra, 1975, p. 1137). During the period 1956-61, the rate of growth of GDP was 3.87 lower than the rate of growth of Korean economy during its pre-consolidation period. The disparities in the rates of growth of the two economies are much more striking in the Plan period, the Korean achievement far excelling India's. Though acceleration of Korean economic growth was traced largely to the shift in industrialisation strategy from import substitution to export promotion in earlysixties and successful implementation of the export-oriented policy thereafter, a number of other factors, economic and non-economic ones, have helped this process (Kim Kwong-suk and Park, 1985, pp. 1-2). In India, the economic and non-economic factors retarded the growth process, which shall be examined later.

Growth Rates and Structural Change

To identify structural change, growth trends in sectoral composition of GNP in both Korean and Indian economies are shown in Table 2.2.

As it can be seen, while in South Korea the structure of the economy changed markedly over the decades, shifting the balance between agriculture and industry radically, such shifts cannot be noticed in case of India. V.K.R.V. Rao, (1983, p. 53), observes

Table 2.2: Sectoral Shares in GNP of Korea and India (at 1970 and 1970-71 constant prices)

Year		*Primary*		*Secondary*		*Tertiary*	
Korea	*India*	*Korea*	*India*	*Korea*	*India*	*Korea*	*India*
—	1950-51	—	59.61	—	14.47	—	25.92
1961	1960-61	44.89	55.14	10.12	17.28	51.70	27.58
1971	1970-71	26.45	48.46	24.42	20.67	49.09	30.87
1981	1980-81	14.92	41.62	44.47	21.57	—	36.81
1985	1984-85	12.75	38.08	—	21.60	—	40.32

Note : Korean data was adjusted to 1970 constant prices.
Source : Korea: MAF: Year Book of Agriculture and Forestry Statistics 1972, 1977 and 1985
India: Indian Institute of Public Opinion, 1986, p. 13.

that during the period 1950-51 to 1979-80, the Indian economy continued to be dominated by the primary sector and by unorganized enterprise. The only similarity between the two economies is the phenomenal rise in the service sector. While industry led the growth of the South Korean economy since 1970, the Indian industrial sector almost remained stagnant.

Changes in the Composition of Work-force

Similar to the differences noted in the sectoral shares in GNP or structure of output, there are marked differences in the structural transformation of the economy in terms of the composition of work-force (Table 2.3).

While both Korea and India had dominant primary sector, followed by tertiary sector in 1950s Korea had only three per cent, of its labour force in the industrial sector as against 10.7 per cent in India. Since 1960s, the transformation in Korea is found to be phenomenal, with a fast decline in the composition of labour force in the primary sector to the nearest minimum of around 23 per cent by 1985, while in India, only in 1981, a slight decline is noted in this respect. The composition of labour force engaged in industrial sector in India showed an insignificant rise in 1980s while in respect of Korea, the share has increased from 3.7 per cent in 1949 to 28.1 per cent by 1987. A similar trend persists in tertiary sector also.

As about the structural shifts in the composition of output and employment in Korea, the occupational structure favourably

Table 2.3 : Changes in the composition of work-force in Korea and India

(in ,000 persons)

Year		*Primary*		*Secondary*		*Tertiary*	
Korea	*India*	*Korea*	*India*	*Korea*	*India*	*Korea*	*India*
1949	1951	6359	—	300	—	1301	—
		(79.9)	(72.1)	(3.7)	(10.7)	(16.4)	(17.2)
1960	1961	7595	135327	658	23006	2246	30239
		(72.3)	(71.8)	(6.3)	(12.2)	(21.4)	(16.0)
1970	1971	4846	130058	1377	20211	3395	30216
		(50.4)	(72.1)	(14.3)	(11.2)	(35.3)	(16.7)
1980	1981	4654	153049	3079	30146	5951	39321
		(34.0)	(68.7)	(22.5)	(13.5)	(43.5)	(17.8)
1985	—	3733	—	3659	—	7578	—
		(24.9)		(24.4)		(50.6)	
1987	—	3580	—	4602	—	8172	—
		(21.9)		(28.1)		(50.0)	

Source : Korea : 1. Woo Ki-Do, 1972, p. 39.
2. EPB, 1988, p. 24.
India : 1. Government of India, 1972.
2. CSO, 1967 pp. 15-18.
3. Government of India, 1975, pp. 18-21.
4. Government of India, 1987 pp.238-41.

responded to the changes in the sectoral shares of GNP over time, while there is no such response in India, though a slight indication in this direction could be noted in respect of the primary sector since 1981.

Performance of Agricultural Sector

To have a glimpse about rural transformation, a comparative picture of the performance of the agricultural sectors of both Korean and Indian economies is relevant. What is the share of agriculture in GDP? What is the agricultural population in actual and percentage terms? and what is the gross value of agricultural output per agricultural population? (Table 2.4).

In understanding the performance of Korean Agriculture, one should not look at 1950 picture seriously because of the Korean war and non-reliability of the data given during the war period. If one leaves 1950, even in the 1960s the agricultural output accounted for a substantial share in GDP and the percentage of

Table 2.4. Comparative performance of agricultural economies of Korea and India–1951-85

Year	*Share of Agriculture in GDP U.S. Dollars 1970*		*Agricultural Population*				*Agricultural output per agricultural Population U.S. Dollars 1970*	
			Number in '000		*Share of Total Population*			
	Korea	*India*	*Korea*	*India*	*Korea*	*India*	*Korea*	*India*
1951	37.00	57.05	12779	251687	63.37	69.7	35.00	52.93
1961	42.40	52.47	14559	301730	58.26	68.7	96.92	59.66
1971	24.62	45.51	14712	382095	44.7	69.7	148.86	61.10
1972	22.66	41.64	14677	—	43.8	—	—	—
1973	19.77	45.35	14645	—	42.9	—	—	—
1974	18.77	42.40	13459	—	38.8	—	—	—
1975	19.12	47.71	13244	—	37.5	—	—	—
1976	17.62	40.95	12785	—	35.7	—	—	—
1977	15.87	45.41	12309	—	33.8	—	—	—
1978	13.82	42.93	11527	—	31.2	—	—	—
1979	13.83	35.21	10883	—	29.0	—	—	—
1980	11.09	41.76	10827	—	28.4	—	—	—
1981	12.76	40.17	9999	454176	25.8	66.4	196.86	60.83
1982	12.45	38.77	9688	—	24.6	—	—	—
1983	11.96	36.43	9475	—	23.7	—	—	—
1984	11.02	37.34	9015	—	22.3	—	—	—
1985	10.34	35.63	8521	—	20.8	—	335.10	—
1986	—	—	8180	—	19.7	—	—	—
1987	—	—	7771	—	18.5	—	—	—

Note : (i) Except population figures, the Indian data relates to the financial years, *i.e.*, 1971 = 1970-71.
(ii) Agricultural population refers to the cultivators and agricultural labour classes and corresponds to the Farm population in Korea.
(iii) Conversion of US \$ in 1970 = 316 Won and Rs. 7.509.

Source : Korea—EPB, 1988 and MAF 1972, 1977 and 1986.
India—CSO, 1976, 1981, 1984.

population engaged in agriculture is also around 60 per cent in both cases. But in terms of Agricultural Gross Domestic Product (AGDP) per capita of agricultural population, in India it formed only little more than 50 per cent of that of Korea.

What is striking is the decline in the relative share of agriculture both in the work-force and in GDP in Korea, in sharp contrast to India. In the case of India, the share of agriculture in GDP is fluctuating though the overall trend is on the decline. But it continues to be high even in 1985 at a level similar to the one in Korea of early 1960s. India witnessed signs of decline in its share of agricultural work-force only in 1981, in sharp contrast to Korea where it began to fall from 1960s itself.

Further there is continuous increase in the absolute number of persons depending on agriculture in India, which almost doubled from 252 million in 1951 to 454 million by 1981. The Korean scenario is in sharp contrast to that of India with decline in the absolute numbers from 1972 itself. Their number declined from 14.7 million in 1972 to 10 million by 1981 and further reduced to 7.8 million by 1987.

Moreover AGDP per capita is almost constant in India during the period; in Korea it increased continuously since 1961 and almost tripled by 1981. The superior performance of agriculture in Korea in terms of higher AGDP per capita cannot be attributed to the declining numbers or to the favourable price policies implemented since 1970s. Korean success on the agricultural front is largely attributable to the technological advances, increase in investments and better water management and cultural practices, as well as the coordinated and integrated efforts of the institutions involved in agricultural development. Even if one concedes that there is an element of truth in what John Halliday said, "South Korea manipulates and conceals statistics to suit its case, particularly in agriculture" (Halliday, 1987, p. 34), still the superior performance of the South Korean agriculture compared to that of India cannot be denied.

The differential growth rates of the two economies and the nature and degree of structural transformation experienced in terms of output as well as occupational composition of labour force have implications to the problems of poverty, equity and quality of life of the people. These aspects need examination as they are relevant in understanding the outcomes of the differential transformation in Korea and India.

Differential Transformation : Implications for Poverty, Equity and Quality of Life

The relationship between growth, transformation, poverty, equity and quality of life is too complex; and nonetheless these complexities received attention of researchers (Lindert and Williamsen, 1985, pp. 341-77). As yet there is no unanimity among economists that the Kuznets curve lies to the right with rise in per capita income (Lindert and Williamsen, 1985, p. 346, Griffin, 1985, p. 49). Further, the two economies of Korea and India are distinctly different in the initial conditions having a bearing on income distribution. Korea had initial favourable conditions that facilitate equity in income distribution (Choo, 1977, pp. 303-30). It also had a population that never considered income distribution to be equal (Yong and Siegel, 1985, p. 403) and a Government that laid stress on rapid growth upto 1980s (Jung, Yong Duck, 1984, pp.147, 151-2; Kwan Tai-Hwan, *et al.*, 1981, p.12). But it is quite different in India, where the basic institutions of the society *viz.*, the joint family, the village and the caste system have been antithetical to the ideal of equality (Tendulkar, 1987, p.110), though concern for growth with social justice has been the main objective of national planning since fifties (Bandopadhyay, 1985, pp.101-4).

Ideally, problems of poverty and growth-equity issues have to be examined in an explicitly historical context of the particular countries (Ahluwalia, 1976, p. 307). But this is thwarted by the absence as well as inadequacies of the data and their comparability over time. The statistical base of Korea is not so comprehensive as that of India. The social statistics survey of Korea, an annual survey designed to provide data for social indicators with focus on one or two selected special issues, was started in 1978 and the first survey was in 1979. Household income has been selected as the major focus of the 1981 survey. The major part of the data on social indicators is drawn from the surveys on household expenditure, farm household economy; the economically active population and labour force information on income and consumption is drawn from the household economy surveys of urban areas. The reliability of data from this source for the study of income distribution is questioned on the ground that the major purpose of the urban household survey is to arrive at weights for computing the consumer price index numbers and to measure the level and behaviour of consumption. Further, it is also questioned on account of too small a sample size, exclusion of both low and high income brackets, lack of consideration of income distribution aspects in the sample design. Similarly, rural household surveys are also not meant to grasp the structure of income distribution. Their sample size is not only small but also excludes very low income households (Kwan Tai, Hwan *et al.* 1981, pp.13 and 18).

In India, despite comprehensive data-base and conduct of household census by the National Sample Survey Organisation (NSS) on a continuous basis since 1951, data on household incomes were not collected on the assumption that income data are unreliable and inclusion of income data effects the relative accuracy of other data. As a result, income distribution statistics in India, as Surjit Bhalla observed, have had to be 'patched up', *i.e.*, information on consumer expenditure (NSS) has to be merged with other data (Bhalla and Vashishtha, 1988, p. 39). Even the data of the National Council of Applied Economics Research (NCAER), the only organisation to collect data on income and expenditure of households, do suffer from limitations of comparability over time. The exclusion of certain items from the definition of income from its All-India Consumer survey for the financial year 1964/65 and presentation of data by 'net income' and 'disposable income' rather than the commonly used definition of gross income in its survey of Income, Savings and Expenditure in the agricultural year July 1967 to June 1968 are the limitations of the NCAER data. However, its survey on household income and disposition for the agricultural year 1975-76 is considered valuable, as it is free from known drawbacks either in terms of definition or coverage and also because 1975-76 is considered as normal 'good' year (*Ibid*, 41-3). Thus, though the Indian data on income distribution are comparatively more comprehensive than Korean it is not suitable for any trend analysis, as the sources, concepts and coverage differ, when one attempts to look at these for fairly long periods.

Relative Disparities in Income Distribution and Consumer Expenditure in Korea and India

Irma Adelman and Sherman Robinson's (1978, pp. 45-6), World Bank Study was one of the earliest studies on Korean income distribution and their estimates are based on rigorous scrutiny, cross-checking and subjecting the data to sensitivity analysis. Their findings that Korean income distribution during 1964-70, a period of rapid growth of 11 per cent per annum remained unchanged and is the best in the developing world are often quoted in praise of equitable income distribution of Korea. Similar findings were made by Oshima who observed that South Korea with an even lower per capita income than Taiwan before 1970s has an index of inequality as low as that of the U.S., and Japan (quoted by Choo, 1977, p. 304). However, these studies reflect on the pre-industrialised Korea. In this context Shong (1989, p. 514), observed that in the pre-industrialised Korea income distribution was equitable because of widespread education, major redistribution of land and assets held by Japanese. In view of this it was argued that what is relevant is whether Korea had more equitable distribution over time rather than, it having more equal income distribution than other developing countries (Shong, 1989, p. 519).

For this reason, data on changing income distribution of Korean hosueholds during 1965-82 compiled from various sources by Kim Kyong Dong (1985, p. 772) are used to observe the trends in income distribution in Korea over time (Table 2.5 and 2.5.1).

As could be seen, the differences in the relative share of the lower 40 per cent and upper 20 per cent are marked without any clear trend in the upward movement of lower 40 per cent and decline in those of the upper strata. The Gini coefficient, which was just 0.34 in 1965 because of redistribution of wealth (Choo, 1977, pp. 303-30), increased to 0.42 by 1969. Though the trend is one of continuous decline since 1974 to 1982, it is still higher compared to the 1965 level. Despite this fluctuating trend and a higher level of inequity in 1982 compared to 1965, there is a progressive trend towards bridging income inequalities in Korea since mid-seventies.

The Gini coefficients series for India are based on NSS data on size distribution of nominal per capita expenditure, while those of Korea are based on income distribution. Even the limited estimates readily available on income distribution in India are for different decile groups and vary with those available for Korea. In spite of these limitations, the broad trends in the changing income distribution in these countries could be discerned (Table 2.5).

The Gini Lorentz Ratio's (GLR) based on size-distribution of nominal per capita household private consumption expenditure derived from NSS data are subject to certain limitations. For example, while 'week' was used as reference period in early rounds, it is 'one month' for later rounds. It also excludes houseless destitutes living on charity (Iyengar and Brahmananda, 1987, p. 84). Further, it is noted that while the relative price movements did not vary much across decile groups during 1952-53 and 1960-61, not only prices increased four times during 1960-61 and 1964-65, compared to the earlier period, but the rate of growth of prices was also considered to be distinctly higher for the bottom 30 per cent of the population than for the top 20 per cent (Tendulkar, 1987, pp.123-4). Given these limitations, the GLRs which are relatively high during fifties both for rural and urban areas, have shown decline by 1960-61. During 1960-61 and 1964-65, while the GLR declined from 0.32 to 0.30 in rural areas, no such trend is noticed in the urban areas. In India, during the deceleration phase of 1964-65 and 1973-74, the GLR declined for the rural population marginally from 0.30 in 1964-65 to 0.28 in 1973-74, and for urban population from 0.36 to 0.33. In 1977-78, the GLRs rose in both rural and urban areas and again declined by 1983. Thus, there is an observed reduction in the GLRs over time, in both rural and urban areas.

One has to look into the income distribution data of NCAER, despite problems of comparability over time. As could be seen, while there are perceptible differences in the relative shares of the bottom 40 per cent and that of top 20 per cent in both rural and urban areas, they are more pronounced in the urban areas (Table 2.5.1). It is hazardous to interpret on the trends over time as the household incomes used are disposable income in 1964-65, net income in 1967-68 and gross income in 1975-76. "The per capita distribution for 1964-65 and 1975-76, if accurate, shows that income distribution was essentially constant for data eleven years apart" (Bhalla and Vashishtha, 1988, p. 56).

Table 2.5 : Gini Coefficient of income distribution in Korea and India

Year	Korea			India	
	Lower 40%	*Upper 20%*	*Gini Co-efficients*	*Rural*	*Urban*
1952	—	—	—	0.340	0.365
1952-53	—	—	—	0.330	0.397
1953-54	—	—	—	0.334	0.371
1954-55	—	—	—	0.350	0.370
1955	—	—	—	0.335	0.371
1955-56	—	—	—	0.344	0.368
1956-57	—	—	—	0.319	0.402
1957	—	—	—	0.331	0.393
1957-58	—	—	—	0.333	0.377
1958-59	—	—	—	0.328	0.348
1959-60	—	—	—	0.314	0.357
1960-61	—	—	—	0.321	0.350
1961-62	—	—	—	0.316	0.362
1962-64	—	—	—	0.300	0.366
1964-65	—	—	—	0.297	0.357
1965	19.25	42.82	0.3428	—	—
1965-66	—	—	—	0.301	0.347
1966-67	—	—	—	0.298	0.349
1967	16.44	46.81	0.3926	—	—
1967-68	—	—	—	0.296	0.348
1968	16.17	50.51	0.4251	—	—
1968-69	—	—	—	0.310	0.346
1969	15.80	50.49	0.4246	—	—
1969-70	—	—	—	0.298	0.362
1970	18.97	44.73	0.3550	—	—
1970-71	—	—	—	0.289	0.352
1971	18.26	45.21	0.3647	—	—
1972-73	—	—	—	0.304	0.348
1972	15.85	46.05	0.4022	—	—
1973-74	—	—	—	0.282	0.310
1974	16.44	46.24	0.3989	—	—
1977-78	—	—	—	0.340	0.352
1976	17.00	47.29	0.3985	—	—
1978	17.25	46.00	0.3878	—	—
1980	18.15	44.23	0.3673	—	—
1982	17.92	43.85	0.3675	—	—
1983	—	—	—	0.296	0.332

Source : Korea : Kim Kyong-Dong, 1985, p. 772.
India : Iyengar and Brahmananda, 1987, p. 101.

Table 2.5.1 : Changes in Income Distribution in India

	1964-65			1967-68			1970-71			1975-76		
	Rural	Urban	India	Rural	Urban	India	Rural	Urban	India	Rural	Urban	India
Bottom 40%	19.3 (18.62)	14.6	17.31	13.0	14.4	13.21	17.1	—	—	— (17.72)	—	15.69
Upper 20%	44.6	53.8	49.50	53.1	52.1	53.25	46.6	—	—	—	—	49.34
Gini Co-efficient	0.37	0.48	—	0.48	0.46	—	0.38	—	—	0.39	—	—

Source : (i) Rural/Urban as well as Gini Coefficient for 1964-65, 1967-68 and 1970-71 are from ADB, 1977, p. 64.

(ii) Figures for India for the years 1964-65, 1967-68 and data for 1975-76 and figures in brackets are from Bhalla and Vashishtha Prem (1988), p. 56.

Table 2.6 : Comparative Picture of Poverty in Korea and India

Year	Korea	India (Percentage of Population in Poverty)						
		Head Count Measure				Planning Commision		
	Korea Development Institute Total	Ahluwalia 1984 Rural	Gupta and Datta 1984 Rural	Urban	Suryanarayana 1986 Rural	Rural	Urban	Total.
	(1)	(2)	(3)	(4)	(5)	(6)	(7)	(8)
1956-57	—	54.1	—	—	—	—	—	—
1957-58	—	50.2	—	—	—	—	—	—
1958-59	—	46.5	—	—	—	—	—	—
1959-60	—	44.4	—	—	—	—	—	—
1960-61	—	38.9	56.8	40.40	—	—	—	—
1961-62	—	39.4	56.2	39.36	38.22	—	—	—
1963-64	—	44.5	53.8	42.52	45.33	—	—	—

	(1)	(2)	(3)	(4)	(5)	(6)	(7)	(8)
1964-65	—	46.8	47.4	(45.74)	45.73	—	—	—
1965	40.9	—	—	—	—	—	—	—
1965-66	—	53.9	49.9	(46.43)	47.21	—	—	—
1966-67	—	56.6	49.2	(48.38)	56.09	—	—	—
1967-68	—	56.5	45.2	48.32	55.79	—	—	—
1968-69	—	51.0	48.4	45.53	52.62	—	—	—
1970	23.4	—	—	—	—	—	—	—
1969-70	—	NA	NA	44.40	49.12	—	—	—
1970-71	—	47.5	46.8	41.50	45.39	—	—	—
1971-72	—	41.2	47.8	NA	—	—	—	—
1972-73	—	43.1	50.5	(44.58)	42.92	54.09	41.22	51.49
1973-74	—	46.1	47.6	38.70	44.90	—	—	—
1976	14.8	—	—	—	—	—	—	—
1977-78	—	39.1	51.5	39.56	40.21	51.20	38.20	48.30
1978	12.0	—	—	—	—	—	—	—
1980	9.8	—	—	—	—	—	—	—
1983	—	(33.2)	—	(34.87)	—	—	—	—
1984-85	—	—	—	—	—	39.90	27.20	36.90
1985	6.8	—	—	—	—	—	—	—
1990-91	—			—	—	28.5	—	—
1991	5.3	—	—	—	—	—	—	—
1994-95	—	—	—	—	—	18.5	—	—
2000	3.9	—	—	—	—	—	—	—

Source : Korea: Juang Yong Duck 1984, 159; EPB 1986, p. 467.

(i) Column 2, 3 and 4 Bhalla, Surjit and Vashishtha, 1988. p. 55.

(ii) Column 4 Tendulkar, 1987, p. 143.

(iii) Column 5 Iyengar and Brahmananda, 1987, p. 103.

(iv) Column 6, 7 and 8 Government of India (Vol. I), 1985, p. 33.

(v) Figures for 1990-91, 1994-95 and 2000 are estimates and are taken from Ministry of Agriculture, Govt. of India, 1988, p. 31.

As is known, trends in the distribution of wealth as significant causes affecting income distribution in developing countries which are populous lie not so much in differential wage and salary levels but stem from uneven distribution of wealth. In this context, the Debt and Investment Surveys of the Reserve Bank of India provide data for size distribution of nominal value of assets of rural households as on 30th June 1962, 1971 and 1981. The Gini Coefficients for these three points are 0.652 (1962), 0.659 (1971) and 0.635 (1981), indicating thereby a marginal reduction over time (Tendulkar, 1987, p.118). As about the structure of land ownership during 1953-54 and 1970-71, the ranks of marginal farmers have swollen sharply; the number of their holdings in the total has increased from 31 per cent in 1953-54 to 44 per cent in 1971-72, though their share in area owned increased insignificantly (Dantwala, 1986, p. 61).

While comparable data on size distribution of wealth in urban areas are not available, the data for 1975-76 indicate that the distribution of wealth is considerably more skewed in urban areas than in rural areas. The Gini Coefficients based on NSS data for 1981-82 is 0.704 for urban households and 0.635 for rural households. This shows that there are considerable degrees of inequalities in tangible wealth in rural and urban areas (Tendulkar, 1987, p.119).

Thus, in India, the absence of any perceptible change in income distribution, marginal decline in the concentration of wealth, viewed in the context of the growing labour force show that growth has not resulted in any notable reduction in the inequalities of income distribution.[4]

Poverty

The data on poverty estimates also pose problems of comparability over time. Owing to differences in the conceptualization of poverty, periods covered as well as methods used in both Korea and India, it is difficult to discern any meaningful trends over time. It is true that Korean Government did not provide the public with any rational standard to measure the minimum costs of living or the 'number of poor' till 1978 (Jung, Yong-Duck, 1984, p.158). In 1978, those whose monthly per capita income fell below $10 for the rural residents or $11 for the urban residents are considered absolutely poor or public assistance needy. There is also criticism that the official standard was neither realistic nor reasonable (Jung Yong-Duck,1984, p.158). In 1985, families with four persons each with less than 1.18 lakh Won or $134 per month were treated as 'absolutely poor families', (EPB, 1986, p. 467). This is more realistic with what was fixed in 1978. Even after allowing for price rise, the norms for defining poor prior to 1978 are hard to get at.

In the case of India, poor are defined as those whose per capita income is less than Rs.15 and Rs. 340 per month at 1960-61 prices in rural and urban areas respectively and poverty estimates are made over time adjusting these to consumer price index numbers for agricultural labourers (rural) and consumer price index numbers for industrial workers (urban) in each year. Owing to non-availability of consumer price indices for making price adjustments, poverty estimates series are available for rural areas from 1956-57 and for urban areas from 1960-61 (Tendulkar, 1987, pp.125-6). Despite these limitations, some useful inferences can be drawn about relative levels of poverty in the two countries and the changing trends over time (Table 2.6).

The Planning Commission's estimates indicate a decline in urban poverty since 1972-73 contrary to the estimates of Gupta and Datta for the same period. On the whole, the available data show that there has been a decline in poverty in India since 1970-71 though this is questioned by Parthasarathy, based on an examination of other circumstantial evidence drawn from across the States for the period 1973-74 to 1980-81 (Parthasarathy, 1989, p.15).

As against the contradictory trends in the available poverty estimates in India, the poverty estimates for Korea provided by the Korea Development Institute and Economic Planning Board (EPB) clearly affirm the miraculous achievement of Korea in reducing the percentage of poor to about a half between 1965 and 1970 and still further since then. The absence of individual estimates on poverty makes it difficult to critically look at Korean data on poverty. Despite this and the limitations cited earlier, one can safely conclude that while both India and Korea started with a sizable percentage of poor in mid-sixties, Indian performance in attacking poverty falls much short of the Korean achievement. Thus, the limited growth in India did not succeed at all in alleviating poverty, while the higher growth in Korea helped to curtail poverty in a significant way. This is evident from the fact that the percentage of poor in India in 1984-85 is almost equal to the Korean situation in 1965, even if analysis were to be limited to the Government estimates on both sides.

Quality of Life

Select social indicators of growth reflecting the quality of life of the people are presented in Table 2.7.

Eventhough data on per capita income are not available for Korea prior to 1950, one can visualise higher income than those prevailing in 1950 as the adverse effects of War undermined economic activity during 1950-53. The per capita GDP is more or less the same in both the countries around 1950. However, during 1961-85, while the per capita GDP in India has not even doubled, there is a five-fold increase in Korea. The per capita calorie intake is less than the optimum as it declined from 91 per cent to 86 per cent in India. In Korea, while calorie intake is not only more than the optimum, it improved from 119 per cent to 126 per cent during the same period. In respect of life expectancy, in 1961, Korea was not only ahead of India but improved significantly during the two decades 1961-81, while India reached to the 1961 level of Korea only in 1981. Much sharper differences are manifested in respect of infant mortality and adult literacy. Not only the infant mortality in 1961 is very high in India, but the rate of decline has been slow in 1982, as it was three times higher than Korea. As mentioned earlier, historically Korea is better placed than India on the educational front. The literacy rate of India in 1981 falls short of literacy level of Korea even in thirties and the rate of growth is also lower. Thus, Korea stands on a higher footing with better performance in respect of all the indicators considered.

Despite certain differences, there are subtle similarities in the

Table 2.7 : Social Indicators Reflecting Quality of Life in Korea and India

Year	*Per capita GDP constant 1970 US $*		*Per capita calorie intake per day*		*Life Expectancy (in years)*		*Infant mortality*		*Adult literacy rate*	
	Korea	*India*	*Korea*	*India*	*Korea*	*India*	*Korea*	*India*	*Korea*	*India*
	(1)	(2)	(3)	(4)	(5)	(6)	(7)	(8)	(9)	(10)
1950	60	65	–	–	–	32	–	–	–	16
1954	147	–	–	–	–	–	69	–	–	–
1961	143	77	–	–	53	42	58	139	71	24
1971	261	89	–	–	–	46.4	–	–	–	29
1975	377	155	12785 (119)	2021 (91)	61.0	50.0	38	122	91	36
1981	513	100	1977 (126)	1906 (86)	66.1	54.1	37	91 (1982)	93	36
1983	–	–	–	157.6	–	–	34.2	–	–	–
1984	647	–	–	–	–	–	–	–	–	–
1985	–	120	2841	2189	–	–	27	89	–	–

Note : Figures in brackets in column 3 and 4 indicate the percentage of calorie intake compared to the optimum.

Source : 1. Figures in Column (1) and (2) are estimated based on GDP at constant prices and exchange rates of currencies in 1970.

2. Columns (3) to (10) are taken from World Bank, 1981, 1983, 1987.

initial conditions of the economies of Korea and India that justify comparison. Trends in growth and structural transformation show that the growth achieved by Korea is remarkable. Korean achievement in attaining swift structural transformation is in marked contrast to almost near stagnancy in India.

While high growth trend and structural transformation Korea experienced helped in bridging income inequalities, significant reduction in poverty and improvement in the living standards of its people, India presents a dismal picture almost comparable to that of Korea in early sixties as its limited growth did not result in alleviating poverty or improving living standards of its people.

What accounts for this differential growth and transformation?

NOTES

1. 'Kolpum' means 'Bone ranks' Under this system, social status would be determined by heredity (Han, Woo-Keun, 1974, 58).
2. In Korea, during the Yi dynasty period (1392-1910), social classes were clearly distinguished and class boundaries strictly enforced on the Confucian ethic that the ruled and rulers must always be distinct from one another. The class system consisted of four classes, *viz.*, (i) the Yangban (meaning two classes: the civil and military officials) were at the top and monopolised political power and wealth; (ii) Chungin (middle people), a relatively small class of petty officials; (iii) Sangmin (common people), who were mostly farmers and formed the bulk of the Korean population; and (iv) Chonmin (low-born people), mostly slaves and butchers. Status in all classes was hereditary and attempt to change one's status was considered as a crime against society and sin against heaven (Han, Woo-Keun, 1974, p. 247).
3. The Kanghwa Treaty of 1876, opened Korean doors for Japanese market (Han, Woo-Keun, 1974, pp. 372-5)
4. Gini Coefficients of income distribution was the same, *i.e.*, 0.39 for India in 1975-76 and for Korea in 1980 (Randhawa, N.S. 1986, p. 8).

3

DETERMINANTS OF GROWTH AND STRUCTURAL TRANSFORMATION IN KOREA AND INDIA

All interrelated sectors of State, Religion, Education, Agriculture, Industry and rural non-agricultural employment have a bearing on agrarian transition and rural transformation. As such, these are grouped into non-economic (Section I) and economic (Section II) factors.

SECTION-I

NON-ECONOMIC FACTORS

Studies pertaining to the growth process of Korea as well as India have dealt with the role of (1) State, (2) Religion, and (3) Education in view of the significance attached to these factors in explaining growth.

The State

It is said that transformations are driven by power, whether concentrated or diffused. The State as power is inescapably involved in rural transformation through directed changes in public law and policy (Herring, 1986, p. 2).

The State in Korean Development

Historically, in Korea there has been intimate interplay of politics and economics (Steinberg, 1988, p.19). The critical factor accounting for high growth rate of around 10 per cent per annum since 1962 in Korea has its prime origin in the leadership's commitment to economic growth (Sakong, 1980, p.104; Jones and Sakong, 1980, Chapter 3; Steinberg, 1988, pp. 21-2). The military Junta that ruled Korea since 1962 forced the Korean people to do what it thought had to be done. President Park successfully mobilised the people through a nation-wide campaign, fighting and eliminating the unwanted (Kim, Jongbin, 1980, pp. 49-56). Perhaps the most important lesson that Korean experience taught is that a strong State need not necessarily be inhibited by advocates of free enterprise (Halliday, 1987, p. 44).

Park's Saemaul Undong is a single-minded Rural Development Movement, which continuously and demonstrably extended its physical base and accrued profit for the individual and the nation to generate an authentic inner momentum (Keon, 1978, p. 95).

Chung Hee Park and Chun Doo Hwan, the two strongmen who were at helm of Korean State affairs, had a strong sense of commitment, greater sense of goal-orientation, willingness and ability to learn and put forth their best for the effective implementation of policies by mobilising all the concerned ministers, bureaucracy, businessmen and public at large.

They preached for improved quality, advanced know-how and increased exports as if it were a new religion (Woronoff, 1983, pp.41-5). The single-minded pursuit of growth goals coupled with authoritarian executive dominance over and above legislative and judicial processes reached the economic targets like a military operation (Bardhan, 1986, p.72).

The Korean planning was successful, rare among less developed countries, free from weaknesses that plagued national planning elsewhere (Caiden Gerald and Jung Yong-Duck, 1985, p. 24) as that country had the benefit of a committed leadership with uncommon dedication to fulfil the tremendous hunger for the economic progress of their countrymen during 1962-86 to realise the 'Korean Miracle'

Role of State in India's Development

Indian State is conditioned by pulls and pressures with little control over the outcome of development. Every plan is crisis-prone. The Planning Commission followed the Government's need to trim its sails to various winds of public and group option (Hanson,1969, p.185).

Further, in the Indian planning process, there are shortfalls in many sectors partly to lack of realism and largely for want of seriousness (Hanson, 1969, pp. 179 and 189). Indian Plans dwell at length on vague ideological issues, waste time in preparing futile perspective plans without any effort at identifying their effectiveness to the attainment of Plan objectives. The Plans are silent when considerations of growth clash with equity (Mahajan, 1987, pp.741-2). Imaginary hurdles stand in the way of an efficient administration and Central funds not allocated but only talked about (Minhas, 1972, pp. 41-2).

The Indian Planners have been unable to meaningfully change the focus of their work, which is largely due to the political compulsions and administrative constraints inhibiting the State at the macro-level. The style of the governing of the independent nation has been what it used to be in the colonial days (Desai, 1979, pp.160-7). "Every time basic structural changes when suggested, used to be defeated, whether it was the Dutt Committee in 1969-70, or the Narasimhan Committee in 1983-84. The bureaucracy and those in political authority agree on the negation; for they both benefit as a result (Paranjape, 1988, p. 2357).

The Nehru era in its initial stage, perhaps rightly addressed itself to promote national integration to bring about national unity. Coming to the economic reforms, despite leadership's unquestioned commitment, the success has been limited. Nehru wanted to build up and guide India towards socialism but elimination of inequalities could not succeed. It is rather difficult to defend Nehru or praise him for his performance (Kanwar Lal, 1970, p. 260).

Though the later Prime Minister, Indira Gandhi, pushed through many reformist programmes of a radical nature, she too could not succeed in making the structure work towards the realisation of the economic goals and programmes. In this context, the findings of the Public Accounts Committee of the Parliament on the activities of the Planning Commission in its 1981-82 Report are noteworthy:

"Not a single project in the irrigation, power and flood control sectors has been completed within the scheduled time and within the estimates....Most projects showed cost overruns of 500 per cent or more and the work done despite enormously increased estimates was 66 per cent against a 100 per cent expenditure" (Ram Gopal, 1986, pp. 299-322).

Indian productive systems at different stages of development are not equally responsive to State policies and direction. The ruling party could not inspire the common masses to participate in the programme of national reconstruction. State economic policies were at variance with their avowed purposes, which resulted in the poor performance of State capitalism in India (Kotwal, O.P., 1979, pp. 43-5).

In India, the dominant doctrine of development relied exclusively on economic factors and neglected critical dimensions of administrative capability and the power structure of society. Governmental bureaucracy had to be the principal agent of change and it was culturally closer to the small group of local industrialists and landed gentry than to the bulk of poor people for whom the plans were supposedly formulated (Rajni Kothari, 1972, pp.1543-5). But the Indian State is constrained by the special features of its administrative and political system afflicting its initiatives at the implementation stage (Wade, 1985, p. 486). 'No doubt, there are good intentions, but only to be followed by inadequate pragmatism' (Veit, 1976, p. 347). Conflicting interest groups, both at the stage of formulation of policy and in its implementation, made a pathetic impact on the outcome (Bardhan, 1986, p. 74). Thus, the State in India, far from being a part of the solution to development, became a part of the problem (Singh Ranadhir, 1989, p. 725).

Though both Korea and India pinned their visions of transformation on State power, the 'strong-State' in Korea succeeded in realising its vision, while the Indian 'soft-State' could not make it. The small size of the country, homogeneity in culture and language made the task easy for the Korean State to play its role effectively in the development process. In India, the vast size of the country, greater diversity in religion, language, culture and regional squabbles limited the scope for the Indian State to pursue development goals with single-minded devotion as Korean military leadership could do. Further, the unitary character of the Korean State also made its task easy. In contrast, the federal character of the Indian State is filled with marked differences in perceptions between the Centre and the States; in the case of Korea, they were influenced by larger perspectives, while in India they were governed by local and intra-regional considerations, standing in the way of timely and effective implementation of the national economic policies.

Religion

In analysing the role of religion in relation to economic development, the focus must be on the religion as understood and practised by the masses rather than what is being written in scriptures. Viewed from this perspective, the six dimensions of religion[2] suggested by Ninian Smart (quoted by Bishop, 1987, p. 7), particularly, the ritual, social and ethical have implications for strengthening or weakening the productive processes in a society.

Though Korea and India are characterised by religious pluralism, Confucianism and Hinduism are the dominant religions discussed in relation to economic development of Korea and India respectively.

Confucianism and Korean Economic Development

Confucianism is designed to produce a peaceful, harmonious and well-ordered society, each individual functioning according to his or her capacity. The supreme virtue stems from 'ren', variously translated as 'goodness', 'love', 'benevolence', 'human-heartedness', or 'humanity' (Smith, 1987, pp. 273 and 275).

Neo-Confucianism stressed on personal morality, filial piety and social responsibility of the Government (Smith, 1981, p. 276). Chu-Hsi (1130-1200 A.D.) modified traditional Confucianism by giving it moral authority and wide ethical interpretation[3] (Bun, Woong Kim, 1976. p. 270).

Though formalities of hierarchical social structure and centralised bureaucracy had attracted the Koryo Dynasty (particularly, An Hyang 1243-1306) that ruled Korea (Bun Woong Kim, 1976, p.270; Henthorn, 1971, p. 130), during the Yi Dynasty (1392-1910) many schools accepted the basic doctrine, though divided on various matters of emphasis and interpretation (Yang and Henderson, 1959, p. 259).

Effect of Confucianism on Korean people is characterised by: (1) hierarchical view of life, (2) authoritarianism on the part of the ruling class, (3) corresponding submissiveness on the part of the ruled, (4) status-oriented consciousness, and (5) well ordered family (Bun Woong Kim, 1976, p. 271).

According to many, Confucianism is an important contributing factor for the Korean achievement as Confucian values permeate Korean society and have had some degree of influence on the development phenomena (Moskowitz, 1982, p. 87). As against this dominant view (Kim Sun-Ung, 1988, pp.76-92), people give credit to the pragmatic attitude of the Koreans rather than to Confucianism. The most important socio-cultural factor that can be considered to be involved in economic development in Korea is the downfall of the traditionally oriented upper class, after which the society was more favourable to the new ideas to bring about change (Lee, Man-gap, 1984, pp. 110-11). It was only when Korea had shed much of its Confucian heritage, modern economic growth took a forward plunge (Woronoff, 1983, p. 81).

As a set of social practices, Korean Confucianism could be lauded for a sense of organisation, a respect for authority, an acceptance of discipline and hard work or love of learning (Woronoff, 1983, p. 70; Kim Sun-Ung, 1988, p. 84), while it certainly did not accord status as a function of economic value or usefulness (Woronoff, 1983, p. 21).

Confucianism remained as an elitist religion and was tolerated during the Japanese rule despite its unproductive nature (Han, Woo-Keun, 1974, p. 470; Lee, Man-gap, 1984, p. 60). However, there was (in fact) cultural co-existence of Confucianism with the religion of the masses, along with the tendency "at society's lower levels to pattern their behaviour after that of aristocrats" (Brandt, 1971,

p. 117). There are some who say that Korean masses have not taken Confucianism seriously (Yi, Hae-Yong and Woo-Keun Han, 1982, p. 168).

An understanding of the evidence in the area shows that positive features of Confucianism in facilitating Korean growth process should not be ignored, while overplaying of Confucian ethic is also equally unwarranted (Woronoff, 1983, p.70). Moreover, it is also not desirable to interpret traditional Korean society from the Confucian perspective alone (Yi Hae-Yong and Woo-Keum Han, 1982, p.177) as it is not so much the 'positive features of Confucianism' *per se,* but the efforts of the Government to make use of the positive features of Confucianism in mobilising Korean masses towards developmental goals.[4] This gets reflected in the work ethos of its people who contributed a lot to achieve development. Koreans are rated high in work ethos, *i.e.,* effort propensity, social efficiency capital and rationality (*see* Alam, 1985, pp. 251-54) .

Hinduism and Indian Economic Development

Opinions diverge on the role of Hinduism in relation to Indian economic development. However, rigidity of caste system among Hindus assumes ascriptive status-orientation, without scope for social mobility, and is considered as a stumbling block to economic development via curbing occupational mobility and stiffling individual initiative. It tends to limit loyalty of individuals, limiting community feeling among people of a region or a nation (Kapp, 1963, p. 64; Foster, 1973, pp.126-8). Others consider its changing character and flexibility, implying thereby that it is not an obstacle to economic development (Nijhawan, 1975, pp. 35 and 36).

Those emphasising the inhibiting effect of Hindu ethics on economic development refer to the low priority given to *Artha* compared to *Dharma* and *Moksha* which promote other worldly values inimical to development (*see* Nijhawan, 1975, p. 30). Even the concept of *Dharma* implies the preservance of the rigid social structure which laid down the pattern of behaviour in every possible contingency without any freedom of choice to the individual

(Dandekar, R.N., 1989, p. 10), even though there is nothing in Hinduism which impedes progress, democracy, science and material prosperity (Murthy, K.S., 1965, p. 81) and *Panchatantra's* attribution that most evils and vices are for want of money (*see* Nijhawan, 1975, p. 30).

On what is written in scriptures, there is total absence of consensus.[5] Most studies do not lend credence to the view that Hindu culture as it is practised by masses or elite is inimical to growth.[6] "Hindu morality is contextual and not absolute ... the self sometimes expands to fuse with the cosmos; but in another moment, it completely withdraws itself from it" (Tripathy, 1988, pp. 321-2). Hindu tradition is resilient and it adjusts itself to any circumstance (Dandekar, 1989, p. 12).

Unlike Confucianism, Hinduism "possesses no single founder, no central doctrine, no unified organization, hierarchy or mission of teaching. Its essential carriers were the bonds of family, caste and village" (King, 1987, p. 186). On the practical side also, Hinduism is immensely diverse, with its local, regional and sectarian traditions.

For Hindus, the essential self of man is in no way involved in doings of this phenomenal world. Life in this world is accordingly to be looked upon merely as a bridge over which, one has, of necessity, to pass in order to reach one's ultimate destination, but on which it would be unwise to build one's house ... However, *Dharma* connotes that while pursuing the 'ideal', man should not overlook the 'actual' (Dandekar, 1989, p. 8). On the philosophical plane, Hinduism aims at securing the material and the spiritual development alike. It prescribes for everybody a set of rites, social practices and ethics. However, adoption of beliefs, practices and rituals of high ranking castes is termed as 'Sanskritisation,'[7] (Srinivas, 1972, p. 6).

Hinduism as a Set of Social Practices

The most important of the Hindu *Dharma Sastras*, 'Law of Manu' (200-100 B.C.) describes human life in terms of *varnashrama dharma*, according to which there is no universal *dharma* for all; and each individual's duty depends on one's *varna* (class) and *ashrama* . Though *varna* is a four-fold one at its ideational form governing Hindu social practices, the system has been undergoing change in its functions, rituals and social practices, but the core of it continues to be intact as evident from the prevalence of endogamous marriages (*see* King, 1987, p. 192).

Even if "Hinduism does not disparage money and hard work necessary for it, Hindu ethos is against the capitalistic spirit as understood by 'the temper of single-minded concentration on pecuniary gain' (Max Weber) and is adverse to take it as the supreme end. Economic ends must be achieved not only lawfully but morally" (Murthy, 1965, pp. 83-4). Further, even if "caste has nothing to do with real Hinduism, just as racism has nothing to do with Christianity or Communism" (Murthy, 1965, p. 69), the fact remains that Indian planners did recognise that the rigidities of caste system act as barriers to economic growth, though nothing much has been done by the Government of India to overcome these obstacles.[8]

Education

The level of education, the skills and discipline it fosters and the optimal utilization of the trained human resources become crucial in economic growth. "The significance of education in accelerating the development process by high labour efficiency, greater factor mobility, increased specialization, imbibing values that facilitate economic change are widely recognized despite disagreements on the means and strategies to be followed to make investments in human capital subserve development needs" (Meier, 1984, pp. 610-4).

While there are many who stress on Education's positive contribution (Mason *et al.*, 1980, p. 366; Moskowitz, 1982, 67), there are some who view that educational development was not that high when economic breakthrough occurred in Korea in sixties.

Role of Education in Korea

"What the Korean model proves, if anything, is that a country can progress economically even without a proper educational system" (Woronoff, 1983, pp. 224-5). Korea had an educational system even in the pre-colonial period. During the period of Yi dynasty (A.D. 1400-70), education was promoted by establishing 'Sodang', (Elementary school), 'Hak tang' (Secondary school) and 'Hyanggyo' (Correspondence institutions) though these are mostly limited to 'Yangban' (aristocratic class). However, the 'Chungin' (middle class) were trained in technical and scientific subjects and in foreign languages by the Government to meet with the administrative needs and large numbers were trained for the hereditary posts of petty Government functionaries" (Han Woo Keun, 1974, pp. 239-40).

The educational reforms initiated by the Japanese, after Konghwa Treaty of February 1876, also helped spread of education to wider sections of Korean society. Disregarding the Korean feelings, Japanese abolished the old examination system which laid emphasis on Confucian classics and replaced it with new subjects. They also started conducting examinations in scientific and technical subjects and abolished class system for recruitment to Government posts. Further, constitutional changes adopted in January 1896 facilitated sending the talented abroad for higher studies. These provisions made it obligatory for the Government to appoint people on the basis of merit only without regard to their social status. These measures facilitated percolation of education into a wider society.

The role played by Korean youth in the eradication of illiteracy as part of their struggle against Japanese imperialism helped spread of education among the Korean masses. Korean students started teaching Hangul (the Korean alphabet), since 1928, to spread literacy in the countryside during their summer vacations and continued their efforts uninterruptedly, till it was stopped by the Japanese. Nonetheless, Koreans also managed to attend private universities in Japan. That by 1930, around 3,000 Koreans obtained university degrees from Japan. The Farm-Household Survey of 1859 indicates spread of education over eight provinces of the present day South Korea. In 1938, only nine per cent of the rural families were illiterate (Ban *et al.*, 1980, p. 312),

Post-Independence Education Development in Korea

Korea did introduce six-year primary education as compulsory in 1949 itself. By 1950, enrolment ratio at the primary level improved to 83 per cent and attained near full enrolment by 1960 (Table 3.1). Though not spectacular, the enrolment at secondary level doubled from 16 per cent in 1950 to 34 per cent in 1965 and 41 per cent by 1970.

Table 3.1 : Education in Korea-1950 to 1986 (select indicators)

Year	*Enrolment ratio*					*Percentage of students reading vocational course at school level*	*No. of students reading vocational course at (Junior) college level*
	Literacy rate	*Primary School*	*Middle School*	*Secondary School*	*Higher Education*		
	(1)	(2)	(3)	(4)	(5)	(6)	(7)
1950	—	83.0	—	16.0	—	—	—
1960	71	96.0	—	29.0	5	—	—
1965	—	95.1	54.3	34.0	6	40.43	7,263
1970	—	97.0	66.0	41.0	—	46.58	23,440
1975	91	97.3	77.2	63.0	10	42.29	58,500
1980	93	97.9	95.8	—	—	45.04	151,199
1985	—	98.6	99.2	91.0	26	41.15	242,114
1986	—	98.8	99.5	95.0	33	40.53	250,652

Source: 1. Column 1 and 5, World Bank, various issues of World Development Reports;
2. Column 2, 3, 4, 6 and 7: 1950 and 1960 data from Hasan and Rao, 1979, p. 151; 1965-86 from EPB, 1984 and 1988.

In addition to the progress in the general education, reforms introduced in school system by President Park since 1962 helped Korea meet the technical manpower requirements of a growing industrial economy. There were several reforms initiated in the school system which were against the tradition, even at the cost of facing accusations of turning the Centres of learning into mere tools of development. Even though the educational system did not appeal to the liberal academics, it helped meet the requirements of a growing industrial economy. The number of vocational high schools, which were around 44 per cent of all high schools in 1964, increased to 57 per cent by 1972. The number of students attending vocational junior colleges also increased almost ten times, *i.e.*, from 4,374 in 1964 to 41,374 by 1972.

The vocational schools also specialised in specified trades like communications, electronics and agriculture and number of vocational colleges and universities were permitted to increase enrolment of students into engineering, medicine, electronics and aeronautics, while putting ceiling limits on others. The companies trained the students without any restriction on their staying with the company after training. All these, apart from the skills that were imparted to thousands of Koreans through military training, helped bring in discipline, cooperation and devotion to work in the labour-force.

Educational attainment of employed population by occupation during 1960-70 can be seen in the percentage of those without education among professional and technical workers declining from 3.2 in 1960 to 1.3 by 1970. Nearly 33.5 per cent of the professional and technical workers had higher education by 1960, *i.e.*, on the eve of Korea's launching of development effort, and their share increased to 55.6 per cent by 1970. Similar change for the better was also evident in respect of the workers employed in production activities. The percentage of illiterates among production workers declined from 26.2 in 1960 to 9.0 by 1970 (Hasan and Rao, 1979, pp.154-5).

The index of labour quality taking into account the position of workers by educational attainment with 1972 as the base is 90.91 in 1960 as Korea was in a better position to usher in economic growth with increased labour productivity (Kim and Park, 1985, pp. 117-20). Till sixties the formal education was ill-equipped both under the Japanese colonial days and under Syngman Rhee regime. Moreover, there was the impact of military training in meeting the skills of the Korean work-force (Woronoff, 1983, pp. 225-8).

An overview of the evidence on role of education in Korean economic development shows that the positive development in education during the pre- and post-Independence period, particularly till seventies, as well as the compulsory military training enabled the Korean youth to acquire technical skills and scientific knowledge in meeting the growing needs of industrial economy and furthering its growth process.

Education in India Prior to Independence

During the colonial period, not only education was neglected and even the limited efforts at promoting education had no national direction. Public expenditure on education in India was 0.2 per cent of the National Income in the Nineteenth Century and never above 0.5 per cent in the Twenticth Century and a too small share of this small share was spent on primary education (Dharmakumar, 1982, p. 937).

The poor investments in education resulted in the decline of literacy during the colonial period with only six per cent literates at the end of the Nineteenth Century. Though during 1901-31, literacy increased by 1½ times, it has not spread to wider population. The percentage of literates among the population aged 10 and above, which was around 6.2 in 1901, increased to 9.2, by 1931 enabling only 10 per cent of the population to read and write (Petrov, 1985, pp. 229-32). The low percentage of students in the total population of India which was around 0.010 in 1871, 0.013 in 1881 and 0.054 in 1941 was far lower than the levels obtained at the starting point of economic development during the Meiji era (1868-1912) of Japan, which was 0.073 in 1881 and 0.140 in 1911 (Heston, 1982, p. 411). "Of the total number of students entering schools in 1945-46, only 40 per cent reached Class IV and the expenditure on the remaining 60 per cent was largely wasted. The experiment of compulsion had not made much progress. The absence of adequate facilities for technical and vocational education resulted in a much larger number of students going in for general education than was justified by the requirements of the country or the tastes and aptitudes of the people" (Chopra, 1975, p. 141).

The system of education obtained before Independence had no national direction. It was by and large mechanical, emphasising memory work. The schools were ill-equipped. In the arts and science colleges, the methods of teaching were hardly conducive to the development of a critical and cultivated mind. The facilities for research at the post-graduate level were meagre. Some reforms had partly begun at the elementary stage without affecting other stages (Chopra, 1975, p.140).

The low literacy and scarcity of skilled labour, because of

limited social investment in human capital had adverse effects on industrialisation in the colonial period. In India, there was limited social investment in human capital. It sharply restricted the spread of even simple literacy, let alone technical training. This slowed down the rate at which superior kinds of labour could be reproduced and also inhibited the rate at which technological innovation could occur (Morris and Luce, 1982, p. 653). Because all workers were illiterate, all tasks of organisation were made very hard (Morris and Luce, 1982, p. 665).

On the eve of Independence, India was in an unenviable position on the educational front with low levels of literacy, high dropout rate, and total neglect of vocational/technical education.

Post-Independence Development in Indian Education

Though the Indian Constitution did not declare education as a Fundamental Right, it was serious about eradication of illiteracy. Article 45 of the Constitution provides for a free and compulsory education for children until they complete the age of 14 years. Certain efforts were made to promote education during the four decades after Independence, number of schools have more than doubled and there was a five-fold increase in the number of universitites. Qualitative improvement along with expansion of educational facilities was aimed. Since 1976, through a Constitutional amendment, education was made the joint responsibility of the Central and State Governments. In the Seventh Plan period, efforts were made in the direction of universal elementary education and eradication of illiteracy in the age-group 15-35 by 1990. Programmes like 'Operation Blackboard' were announced. These were all announcements without proper realisation.

The progress of education in terms of literacy levels and enrolment ratios at different levels are presented in Table 3.2.

The Indian State could not succeed in achieving free and compulsory education by 1960 as originally conceived. The data provided in Table 3.2 are at variance with the estimates made by scholars in the field. In 1981, John Kurien (1981, pp. 1609,

Table 3.2 : Education in India 1950 to 1986 (Select Indicators)

Year	Enrolment ratio					Percentage of students reading science at University level
	Literacy rate	*Primary School 6-11 years*	*Middle School 11-14 years*	*Secondary School 14-17 years*	*Higher Education 17-23 years*	
	(1)	(2)	(3)	(4)	(5)	(6)
1950-51	16.7	42.6	12.7	5.30	0.8	37.8
1960-61	24.0	62.4	22.5	1.06	1.8	28.9
1968-69	29.5[1]	78.1	33.5	18.30	3.3	23.0
1978-79	—	81.6	38.0	18.80	4.9	18.0
1979-80	36.2[1]	82.7	39.4	—	—	24.0
1982-83[2]	—	87.2[3]	43.9[3]	24.6	—	23.4
1983-84[2]	—	91.8	48.4	32.5	—	22.7
1984-85[2]	—	94.1	49.8	32.4	—	21.9
1985-86	—	93.09	52.01	—	—	21.5

Note: 1. Figures stand for 1971 and 1981 respectively
2. Figures are provisional includes below degree level institutions also.
3. Percentage is based on projected population for 1983.

Source : Government of India, 1987, pp. 11 and 73.

1616-17) observed that the enrolment ratios for standards I to V (6 to 11 years), show that only 32.7 per cent of the students in this age group were enrolled by 1950-51 and increased to 62.6 per cent by 1975-76. At the secondary level, that is, standard VI to VIII (11 to 14 years), it increased from 7.0 per cent to 21.7 per cent by 1975-76. About efforts at implementing universal elementary education, John Kurien observes: 'It will be impossible to achieve universal elementary education for many decades to come. Certainly, it will be impossible in the Twentieth Century. It is relatively easy to provide schooling facilities, but the more difficult problem remains to ensure children enrol and attend school regularly for a few years continuously'.

Without belittling the efforts at eradicating illiteracy in post-Independent India, it is to be noted that even by 1981, only one-third of the population can read and write; the written word continues to be out of reach of two-thirds of the Republic's citizens. On the territory of today's India in 1650, there were probably more than 70 million illiterates; in 1750, more than 100 million; in 1850, more than 150 million; in 1901, evidently approximately 230 million; in 1961, 334 million; in 1971, 387 million; and in 1981,

436 million illiterates. From 1951 to 1961 alone, the number of illiterates in India increased by 30 million; in 1961-71 by 53 million, and in 1971-81 by 49 million. It is obvious from these figures that illiteracy in India today is not being eliminated swiftly enough (Petrov, 1985, pp. 234-5).

The possibilities of eradicating illiteracy in India even by the turn of this Century are bleak is evident from the perspectives of the Eighth Five-Year Plan which notices that an investment of Rs. 46,000 crores have to be allotted for primary education alone to eradicate illiteracy by the end of the Plan period and this amount is equivalent to the total planned era up to the Seventh Five-Year Plan and as such was given up because of the problem of resource constraints.

Coming to the content of education, no significant status of technical orientation at the secondary and higher levels of education has been existing in India even in sixties.[9] The percentage of those enrolled for technical subjects at higher education level during sixties was far lower than other developing countries like Sri Lanka, Taiwan, Philippines, Malaysia and that of Japan in 1910. In India, proportions of those enrolling into technical subjects at secondary level is 3.8 and for those at higher education level it is 10.1. These are far lower compared to South Korea, where 13 per cent at secondary level and 28 per cent at higher education level enrolled into technical subjects in 1962 (Bhatawdekar, 1972, p.1798).

The Seventh Five-Year Plan contains the observation that although the Indian education scene since Independence has been characterised by massive quantitative expansion at all levels, it is still to undergo the kind of transformation envisaged in the national policy. It is faced with a staggering backlog, the level of illiteracy is as high as 63 per cent to achieve universal elementary education as enjoined by the Constitution. There will be need to enrol 50 million more children; vocationalisation of secondary education has, yet to make a headway;[10] there is very significant pressure on the higher education system and a decline in the standards of quality (Planning Commission, Vol. II, 1985, p. 252).

Since Independence, the stress has been on higher education rather than on imparting technical skills at secondary levels. This is evident from the fact that of the total men workers, only one per cent of the work-force had a technical diploma; those with technical degrees formed two per cent of the total work-force (Government of India, 1988, pp. 404-7). Apart from technical skills, even in terms of mere literacy, the work-force in India is far lower than South Korean work-force. The percentage of work-force in India with primary and secondary education in 1981 (45) was lower than the literacy levels of South Korean work-force in 1960 (52.8).

This subscribes to the view that it has been seriously contemplated to alter the legacy of colonial educational system inherited at the time of Independence.

Till seventies most of our University courses are dominated by ancient and academic trivia and theory. This is true also of the professional courses. Work in the farm, factory, workshop or in the field of operation is at present only nominal and ornamental. When could this be reversed both for teachers and the students? (Kaul, 1972, p.1651). This holds good to describe the situation prevailing even till mid-1980s.

Scientific education continues to be fettered by the colonial exploitation (Bhattacharya, 1972, p.1838). There was reluctance on the part of the educational planners to change the Indian tradition of having more and more B.As. This view was forcefully expressed at the Central Advisory Board of Education, the country's top policy-making body in education, while examining the draft Fifth Five-Year Plan proposals (Malcolm Adiseshaiah, 1972, p. 2106).

The distortions in the educational planning, in not tuning it to the developmental needs of the country, through eradication of illiteracy and development of skilled manpower, are not due to the low percentage of GNP expenditure on education but because of the failure to conceive a right mix-up of levels of primary, secondary and higher education in accordance with the stage of development and needs of the country. It can be seen that Japan by investing only around three per cent of her GNP on education in 1910, a situation similar to the one faced by many developing countries like India, could achieve a stage of self-sustained growth largely because of her emphasis on universalisation of primary education, technical bent to secondary education, expansion of vocational education and promoting higher education in technical subjects as well as limiting enrolment at higher education level. The percentage of enrolment at higher education level of the corresponding age-group was 1.0 in Japan in 1910, whereas it is 3.7 in India and 5.6 in South Korea around Sixties, (Bhatawdekar,1972, pp. 1793-1801).

The Indian educational system is in essence still colonial; has over the years come into pressures for corresponding higher education; has almost forgotten the Constitutional mandate for the spread of literacy and primary education; and has failed to perform any policy for the creation of intermediate skills that are still in scarce supply in the country. The result has been a bloating of the ranks of the educated unemployed on the one hand and a very large mass of wholly illiterate and unskilled people on the other (Rajni Kothari, 1972, p.1549).

It can thus be noticed that the educational system inherited by India is not only devoid of some of the best elements of the Japanese system incorporated into South Korea, nor the post-Independence education reforms geared so much to make education a hand-maid of industry as Park Chung. Hee has done in Korea in early sixties.

In India, the heritage of colonialism is very much dominant in the spheres of literacy and education. It could not yet by any means be done away with. Mass level illiteracy complicated the resolution of such vital tasks as raising productivity and mastering modern technology (Petrov, 1985, p. 242).

SECTION-II

ECONOMIC FACTORS

The economic factors examined to understand the differential transformation in the two countries are: (i) structural changes in Agriculture, (ii) role of Agriculture in economic growth, (iii) terms of trade, and (iv) growth of non-Agriculture sector and rural non-Agriculture employment.

Structural Changes in Agriculture

Structural reforms in agriculture are considered as a pre-condition for technical progress. In the words of Parson "increasing man's control over physical nature is only half of the problem of agricultural development; the other half is increasing the effectiveness of man's participation in the rural economy by measures which enhance his abilities as well as by arrangements which are provided for him to use those abilities" (UNO, 1951).

Agrarian Structure on the Eve of Korean Independence

On the eve of liberation from Japanese domination in 1945, Korea inherited a highly inegalitarian agrarian structure with oppressive tenancy. "In 1930, 3.6 per cent of the landlords owned 66.6 per cent of paddy fields and 49.1 per cent of dry land and controlled owner-tenant-farmers who constituted 77.5 per cent of total agricultural household population" (Shin Yong-ha, 1971, p.1).

The inegalitarian character of the agrarian structure could be seen from the fact that in 1945, a small minority of the landlord class, accounting for a mere one per cent of the rural households, enjoyed little more than one-fourth of the cultivated land, while nearly two-thirds of the rural households were left with just, one-tenth of the land (Table 3.3).

Table 3.3 : Distribution of Farm-Households and Area by Size of Cultivated Land, Korea 1937-1960

(In Percentages)

Year	Below 0.3 ha	0.3 to 0.5 ha	0.5 to 1.0 ha	1.0 to 2.0 ha	2.0 to 3.0 ha	3.0 and above	Total
			Farm Households				
1937	—	48.8	27.6	16.6	—	7.0	100
1945	—	72.1	—	23.8	—	4.1	100
1955	19.0	24.1	31.1	20.1	5.5	0.2	100
1960	19.7	23.2	30.1	20.7	6.0	0.3	100
			Cultivated Area				
1945	—	10.4	—	40.0	—	26.4	100
1955	5.8	12.2	29.2	35.9	15.9	1.0	100
1960	5.3	11.4	27.9	36.9	17.3	1.2	100

Note : ' —'Indicates non-availability of Data.
Source : Ban *et al*., (1980, p.294-6).

The problem of tenancy was also very acute, involving significant numbers as well as considerable area (Table 3.4). In

1945, tenant farm-households formed around 86 per cent of the total farm households. Nearly 67 per cent of the cultivated area was under tenancy.

The terms and conditions governing tenancy were also very oppressive with high degree of insecurity and oppressive rents. As about the tenancy situation during the Japanese period; only in 60 per cent of the cases, contracts were made for one year (Lee, Woo-Jae, 1974, p. 66). Though the methods of rent fixation varied, rents formed 55 to 60 per cent of the gross produce and more than 90 per cent of it was collected in kind during the colonial period (Shin, Yong-Ha, 1971. pp. 5-6).

Table 3.4 : Trends in Land Tenancy in Korea 1945-1960

Year	*Farm Households in thousands*			*Cultivated Area in thounsad hectares*		
	Total farm H.H	*Tenant H.H*	*Percentage of Tenant H.H*	*Total Area*	*Area under Tenancy*	*Percentage of Area under Tenancy*
1945	1,999	1,723	86.2	2,207	1,407	66.7
1960	2,329	615	26.4	2,025	273	13.5

Source : Pak, Ki-Hyuk, 1983, p. 15.

Thus, on the eve of Liberation from Japanese rule, Korea inherited a highly inegalitarian agrarian structure, with a system of oppressive tenancy.

Agrarian Reforms and Structural Change in Korean Agriculture

The change from semi-feudalistic land ownership into one based on the principle of land-to-the-tiller was ushered in by the Farm Land Reform Law on June 21, 1948 in Korea.

Unlike in many cases, where such reforms got initiated with reluctance and allowed to fail for want of political will, the Korean experiment in land reforms is a unique example outside the Communist World. Not only the ceiling limit was fixed at a relatively low level of three hectares; but even the compensation paid was also low. It was fixed at 1.2 times the gross value of produce through an amendment to the New Land Reforms Act of 1949. Even this was paid in Government bonds payable in terms of rice, not in cash. The Government's concern for keeping its promise of providing control over land to the tillers, and the weakened position of the landlord class, which mostly identified itself with the Japanese, helped effective implementation of these radical reforms.

The land reform programme designed and carried on mainly to achieve an equitable distribution of farm land, adopting a strict land-to-the-tiller policy, can be considered as a success. These reforms transformed the Korean agrarian structure from one dominated by landlord class to one of peasant proprietorship. This is evident from nearly two-fold increase in the share of those owning around 0.5 hectare and less during 1945 and 1955, and sharp fall in the share of the landlord class. It declined from 26.4 per cent in 1945 to one per cent by 1955, in a short span of just one decade (Table 3.3). As a result of this, the Korean rural society became more equitable, more democratic and more egalitarian, though it is not free from shortcomings with regard to tenancy[11] (Pak, Ki-Hyuk, 1983, p. 11).

With respect to tenancy also, the achievements are remarkable. The percentage of area under tenancy has declined from 66.7 in 1945 to 13.5 by 1960 and the tenants among the farm households declined from 86.2 per cent to 26.4 per cent. However, for want of follow-up, tenancy began to increase from mid-fifties. Some of its oppressive features like insecurity and higher rents have emerged over time.[12]

Thus, Korea had the advantage of an equitable agrarian structure that facilitated effective functioning of rural institutions in promoting agricultural growth, a rare feature in many developing countries.

Agrarian Structure on the Eve of Indian Independence

The colonial heritage of agrarian structure of India is no better than what Korea inherited from the Japanese. It was even worse with an increasing class of landless agricultural labour. It is difficult to clearly depict the agrarian structure in a vast country like India. The Indian agrarian structure prior to Independence was equally inegalitarian, with a small number enjoying a disproportionate share of agricultural land, at the expense of a substantial class of small peasants who were eking out their livelihood on fragmented holdings (Table 3.5), and a large army of landless agricultural labour, whose living conditions were worse than small peasants. The area under tenancy was also high in 1950.

The tenurial conditions were also much worse with a large number of intermediaries between the State and the tiller of the land in the Zamindari areas which covered nearly one-half of the country at the time of Independence. Even in Ryotwari areas, though legally a direct relationship between the State and the landholders existed it was not free from intermediaries and exploitative tenurial conditions with no security of tenure (Appu, P.S., 1974, pp.70-1).

The structure of ownership holdings in 1953-54 and the share of tenant holdings in operational holdings affirm the above observations (Tables 3.5 and 3.6).

Table 3.5 : Distribution of Rural Households and Area owned by size of owned Land–India

(In Percentages)

Year	*Marginal (less than 1.0 ha.)*	*Small (1.01-2.02 ha.)*	*Semi-Medium 2.03-4.04 ha.)*	*Medium (4.05-10.12 ha.*	*Large (10.13 ha. and above)*	*Total*
			Rural Households			
1953-54	60.76	13.66	12.87	9.21	3.50	100
1961-62	60.06	15.16	12.86	9.07	2.85	100
1971-72	62.62	15.49	11.94	7.83	2.12	100
1982	66.64	14.70	10.78	6.45	1.42	100
			Owned Area			
1953-54	6.31	10.46	19.22	29.74	34.27	100
1961-62	7.59	12.40	20.54	31.23	28.24	100
1971-72	9.76	14.68	21.92	30.73	22.91	100
1982	12.22	16.49	23.38	29.83	18.07	100

Source : NSS, (1961, p. 13; 1987, p. 13).

Table 3.6 : Percentage of Operational Holdings with Leased-in Area and Leased-in Area to Operated Area—India

(In percentages)

Year	*Holdings*	*Leased in Area*
	Rural	
1953-54 (NSS 8th round)	39.85	20.34
1960-61 (" 17th round)	23.47	10.70
1970-71 (" 26th round)	25.18	10.57
1981-82 (" 37th round)	14.70	7.18

Source: 1. NSS, (1961, p.18).
2. Sarvekshana, (1988, p. 29).

Agrarian Reform—Indian Experience

Prior to Independence also, the ruling party, Congress was seized of the defective agrarian structure and exploitative relationships. It advocated policies for abolition of *Zamindari* system, conferring ownership rights to tenants and imposition of ceilings on land holdings.

The first set of agrarian reforms, focused attention on abolition of intermediaries and to bring tenancy reforms aimed at ensuring fair rent, security of tenure and conferring ownership rights on tenants. The successful implementation of *Zamindari* reforms, helped abolition of the system by mid-fifties. It facilitated acquisition of 173 million acres of land involving a compensation of Rs. 530.60 crores.

However, this was not the case with respect to tenancy reforms initiated in mid-fifties and ceilings law of early sixties. The tenancy reforms resulted in large-scale eviction of tenants as is evident from the decline of the area under tenancy (Table 3.6). As about the effectiveness of early tenancy reforms in 1957-58, Dantwala comments : "Both official and non-official opinion accept the fact that a large number of tenants pay much higher rents than those prescribed by Law. As for the security of the tenure, there have been more evictions and changes of tenants during the years following the tenancy legislation than in the previous period in recent history" (Cited by Parthasarathy, 1989, p. 150).

The ceilings legislation prior to 1972, with family as a unit with higher ceiling limits, wide range of exemptions and wide publicity preceding the legislation failed to serve the purpose. The ceiling legislation prior to 1972 was aptly described by Parthasarathy (1989, p. 151) as "a legislation without political will". This gets reflected in the absence of any notable shifts in the control over land among different size groups of farms (Table 3.5). "In the Nehru era, the transformation of agrarian relations did not proceed very far, the elimination of tax collecting intermediaries weakened the feudal structure without however destroying it. A section of cultivating peasants did get title to the land and consequently were able to accumulate more. But, on the whole, in the place of very large landlordism of the British period, there came into being a smaller, village level landlordism, a landlordism that was connected with money-lending" (DN, 1988, p. 2460).

The political compulsions since mid-sixties and early seventies resulted in moves towards more radical tenancy legislation as well as radical ceiling laws. While the pre-1972 reforms outlived their purpose at the conception stage itself; the so-called post-1972 reforms suffered for want of political will[13] on the part of leadership at the Centre and in majority of the States, with the exception of Kerala and West Bengal and to some extent, in conferring ownership rights on tenants in parts of Gujarat and Maharashtra (Tables 3.5 and 3.6). With regard to post-1972 ceilings legislation, "at best, the effect of radical legislation was a little more diffusion of ownership among top groups of the rural society" (Parthasarathy, 1989, p. 155).

Failure of land-reform laws in early seventies is seen by the Task Force on Agrarian Relations as: "With resolute and unambiguous political will, all other shortcomings and difficulties could have been overcome; in the absence of such a will, even minor obstacles become formidable road-blocks in the path of Indian land-reforms". That was in summer of 1983. "The statement remains substantially valid in the spring of 1986" (Bandyopadhyay, 1986, p. A 56). The NSS data on size-distribution of households and area owned (Table 3.5) show that structural inequalities in land-ownership continue to persist though little buttressed. During the 20-year period (1961-62 to 1982), the percentage of large holdings owning 10 hectares and above though declined from 2.85 to 1.42, there is no corresponding decline in their share of land owned; while this group owned 28.24 per cent of arable land in 1961-62, it declined to 18.07 per cent in 1982. At the other end of the spectrum, the proportion of marginal holdings owning one hectare and above, which are around 60 per cent in 1961-62, increased to 66 per cent by 1982 and their share in land from 7.59 per cent to 12.22.

With regard to tenancy, the NSS estimates show decline both in the percentage of operated holdings reporting leasing-in as well as area leased-in. The operational holdings reported leasing-in declined from 39.85 per cent during 1953-54 to 14.70 per cent by 1981-82 and that of leased-in area from 20.34 per cent to 7.18 per cent during the same period (Table 3.6). Though the 1981-82 estimates are considered under-estimates due to conceptual changes,[14] this decline in tenancy is partly due to resumption of land for personal cultivation by the absentee landlords as well as due to structural stagnation in the economy.

Successful implementation of structural reforms in Korea helped establishing an egalitarian rural society, which had a positive impact in facilitating successful functioning of rural institutions and in furthering agricultural growth. In India, the unsuccessful attempts to alter the agrarian structure had not only failed to exert such favourable impact on agricultural growth, but also stood in the way of successful working of rural institutions (*see* Chapter 4).

Role of Agriculture in Economic Growth

The Korean Case

"The importance of agriculture in different stages of economic growth is well recognised" (Rostow, 1960, p. 179). Agriculture plays a vital role in the pre-take-off and take-off stages, through increased food supplies, transfer of manpower to industry, increased capital accumulation and meeting the demand for industrial products. In Korea, the agricultural sector was 'pulled along' by a dynamic industrial sector and the "switching point" (when a natural resource-poor region switches from being a net exporter to being a net importer of agricultural commodities) preceded the "reversal point" (when the agricultural labour force begins to decline absolutely) by a substantial margin (Hayami and Ruttan, 1985, p. 32). Still agriculture's contributions to the Korean economic growth has been significant, particularly, in releasing labour to the capital-growing industrial sector. Given the rapidity and smoothness of sectoral transition in Korea in a short span of 30 years, the interaction between the agriculture and industrial sector is significant.

The share of agriculture in Korean GNP at 1970 constant prices declined from 45.5 per cent to 19.2 per cent by 1975. Its relatively small and declining contribution between 1955-77 was traced to the unfavourable factor endowments. This could be seen from the low per capita of land which was just 0.134 hectare (Ban, *et al.*, 1980, p. 17). Korean agriculture did not contribute more to overall economic growth, not because farmers failed to respond to stimuli or even because of Government's neglect, although prior to the seventies there was some of that, but because of a basically unfavourable factor endowment (Ban, 1980, p.13). As in the case of GNP, agriculture's contribution to capital accumulation via savings and taxes is also consistently insignificant and never exceeded 10 per cent of the total capital formation, particularly, after 1965. While farmers could save a respectable proportion of their income in sixties, but not in late fifties, relatively little of this income found its way into the modern sector, and have gone into household means, farm equipment and the like. Between fifties and sixties the farmers had a negative cash flow (Ban *et al.,* 1980, pp. 21-23); Moon, 1979, p. 165).

However, farmers were forced to sell grain between 1950 and 1960 at prices far below the cost of production.[15] Gap between the cost of production and the actual price received may imply the income transfer out of agriculture so that it might support low wage levels prevalent in the industrial sector (Moon, 1979, p. 163). There was massive transfer of around nine to 10 million labour force from farms to industries. Education of rural population is the most significant role Korean agriculture played in the process of economic growth (Moon, 1979, p.169; Ban. *et al.*, 1980, p. 24). Korean agriculture's major contribution to the growth process has to be seen in its ability to cope with rapid movement of labour out of agriculture since sixties and yet improving labour productivity without adverse mechanization (Ban *et al.* , 1980, pp.71-9). This is particularly significant as the movement of labour out of Korean agriculture since sixties was considered far higher than any other Third World country witnessed at a similar stage of development (Song Byung-Nak, 1980, p. 343). Korean agriculture also contributed to the growth process by containing food imports, particularly rice, since 1971 (*see* Braverman, *et al.*, 1983, p. 94).

The Indian Case

Indian agriculture continues to be a dominant sector in terms of numbers employed and in its contribution to GNP. Though its share in GNP declined over time, it was 37 per cent in 1982-83. It is also the main supplier of raw materials to important agro-based industries like jute, cotton, sugar and oilseeds. Its contribution to foreign exchange earnings is also not insignificant. The share of agriculture in exports is also significant though declined from around 42 per cent in 1965-66 to around 35 per cent by 1979-80. Both through exports and imports substitution, agriculture has contributed to the earnings and conservation of foreign exchange (Jakhade and Sundaram, 1986, p. 20). However, the relative contribution of rural savings to aggregate savings of household sector declined from 37 per cent in 1972-73 to 21 per cent in 1978-79. Indian agriculture's contribution to growth is limited via terms of trade favourable to agriculture till mid-seventies. This is in sharp contrast to Korea, where terms of trade were adverse to farmers almost till mid-seventies

As in Korea, Indian agriculture contributed to the growth process by containing food imports. The rate of growth of Indian agriculture at 2.5 per cent per annum since sixties is on par with that of Korea. But it must be noted that agricultural productivity per hectare of cropped land and per agricultural worker was far higher in Korea since fifties or earlier. The increase in value added both per hectare of cropped area and per agricultural worker is relatively higher in Korea compared to Andhra (Table 3.7). This is particularly striking in respect of value added per agricultural worker.

Domestic Terms of Trade and Agricultural Growth

Terms of trade refer to the number of units of non-agriculture goods which can be obtained by a farmer for one unit of agricultural goods. As terms of trade improve the farmer is induced to produce more and offer more marketable surplus to the market. But the income terms of trade depend not merely on price but also productivity.

Table 3.7 : Trends in Value of Agricultural Productivity in Korea and India

Year	*Korea (in '000 Won, 1970 prices)* Per hectare	*Korea (in '000 Won, 1970 prices)* Per worker	Year	*India (in rupees at 1970-71 prices)* Per hectare	*India (in rupees at 1970-71 prices)* Per worker
1953	198.4	50.8	1950-51	758	961
	(627)	(161)		(101)	(128)
1960	222.4	56.5	1960-61	885	953
	(704)	(179)		(118)	(127)
1970	292.7	93.7	1970-71	1056	1347
	(926)	(296)		(141)	(179)
1981	379.9	155.4	1980-81	1418	1606
	(1202)	(492)		(189)	(214)

Note : Figures in brackets are in U.S. dollars at 1970.
Exchange rates U.S. $ = 316 Won or 7.056 rupees.

Source : Korea 1953-70 Ban *et al.*, 1980, p. 77.
Details for Korea 1980 and India are computed based on the data presented in Chapter II of this study.

Yet it assumes significance as it reflects on incentives for production and income distribution between agriculture and non-agricultural sectors.

This issue of farm prices (Subba Rao, 1986, pp. 373-84) and whether or not the terms of trade moved in favour of agriculture is a much debated issue in India (*see* Mitra, 1977; Rath, 1985; Thamarajaskshi, 1969; Sidhu and Singh, 1979; Kahlan and Tyagi, 1980) compared to Korea.

Korean Experience

Korean agricultural price policy during fifties and sixties was marked by its concern for maintaining low prices for urban consumers, preventing wide seasonal fluctuations rather than maintaining an adequate price for farm product (Moon, 1977, p. 22). As a result, terms of trade for the farmer have been unfavourable throughout fifties and sixties except for one or two years. Yet Korean agricultural growth did not suffer during the period as policies were also oriented towards improvement in agricultural productivity.

However, there was a shift from compulsory levy on the farmers in fifties and sixties to open market purchases since seventies.

Further, the price at which government purchased in seventies exceeded the cost of production while it was less than the cost in fifties and sixties. Thus, the period 1970-80 was marked by shift in terms of trade in favour of agriculture (Table 3.8). This was also associated with a rapid rise in grain production. However, since eighties the situation again reverted back to the pre-seventies position because of mounting deficits both in Grain Management Fund and Fertilizer Fund on the one hand and growing burden on the urban consumers. The World Bank's Study (1983) on agricultural pricing policies in Korea noted that in 1979, fertilizer prices were about 20 per cent higher than international prices and fertilizer subsidies are really a tax on the farmer and a transfer to the fertilizer firms. Further it was observed that the subsidised prices of rice and barley are really a tax on the urban consumers with the rural and urban prices of rice approximately 65 per cent and 50 per cent respectively than the international prices (Braverman *et al.*, 1983, pp. 5-6; also *see* Anderson Kym, 1983, pp. 43-57 on Korean Fertilizer Policies).

Thus, the Korean policy prior to seventies reflected less reliance on terms of trade and more on non-price factors. The shift to price factors since seventies was to reduce the rural-urban income gap and also in recognition of the need for price incentives to promote grain production. Further, by this period the State was in a position to meet the subsidies on food prices for the urban people. By eighties however, the subsidies escalated and it was not considered desirable to promote high cost agriculture and the terms of trade shifted in agriculture.

Indian Experience

In India agricultural policies since 1950s are more guided by consideration of augmenting agricultural production to growing millions in the country. However, since mid-sixties a policy of minimum support and procurement prices for important agricultural commodities were fixed on the recommendations of the Central Agricultural Price Commission. Over time, there have been efforts to bridge the differences in the cost of production and minimum support or procurement price (Sidhu 1986, pp. 310-26).

The data on prices received and paid by the farmers and parity ratios for the period 1952-53 to 1983-84 estimated by Tyagi in 1986 (quoted by Bhalla G.S., 1987) are considered to examine the terms of trade in Indian Agriculture. The data show that the terms of trade were unfavourable to agriculture in the pre-green revolution period. However, agricultural sector enjoyed favourable terms of trade during 1965-66 to 1975-76 though it faced unfavourable situations since mid-seventies with an average ratio of 86.5 for the period 1975-76 to 1983-84 (Table 3.8).

Table 3.8: Indices of prices received and paid and Terms of Trade for Farmers in Korea and India. Korea (1980=100); India (Triennium ending 1971-73=100)

	Korea				India		
Year	*Prices received*	*Prices paid*	*Terms of Trade Col.1/2=100*	*Year*	*Prices received*	*Prices paid*	*Terms of Trade Col.4/5=100*
				1952-53 to 1963-64 Average	40.3	58.5	68.5
1966	8.1	9.0	90.0	1964-65	67.2	71.5	93.9
1967	9.3	10.3	90.3	1965-66	77.7	75.5	102.9
1968	10.9	12.3	88.6	1966-67	93.7	83.0	112.9
1969	12.4	13.5	91.9	1967-68	100.2	86.7	115.6
1970	14.7	15.6	94.2	1968-69	92.7	88.2	105.1
1971	17.8	17.8	100.0	1969-70	96.1	94.4	101.8
1972	21.7	20.4	106.4	1970-71	100.5	100.5	100.0
1973	24.1	22.3	108.1	1971-72	102.5	105.1	97.5
1974	31.6	30.0	105.3	1972-73	116.9	112.9	103.5
1975	39.2	37.1	105.7	1973-74	145.0	132.3	109.6
1976	47.7	46.3	105.2	1974-75	166.8	166.9	99.9
				Average	105.4	101.5	103.8
1977	56.8	54.2	104.8	1975-76	142.4	160.3	88.8
1978	74.0	70.5	105.0	1976-77	157.0	173.2	90.7
1979	82.1	80.2	102.4	1977-78	164.6	181.6	90.6
1980	100.0	100.0	100.0	1978-79	157.1	183.9	85.4
1981	128.2	128.5	99.8	1979-80	185.4	209.3	88.6
1982	137.1	144.3	95.0	1980-81	213.6	244.8	87.3
1983	140.3	156.2	89.8	1981-82	224.2	270.5	82.9
				1982-83	237.2	279.9	84.7
				1983-84	260.4	302.6	86.1
				Average	193.6	223.8	86.5

Source: South Korea, EPB, 1984, p. 201.
India, Bhalla, G.S. , 1987, p. 264-6.

The above analysis showed that Korea had succeeded in obtaining agricultural surplus for non-agricultural development in the early stage of development even while keeping the terms of trade unfavourable to agriculture. In the later stages of development when reduction of rural-urban income disparity and maintaining high rates of growth were needed State policy contributed to a shift in terms of trade in favour of agriculture. Thus, Korean policy in relation to terms of trade have been appropriate to stage of development. On the other hand, in Indian situation the requirements of self-reliance in foodgrain production along with the need for food security to large masses below poverty line both in rural and urban areas guided the price policy. The emphasis was more on subsidised inputs and minimum support prices rather than on terms of trade. In so far as the objective of the price and procurement policy has been to avert adverse consequences of severe droughts as in 1973-74, the policy should be said to have been successful. But a policy relating to non-farm sector *vis-a-vis* the farm sector is yet to evolve though there are increasing pressures from the farm lobby for such a policy.

Growth of Non-Agricultural Sector

In Korea

The peaceful sectoral transition in Korea was made possible by the growth of a strong non-agricultural sector. While the complementarity between various sectors is necessary for a sustained and balanced economic progress, the relative priorities differ depending upon national policies and relative resource endowments of different sectors. Because of poor resource-base of agriculture on the eve of the planned development of the country beginning in 1962, Korea followed industrialisation, as the first strategy and never deviated from this path. However, it took care of the agricultural sector since mid-sixties and particularly from seventies both to reduce the dependence on imports for basic sustenance and to bridge the inequalities between agricultural and non-agricultural incomes. The Korean Government consciously aimed at promoting industrial growth rather than employment and equality (Bagchi, 1987, pp. 59-60). (For an exposition of evolution of industrial policies in Korea, see Woronoff, 1983, Chapter 5 and 6; Leipziger and Petri, 1986).

The growth of a strong non-agricultural sector in Korea helped agriculture to relieve its surplus labour till mid-sixties. It was also responsible for facilitating agricultural modernisation to sustain the tempo of agricultural growth. Korea adopted a favourable agricultural price policy and other incentives to bridge the rural-urban income inequalities. Korea's industrialization has contributed in a major way to the rising farm agricultural output and farm incomes in the late-sixties and the first-half of the seventies by increasing farm product demand, by making possible the import of key inputs and by allowing Government to avoid policies that would have hurt farm incentives. Agriculture thus became a major beneficiary of the Korean economic growth as against cause of that growth (Ban, *et al.*, 1980, p. 31). The growing industrial sector has also facilitated off-farm migration (movement of farm population into non-farm occupations without migration from the rural sector) and also contributed to rural incomes. However, such facilities were largely concentrated around few metropolitan regions (Ban, *et al.*, 1980, Chapter 12).

In India

Indian planning strategy originally aimed at balanced development of both the agricultural and industrial sectors. This is evident from the emphasis laid on agriculture in the First Five-Year Plan, while taking cognizance of the need for development of industrial sector to tackle problems of mass- poverty and unemployment (Dantwala, 1986, p. 2). The emphasis has been shifted to industrialization during the Second Five-Year Plan, while in the subsequent plans though a sizeable share was allotted to the agricultural sector, it did not receive the attention it deserved. What is relevant is not simply investment in agriculture. Throughout the process of modernisation agriculture in India suffered from the shortage of fertilizers, pesticides, electricity, diesel oil and cement for irrigation projects. Even though there is no justification in placing agriculture next to industry, there is no deliberate neglect of agriculture in planning. But accent on heavy industry did not allow sufficient attention to agriculture.

The relative priority to industrial sector, though helped in strengthening self-reliance through promotion of key and basic industries, industrial growth was limited as comparatively high capital-output ratios failed either to make any positive impact on structural composition of the labour force or to promote agricultural growth in a big way. The experience of over three decades of planned economic development in India has brought out one of the major puzzles in development experience, *viz*., the continuous sluggishness in the performance of industry, despite the relatively easy availability of foodgrains and key agricultural raw materials (Bhattacharya and Hanumantha Rao, 1986, p. 55).

Capital-Output Ratios : The Korean Achievement

Starting with the planned development since 1962, Korea has followed labour-intensive techniques of growth in all its major sub-sectors of the economy. It has consistently kept its capital-output ratios far lower during the period 1963-82. Korean growth during the past two decades was largely attributable to increase in employment and average working hours and the contribution of capital inputs was far lower than that of both Japan and USA. The relative contribution of 'changes in working hours and characteristics of labour except education' to Korean growth was much higher than to Japan and the USA (Kim and Park, 1985, pp. 167-71).

The incremental capital-output ratios (ICOR) for the primary sector showed a continuous rise from 0.8 during 1954-62 to 1.1 during 1963-72. It was 3.9 during 1973-82 and during 1954-82, it was 2.3. The ICOR for the manufacturing sector declined from 3.4 during 1954-62 to 2.3 during 1963-72. However, its rise to 2.7 during 1973-82 was due to increase of investment in heavy and chemical industries. The overall ICOR for the economy slightly increased from 2.3 during 1954-62 to 2.5 in 1963-72. It sharply rose to 4.7 only during 1973-82 (Kim and Park, 1985, pp. 25-6). There was acceleration in the growth of the manufacturing sector since early sixties to rapid expansion of investment and increase in the rate of utilization of the invested capital stocks (Kim and Park, 1985, p. 25)

Thus, the labour-intensive techniques of production adopted by Korea in its early stages of industrialisation and the effective use of the invested capital stocks helped the country to maintain favourable capital-output ratios, which furthered its growth process.

Capital-Output Ratios : The Indian Situation

In the case of India, factors accounting for the slow growth of the economy, particularly in the industrial sector, refer to the high capital-output ratios. Views differ on the factors accounting for the high capital-output ratios. Some trace it to the gestation lags and bulk of unfinished projects (Vaidyanathan, 1977, p.1647). There are others who trace it to the excessive private investment in luxury consumer goods with excess capacity (Bagchi, 1977, p. 223; Nayyar, 1978, pp. 1273-5 and Shetty, 1978, p. 218). During 1950-78, capital-output ratios in India have generally been high by international standards. The ICOR in registered industry at constant 1970-71 prices was 7.5 in the Second Five-Year Plan period and 5.6 in the Third Plan. In the following 10 years, however, it jumped up to about 12 (Desai, A.V., 1981, p. 389). There were social responsibilities borne by public sector plants, like workers' and officers, housing, subsidised canteens etc. Indisputably, consumer goods and services were supplied by public enterprises to their employees at subsidised prices. The major problems of public sector undertakings are largely due to under-utilisation of existing labour, resulting in emergence of a work ethic where every one worked less than one could and under-employment of labour resulted in under-utilization of the machines (Desai, 1981, pp. 389-91).

During seventies the increase in domestic savings has been somewhat primarily due to compulsory deposits and foreign inward remittances. These savings have been absorbed by unprecedented increase in the financial costs of projects. This way, the economic system could not take advantage of the increased domestic savings.

The present situation is one where for want of effective demand for investment goods and mass consumer goods, the growth momentum is contained (Shetty and Menon, 1980, p. 935).

As about trends in savings, capital formation and national income from 1951-52 to 1976-77, there has been rise in *incremental capital-output ratios* as being due to the increase in investment costs, along with the low rates of capacity utilisation (Rao, V.K.R.V., 1980, p. 974). Increase in the incremental capital-output ratios at constant prices is bad enough for our economic development, especially in the light of the general shortage of capacity in our factor resources (Rao, 1980, p. 974).

It looks as though that the relatively capital intensive strategies adopted in the early stages of industrialisation in India with thrust on development of basic and heavy industries and under-utilisation of capital stocks resulted in high *capital-output ratios* with adverse effects on growth.

The savings and investment rates show that low growth and comparatively low level of equity in India, compared to Korea, is not due to failure of the economy to generate savings and investment at the rate of 15 to 20 per cent of GNP (as prescribed by Rostow) to enter the take-off stage, but largely because of the failure to bring about (what Todaro calls) "corresponding changes in the social, political and economic institutions" (Todaro, 1981, p. 29).

But, the Korean experience shows that, given the capital, much could be achieved, if structural, institutional and attitudinal conditions are brought about and various groups are involved in the developmental process.

Thus, it can be seen that even though the determinants of growth are more or less identical for Korea and India, structural transformation of the former is considered a miracle, while in the case of latter, it is still elusive.

Rural Non-Farm Activities

The term 'rural' in Korea covers population up to 50,000, whereas in India in some cases even areas with a population of even 5,000 are considered urban. These differences must be taken into consideration.

As a source of earning, rural non-farm activities facilitate structural change from rural-agricultural to urban-industrial sectors in contributing to development (World Bank, 1978, pp.7-9; Anderson and Leiserson, 1980, p. 236).

While Korea had no traditions of rural non-farm activities, in India, these played a significant role in the rural economy, even though sharply declined during the colonial period. However, in the Indian post-Independence period, some attempts were made for their promotion through various policy instruments and programmes.[16]

Rural Non-Farm Activities in Korea

Korea had no rural industries except the traditional handicrafts located near raw material producing centres and industrial locations centred round urban areas during the Japanese colonial rule with their accent on military goods (Yong Ill Chung, 1981, p. 38). For Korean farmers there are no opportunities for non-agricultural employment, apart from seasonal inter-regional agricultural labour migration (Ban, *et al.*, 1980, p. 373). With hardly 10 km of paved roads per 100 sq km in 1960 and only 13 per cent of farm-households having electricity in 1964, without any significant increase in agricultural productivity during 1947-62 (Ho, 1982, pp. 983-4), conditions are not conducive for the development of rural industry in Korea till 1965. In 1960, rural industrial establishments accounted for 10.5 per cent of the total industrial establishments, 5.2 per cent of industrial labour force and 0.6 per cent of value added by industry (Chung, 1981, p. 43). There was a high degree of annual volume of off-farm migration as it more than doubled between 1960-66 and 1966-70 (Ban, *et al.*, 1980, p. 377). Further, industrialisation in Korea till seventies was carried on without any consideration for agriculture or rural development (Lee, Man-Gap, 1984, p. 24).

The Significance of Rural Non-Farm Employment in the Incomes of Rural Households in Korea

Non-farm activities contributing to the incomes of the rural households in Korea are over-stated (World Bank, 1978, p. 22).

These should include salary, wages for hired non-farm work, selling of animals, plants, crops, home made goods (World Bank, 1983, p. 30). However, in the annual Farm-Household Income Surveys carried out by the Ministry of Agriculture, Forestry and Fishery, the concepts of 'Non-Agricultural Income' (1956-58), 'Business other than Farming' (1962-67), 'Side Business Income', 'Other Side Business Income' (1976-86) include farm wages, income from hiring out agricultural machinery, rents, subsidies and remittances. As such, available data do not permit re-classification. The share of non-farm income in the total income of farm households from 1962 to 1985 is shown in Table 3.9 while non-farm income excluding farm wages, remittances etc., for 1975-85 is shown in Table 3.10.

As per the classification of the non-farm income by the Ministry, the share of non-farm income increased from 20 per cent in 1962 to around 35 per cent by 1985, as against the Government policy of increasing it to 50 per cent by 1986. If one adopts a restrictive concept of non-farm income covering commerce, industry, non-agricultural wages, salary and services as shown in Table 3.8, the share of non-farm income formed only eight per cent in 1975 and remained at 13.5 per cent during 1980-85. In 1981, nearly half of the off-farm income accounts for donation and subsidy sent from family members and relatives living in urban areas (Chung, 1981, p. 48).

Rural Non-Farm Activities in India

In the pre-colonial period, rural communities in India had a sizeable percentage engaged in non-farm employment particularly, weaving. During the colonial period, many of those engaged in weaving were forced to quit and join the ranks of agricultural labour, unable to withstand competition from mill-made cloth dumped by the British.

Significance of Rural Non-Farm Employment in India

Decennial Population Census, quinquennial NSS Enquiries on Employment and Unemployment as well as Economic Census

Table 3.9 : Composition of Non-Agricultural Income of Korean Farm Households—1962-1985

(Amount in Won)

Year	Farm Household Income	*Non-Agricultural Income* — Side Business Income of which Income from: Handi-crafts	Commerce, Industry, & Mining	General Service & others	Total Side Business income	Non-Business Income	Transfer Income	Total Non-Agri-Income	Share of Non-Ag. Income to Total Farm Household Income (Percentage)
1962	67,885	—	—	—	2,597	11,262	—	13,859	20.42
1965	112,201	—	—	—	3,897	19,492	—	23,389	20.84
1970	255,804	—	—	—	9,599	52,168	—	61,767	24.15
1975	872,933	—	—	—	21,863	84,418	51,814	158,095	18.11
1980	2,693,110	—	26,030	26,030	66,603	488,945	382,746	938,294	34.84
1985	5,736,246	11,086	53,978	65,064	214,442	845,545	977,323	2,037,310	35.52

Note : Transfer income was separated from Non-Business Income since 1983.

Source : MAF, 1963, 1966, 1971, 1976, 1981, and 1986.

Table 3.10 : Non-Farm Income of Korean Farm-Households excluding Farm Wages and Remittances, 1975-85

(Amount in Won)

Year	*Handi-crafts*	*Commerce, Industry & Mining*	*Non-Ag. Wages*	*Salary, Pension*	*General Services*	*Total Non-farm Income*	*Total Household Income*
	(1)	(2)	(3)	(4)	(5)	(6)	(7)
1975	—	5,362	17,830	40,609	6,743	70,544	872,933 (8.08)
1980	—	26,030	89,959	217,928	29,413	363,330	2,693,110 (13.49)
1985	11,086	53,978	177,853	471,722	61,344*	775,983	5,736,246 (13.53)

*Estimates at 1983 ratio of General Other Services.

Note : Figures in brackets indicate share of non-agricultral income in the total income of farm-household.

Source : M.A.F., 1976, 1985,1986.

provide data on persons engaged in non-agricultural employment in rural areas in India. The data do not adequately capture part-time involvement of several cultivator and agricultural labour households engaged in rural non-farm activities (Vyas and Mathai, 1978, p. 343).

Non-agricultural employment in the rural areas is taken from 1971 and 1981 Census data and is shown in Table 3.11.

The rural work-force engaged in non-farm employment is a little less than one-fifth of the total work-force in the country. Their share increased from 15.16 per cent in 1971 to 16.64 per cent in 1981, manufacturing, other services, trade and commerce being major sources. The decline in the share of household industry was considered much more severe between 1961-71 and is estimated at over 45 per cent (Jain, 1986, p. 881).

National Sample Survey (NSS) 1977-78 Estimates show that in terms of 'usual status', nearly 20 per cent of male workers and around 12 per cent of female workers in rural India are employed in non-agricultural activities. There are wide inter-State variations in rural non-farm employment as well as the possible contributing factors for this phenomenon (Vaidyanathan, 1986, pp. A 137-46).

Economic Census of 1980 shows that of the 4.7 million non-

Table 3.11 : Occupational structure of Rural Work-force in India , 1971-1981

(No. of workers in thousands)

Sl. No.	*Classification*	1971		1981	
		No. of workers	*Percentage*	*No. of workers*	*Percentage*
	Total Rural Workers	148,478	100.00	176,435	100.00
1.	Cultivators	76,635	51.62	90,157	51.10
2.	Agricultural Labourers	45,574	30.69	52,713	29.88
3.	Livestock, Forestry, Fishing etc.	3,759	2.53	4,196	2.38
	Total Agricultural Workers	125,968	84.84	147,065	83.36
4.	Mining and Quarrying	602	0.40	793	0.45
5.	(a) Household Industry	4,763	3.21	5,433	3.08
	(b) Other than Household Industry	3,402	2.29	6,059	3.43
6.	Construction	1,099	0.74	1,819	1.03
7.	Trade & Commerce	3,624	2.44	4,920	2.79
8.	Transport	1,211	0.82	1,947	1.10
9.	Other Services	7,809	5.26	8,398	4.76
	Total Non-Agricultural Workers	22,510	15.16	29,369	16.64

Source: 1. Census of India, 1971, Series I India, General Economic Tables, Part-II B (i), pp. 20-5.
2. Census of India, 1981, Series I India, General Economic Tables, Part-III A (i), pp. 238-41.

agricultural establishments in the country, 2.3 million or 48 per cent are located in rural areas, but of the 28.9 million hired workers, those hired by rural establishments are only 9.5 million, *i.e.*, 33 per cent. Of the 9.8 million non-agricultural enterprises located in rural areas in 1980, those in manufacturing and repair formed 38.87 per cent; sale and retail trade 31.27 per cent and community and personal services 20.60 per cent (Hazari, 1987, pp. 294-7).

Share of Rural Non-Farm Incomes in the Income of Farm Households in India

Unlike in Korea, systematic data on rural non-farm activities and their share in the incomes of different strata of rural households are not compiled in India. Even the Farm Management Studies, occasionally sponsored by the Ministry of Agriculture, focus attention on the income from crops and allied activities like dairying by the farm-households. This is possibly due to the fact that rural industrialisation policy was pursued in the country mostly to provide sustenance to those engaged in rural arts and crafts and household industry. The dispersal of industry into rural areas was meant mostly to tackle the problem of rural unemployment and certainly not with the objective of maintaining parity between rural and urban incomes as professed by Korea. As such, it is difficult to meaningfully assess the significance of non-farm income in the gross incomes of the farm-households in India.

Data available in respect of 72 village studies conducted since 1954 by the Agro-Economic Research Centres show that around 5.97 per cent of workers are engaged in manufacturing activity and the income derived from manufacturing is around 7.54 per cent (Papola and Misra, 1980, pp.1739-45). Factories employing 5 to 200 workers in Bulsar sub-district of Gujarat in 1974 paid wages similar to those of agricultural labour (Hein Strefkerk, 1981, p. 665).

Farm Management Studies conducted at Andhra University for West Godavari during 1957-60 and for Nagarjuna Sagar Command Area during 1981-84 showed that off-farm incomes (only dairying) formed around 5.05 and 5.44 per cent (Sarveswara Rao, 1960, p. 197 and Prasada Rao and Mohan Rao, 1988, p.93). These two sources do not reflect upon other non-farm incomes. There is positive impact of agricultural development on rural non-farm employment. As a 1979 study on savings and investment behaviour of rural households in coastal Andhra districts show that the share of non-farm incomes (income from agricultural wages, dairying, etc.) in farm-household income for all groups formed around 13.74, 19.23 and 24.67 per cent for Krishna, Nellore and Srikakulam districts respectively (Rami Reddy and Murthy, 1987, p.142). The higher share of the less prosperous Srikakulam district is attributable to higher share of income from cultivation.

The limited data that are available do not warrant any firm conclusions either on the significance of non-farm incomes in farm-household income or to attempt at comparisons between Korea and India.

Rēsumē on Rural Non-Farm Employment and Incomes in Korea and India

For comparable rural areas, non-agricultural employment in Korea is no better than India, despite its developed industrial sector, agricultural affluence, skilled and educated work-force and relatively developed infrastructural facilities. This is probably because of small size of the Korean village, which is comparable to a tribal settlement in India, with scarcity of labour. Also, Korea had neither a tradition of rural industry nor pursued a policy in that direction till seventies when she thought of dispersal of industries into small towns. However, in India, with an established tradition of rural industries in the pre-colonial period, there has been an avowed policy in favour of village and small industries since Independence. Consequently, a wide network of institutional infrastructure side by side with a large volume of rural underemployed and unemployed in relatively big villages, there has been a near stagnancy in the work-force engaged in rural non-farm employment opportunities in India. This is a matter for grave concern.

If one considers the non-farm incomes alone (excluding remittances, rentals, interest and off-farm incomes) and if the Coastal Andhra data could be relied upon, there are no significant differences in the share of non-farm income in the farm-household incomes of Korea and India. However, industrialisation in Korea helped rural areas to get sizeable remittances as in Punjab in India. In addition, rental incomes from land and other sources and interest on capital since eighties, have helped the Korean farm-households to supplement crop incomes to the tune of around one-third.

It can be inferred that it is a hard task to increase employment levels and thus incomes through rural non-farm activities, which Korea herself could not succeed. As such, policy stress should be on favouring dispersal of industry to small towns and linking subsidies and concessions to such industries with employment potential rather than on their mere location in a backward area.

To conclude

There are certain unique features of Korea, when it planned

development without many hurdles that confront many developing countries, *viz*., inegalitarian social and agrarian structures, high level of illiteracy, poverty and a significant class of landless poor. Korea is also relatively free from a class of vested interests that thwart development. These are the resultant outcomes of changes over time, in Korea, starting from the pre-colonial era, the Japanese rule, the social turmoil during the Korean war and the compulsions for reform in the wake of communist threat from the North. As already mentioned, Korea also had access to the U.S. aid and liberal credit from international funding agencies. Korean experience points out that the State emerged as a crucial determinant in ushering in and achieving transformation undeterred by other factors and considerations.

Apart from the above unique features, Korean experience has also brought to light some distinct factors that influenced growth and diffusion of benefits of growth. Its emphasis on primary and vocational education and inculcating work ethics and moral values as part of the reforms in school education, paid rich dividends to Korea. It facilitated easy absorption of rural people into its fast growing industrial sector in addition to the positive impact it exerts in gaining equitable access to rural institutions. Korean religious values, attitudes and rituals did not obstruct growth process, even if one does not agree upon the positive contributions of Confucianism. Korean success in land reforms despite shortcomings in the initial stage also contributed in a great measure to the remarkably smooth agrarian transition without class conflicts.

India had to usher in transformation with a legacy of an unfavourable set of institutions and an unenviable human resource, which is largely illiterate. Many people are without vocational skills, fettered by religious beliefs and caste prejudices. India's vast size as that of a sub-continent with diverse linguistic and religious groups marked regional imbalances often interrupting development priorities, slowed down growth processes. India had to contain its developmental destiny with limited aid from international funding agencies, out of its own choice of adopting a framework of a mixed economy of competing private and public sectors with a policy of non-alignment, striving for a balancing act between conflicts, power blocs in its international relations.

The pre-occupation of the Indian State with vital issues of national integration in the early stages of its Independence stood in the way of concentrating its efforts on developmental aspects. The compulsions of a democratic 'soft-State' to reconcile contradictory goals, regional and sectional interests and the purposefully peaceful and evolutionary transition it opted for also explains for the limited growth effort it had put up as also achieving distortions in the diffusion of benefits of limited growth to the various strata of the society at large.

NOTES

1. Veit observed, "the chief executives in their political role have surmounted a host of serious internal and external threats to national integrity but they have not succeeded very well in bettering the living conditions of the poor" (Veit, 1976, p. 372).
2. To distinguish between ideology and religion Ninian Smart identified six dimensions of religion *viz.*, ritual (expressed in worship, sacrifice and other sacred acts), mythological (stories which encapsulate fundamental beliefs of a group), doctrinal (systematisation of beliefs and experiences), ethical (moral codes and guides to behaviour), social (institutional forms of religion) and experiential (personal spiritual experiences) (Bishop and Darton, 1987, pp. 7-8).
3. Kim, Mahn-Kee cites, "According to Kim Chang-Tae, in the historical religious tradition of Korea, Confucianism led the formation of culture in upper class and Shamanism in lower class while they were interacting with each other in co-existence. While Confucianism provided Korea with principles of ruling and normative system, Shamanistic practices became folk-faith rooted deeply among the grassroots based on the primitive faith, prevalent in North East Asia." (Kim, Mahn-Kee, 1983, 120)
4. Fingarette observed that, "to obey the whip is to be not much more than a domestic animal, but to be loyal and faithful to those who rightly govern, to serve them and thus to serve the human community, to do this out of one's own heart and nature— this is to be a true citizen one's own community" (Fingarette 1972, p. 76). Values such as these not only facilitate stability as long as the rulers are considered as doing their best in the interest of people at large, but also help motivate people through secular preachings as sacred which goes a long way in ushering in development.
5. For a review of the observations of various writers on Hinduism in relation to economic development (*see* Nijhawan, 1975, pp. 23-42).
6. For instance Milton Singer's study on Enterpreneurs in Madras city suggests that Hindu religious attitudes are not counter. productive (Singer, 1972, p. 345).
7. According to Srinivas Sanskritization is the process by which 'low' Hindu caste, or tribal or other group, changes its customs, ritual, ideology and way

of life in the direction of a high and frequently 'twice born' caste", (Srinivas, 1972, p. 6).

8. Hanson observed, "The social obstacles to economic development in India are so serious that to undertake a continuous and scientific investigation of them in order to plan their circumvention would seem to be an elementary requirement".
   He further commented, "lack of sociological realism has characterised a great deal of Indian Planning", (Hanson, 1959, pp.182-3).
9. See Chopra (1975, p. 148, Table XVII).
10. Vocationalisation of school education and updating courses in technical education has not received much attention till the end of the VI Plan period. This could be gauged from the VII Plan observations. It emphasised, "a major task in the VII Plan will be the removal of obsolence in equipment and revision of courses in all technical educational institutions, many of which were drawn up more than two decades ago" (Planning Commission, Vol. II, 1985, p. 260).
11. There is the criticism that the land reform programme in Korea ended up with mere redistribution of farm land and 'was not followed by supporting programmes till mid sixties (Pak, 1983, p. 12). The major criticism relates to the failure to completely distribute the land as well as failure to arrest growth of illicit tenancy. It is said that over 40 per cent of the land scheduled for redistribution was omitted out of the reform purview at the implementation stage due to socio-political reasons. Clandestine, disguised transfers and registrations were allowed to go unchecked. Between 1945 and 1951 the land privately sold by landlords was 5.73 lakh chongbo (one chongbo = 0.992 Ha.), whereas the farm land distributed by the Government in accordance with 1949 Reform Act was only 3.32 lakh chongbo (Ban *et. al.*, 1980, pp. 285-6).
12. The failure of tenancy reform not only resulted in increase in tenancy, but also failed to provide both security of tenure to the tenants as well as fair rents. Pak Ki Hyuk observed that the number of tenant farms and the area of land cultivated by tenants. have increased by 150 per cent between sixties and eighties. The proportion of tenant farms increased from 26.4 per cent in 1960 to 37.1 in 1980 and between 1980 and 1981, the percentage of tenant farms increased by 9.3 per cent (Pak, 1983, pp. 12-4). The percentage of area under tenancy increased to 30.5 and the number of tenant farms (owner tenants and pure tenants) increased to 62.7 by 1985 as against 66 per cent of area under tenancy and 85.9 of tenant farms at the pre-reform period of 1945. (Kim, Woon-Keun, 1986, p.18). See also Lee, Woo Jae, 1974, pp. 64-6).
13. The Sixth Five Year Plan of India (1980-85) stated, "If the progress of land reform programme is less than satisfactory, it has not been due to flaws in policy but due to indifferent implementation. Often, the necessary determination has been lacking to effectively undertake action, particularly in the matter of implementation of ceiling laws, consolidation of holdings and in not vigorously pursuing concealed tenancies and having them vested with tenancy occupancy rights as enjoined under the law" (Quoted by Bandyopadhyay, 1986, p. A50).

14. See Sanyal, 1976 and NSS 1986.
15. The losses incurred by Korean farm-households due to the Government rice price policy during 1952-60 are estimated by Moon, Pal-yong. See Moon, Pal-yong, 1979, p. 163.
16. For details on the policies towards promotion of rural non-form activities, their impact on rural non-farm employment and incomes and the factors affecting rural non-farm employment, the readers may look into the following sources:

    For Korea : EPB, 1985, Singurdsen and Kim Young Chul, 1981; Kada Ryoha, 1981; Chung Yong Ill, 1981; Choe Yang Boo and Kim Tae Myung, 1981; Choe Yong Boo and Lee Yong Mahn, 1980.

    For India; Alexander, 1963; Vyas and Mathi, 1978; Bhattacharya, 1980; Kurien, 1978; Jain L.C., 1980, 1985, 1986; Nasir Tyabji, 1980; Papola and Misra, 1980; Planning Commission, 1985; Rao, V.M., and Errappa, 1987; Rama Swamy, 1987; Sandesara, 1986; Vepa Ram K. 1987.

PART-II

RURAL TRANSFORMATION IN KOREA AND COASTAL ANDHRA—A MICRO PERSPECTIVE

This Part, comprises of Chapter 4, Chapter 5 and Chapter 6, examines the extent to which the macro picture observed in Part-I gets reflected in the rural scene particularly at the micro level. To make comparison more meaningful, micro study was limited to comparable rice regions in Korea and Coastal Andhra. Chapter 4 presents an overview of the rural development administration, rural institutions like land tenure, agriculture extension systems and cooperatives. This Chapter also examines the extent to which they facilitate diffusion of benefits of growth. The other two Chapters of this Part present the results of the field data on the economy and life of rural households, farm economy of sample households in two selected villages of Korea and two selected villages of Coastal Andhra.

4

ROLE OF RURAL INSTITUTIONS IN RURAL TRANSFORMATION

A Comparative Picture of Rice Growing Regions of Korea and India (Coastal Andhra)

Introduction

Every economic problem requires a social institution to solve it (Schotter, 1981, p. 31). Institutions by themselves do not add resources to the economy but they so structure the environment in which factors of production meet in such a way that it may stall, decelerate or accelerate the development process. This they do by stimulating or impeding those kinds of behaviour pertinent to growth by their effect on: (i) the direct calculation of costs and benefits; (ii) the relationship between production and distribution; (iii) the order, predictability and probability of economic relationships; (iv) the knowledge of economic opportunities; and (v) motivation and values (Wolf, 1955; pp. 867-9). In view of this, changes in institutional order are considered vital for ushering in growth in early stages of development (Hoselitz, 1957, p. 29). They are equally important in the later stages as technologies are embedded in an institutional framework and for identical technology different institutional matrices produce different distributive outputs (Race, 1976, 49).

Institutional Constraints as Obstacles to Transformation

In most developing countries, the average producer does not have access to proper quality of institutions and services to increase his production and income (FAO, 1970, Vol. II, p. 375). The Second Asian Agricultural Survey, which reviewed the Asian agriculture for a decade preceding 1976 and identified areas of major concern during 1978-88, observed that progress towards modernization of agriculture is of necessity, evolutionary and that the rate of progress is not constrained by the attitude of farmers, but by the lack of availability of suitable technology and the unfavourable institutional environment in which farmers operate (ADB, 1977, p. 82).

Despite efforts of international agencies in drawing the attention of the developing countries to the institutional bottlenecks impeding agricultural and rural development activities, the position seems to have not altered much. This is evident from the observations of Naya (1983, p. 30) and Vyas (1983, p. 44). Vyas emphasized, "success in future will depend on the renewed thrust in technology, infrastructure, human resource development and appropriate organizational interventions to support the small farmers and landless workers" (Vyas, 1983, p. 44). Attention to these aspects becomes imminent if Third World agriculture has to advance without explosive social tensions resulting from unacceptable levels of inequality (Race, 1976, p. 43).

Thus, there is enough evidence indicating that appropriate institutions go a long way in achieving rural transformation and in enabling the small and marginal farmers and landless labourers in overcoming the relative deprivation they suffer and the differential access to institutions they often undergo. What is keeping rural transformation at bay is not so much the absence of motivation for development, unwillingness to innovate on the part of people involved, lack of capital or appropriate technology *per se*, but is due to absence of appropriate institutions that really work to deliver the goods in 'the complex and uncertain world of economic relations' (Hayami and Ruttan, 1985, p. 95).

In the context of new technology, Dantwala, (1978, pp. 1305-6) observed that gains are likely to remain confined to narrow enclaves unless institutional barriers to their spread caused by land tenure, credit, marketing and extension services are removed. As both countries have ushered in Green Revolution, the extent to which they succeeded in removing these barriers assumes significance for equitable transformation. For this reason attention is focused on three major institutions *viz.*, agrarian structure, agricultural extension and cooperatives. The people's participation in the use of cooperatives is also examined.

For convenience, this Chapter is divided into three sections. Section I presents an overview of rural development administration in Korea and Andhra; Section II highlights on the land tenure institutions, agricultural extension services and cooperatives; and finally people's participation in the use of the cooperatives is examined in Section III.

The Concept of Institution

The term 'institution' is defined in many ways depending on discipline, purpose or problem under study (Wolf, 1955, pp. 867-9; Smith, 1964, p. 204; FAO, 1970, Vol. II, Chapter 10; Race, 1976, p. 45; Taylor, 1980, p. 3; Schotter, 1981, pp. 9-11; and Hayami and Ruttan, 1985, p. 94). An overview of the differing conceptions of institution reveals that in most cases, the stress is on a dimension of it and common to all these is the regularity and its established nature.

In this study, the term 'institution' is used as 'established forms or conditions of procedure of group activity' as defined by MacIver and Page (1965, p. 15).

SECTION – I

RURAL DEVELOPMENT ADMINISTRATION IN KOREA AND ANDHRA : AN OVERVIEW

In Korea

In Korea most of the institutional structures connected with rural development are integrated with the Ministry of Agriculture and Forestry (MAF). In India, both at the national and State levels, there are many independent structures, even for a single activity like agricultural development, let alone the multiplicity of structures for rural development activities.

In Korea, problems of coordination persisted at all levels, particularly at lower levels, in the Community Development Projects (CDPs) stage. Absence of scope for development of local initiative, feeling of loss of status among extension personnel, poor coordination among the public agencies at the county and provincial levels limited the rural development process in Korea in the CDP stage (Moon *et al.*, 1968, pp. 116-8).

Under Saemaul Undong (New Community Development Programme), while vertical coordination has been achieved, horizontal coordination was not as expected in early seventies. However, these are said to have been overcome by fixing up responsibilities and through continuous evaluation of officials' performance with measurable targets *i.e.*, timely delivery of materials, increase in rural production or an improvement in rural life in the communities for which Government services have been delivered. It was said that community performance highly correlates with administrative inputs and support extended by Government officials. Township or Myon level officials shouldered responsibility for implementation of Saemaul Undong in identified villages (Whang, 1980, pp. 183-6) and are accountable for its success (Goldsmith, 1981, p. 455).

In India

Indian Community Development Programme faced teething troubles till sixties. It suffered on account of undue stress on individual programme without an integrated approach and virtual absence of coordination among the concerned departments (Paranjape, 1984, p. 134). Block level coordination meetings are used often to communicate instructions to the staff rather than identifying bottlenecks and arriving at solutions (Mohan Rao, 1963, p. 92).

In the post-sixties vertical coordination is being ensured, with a multiplicity of centrally sponsored programmes under direct departmental line of control. But it eluded horizontal coordination at district and block levels. The Rural Development and Poverty Alleviation Programmes implemented since early seventies are also not free from pitfalls of earlier programmes. Creation of new programme-oriented overlapping structures resulted in strengthening independent line functioning as opposed to integration. It is observed that by late Seventies the block machinery was almost in shambles while at the district level virtual competition prevailed among the multiplicity of sectoral institutions intended to serve the same target group (Department of Rural Development, 1985, p. 16).

To overcome the above problems District Rural Development Agencies (DRDAs) were created through amalgamation of various agencies but without any sound mechanism for coordination. There was no administrative control for DRDA over Block/Mandal officers. There were no inter-sectoral linkages at block level (Department of Rural Development, 1985, pp. 21-2). As things stand the present arrangements between DRDA and Block agency created more problems than solutions for effective implementation of development programmes in the rural areas (Parthasarathy, 1989, p. 140).

A review of village level institutions in Andhra shows that the number of traditional, village based voluntary institutions and institutionalised practices of material aid and cooperation are rather limited. Even these exclude certain social groups and are constrained by institutions like caste. Further, they failed to adapt themselves to the changing times. This is evident from the erosion of most of rural institutions except caste, which has transformed itself more as a divisive rather than a cementing force in society.

The institutions created with external initiative like Panchayats and Cooperatives are vitiated by the factional environment. The other voluntary organisations like Youth Clubs and Mahila Mandals are limited to a small fraction of villagers, and to elitist groups, often are going into oblivion with erosion of subsidies or Government assistance. Thus, the village level institutional framework in Andhra is not only inadequate in terms of number but also is constrained by such divisive forces like caste and factions.

The operational strategies evolved for effective implementation of programmes at the village level in Korea are also noteworthy.

First, villages are classified on the basis of objective criterion for purpose of deciding the type of assistance to be given to make them self-reliant. Secondly, villages are constantly evaluated for their capacity to attain self-reliance before extending Government assistance and support. These measures helped build-in a discipline among villagers to successfully complete the earlier projects to avoid losing future programmes of assistance. Such clear-cut strategies for extending assistance based on objective norms and evaluation, or such imposing measures of discipline before extending further assistance was never a part of Indian experience in Rural Development. An ethos of dependency emerged against self-reliance.

In a way, apart from the differences in the political system and forms of Government, the facilitating factor seems to be the strategy of administration by identification and fixing responsibilities for given tasks and linking promotion to performance in Korea. In India, despite elaborate guide-lines, uncertain organizational linkages, and absence of a measure of discipline did not help ensure the desired coordination among the bureaucratic structures.

Field Level Experiences

To understand the general situation of coordination prevailing among administrative structures and village level institutions, we have to know about the means of coordination among various institutions as well as their effectiveness in providing services to the rural people. Towards this end, a structured questionnaire was canvassed among the institutions involved in rural development at the district, Myon, Mandal and village levels.

District Level

In Korea, information collected was ascertained from the District Administrative Office, Rural Development Administration (ORD), Offices of Farm Land Improvement Association and district branches of NACF (National Agricultural Co-operative Federation). In Andhra, Collectorates, Offices of the Zilla Praja Parishads,

Deputy Directors of Agriculture, Assistant Directors of Industries, DRDA, Lead Bank Cells, District Cooperative Marketing Societies and District Cooperative Central Banks were authenticated.

Orientation of District Administration

In Korea, the General Administration Office (GAO), at the district level is structured to carry on many developmental functions. The organisational structure of the GAO has nine departments, *viz.*, Information, Home Affairs, Saemaul, Fiscal, Social, Agricultural Production, Increase of Production, Production of Fishery and Forestry, Construction and Civil Defence. Through these various departments, it oversees and coordinates functions of other departments connected with the accomplishment of a given task or tasks.

In Andhra, the General Administration Department (GAD) at the district level is basically structured to carry on the traditional function of land revenue administration, and miscellaneous tasks for which there are no departments at the district level. Though the District Collector is the key-figure in the district administration and is endowed with the developmental functions as ex-officio Chairman of the Zilla Praja Parishad, Chairman of the DRDA etc., he does not have an organisational structure under his control like the district chief in Korea. By virtue of his position as administrative head of the district, he can always use his good offices to deal with other departments in exceptional circumstances. Normally, he has no statutory responsibility for the omissions and commissions of other departments at the district level unlike his Korean counterpart who is answerable to the higher-ups in matters like increase in food production, increasing income, diffusion of Saemaul Movement, promotion of traditional culture and sports, exploitation of the production potential of the region, development of tourist places and construction activities in the district.

Degree of Vertical Coordination

In ensuring vertical coordination with higher and lower level structures also, there are differences between Korea and Andhra. In Korea, district level functionaries are called for monthly meetings at the provincial level, while the frequency of such meetings is rather occasional in Andhra. Further, visits to the district level offices by the provincial level staff, and *vice-versa* are reported as other means of coordination between the district and provincial levels in Korea. In Andhra such visits serve the coordination function, though the visits *per se* are not for coordination.

Horizontal Coordination

Both in Korea and Andhra, there are no formal contacts in the sense that there are no statutory obligation of coordinating with one another. However, while monthly coordination meetings are the only forum for interaction among different departmental heads in Andhra, Korean responses indicate almost daily contacts between District Administrative Office, Rural Development Administration (RDA), NACF, NLCF (National Livestock Cooperative Federation) and NFCF (National Fisheries Cooperative Federation). The frequency of contacts between NACF and RDA is more than once in a month. Absence of horizontal coordination was never felt in Korea, as strict vigilance by the GAO ensures horizontal coordination among the related organisations in Korea.

In Andhra, problems if any, will be brought to the attention of the Collector. The monthly coordination meetings of district and mandal level officers convened by the Collector in West Godavari focused mostly on IRDP and distribution of house sites. It also revealed the recalcitrance of some of the Mandal Revenue Officers in cooperating with the Mandal Development Officers, in enabling the latter with appropriate documents relating to land particulars, despite instructions to that effect in the previous monthly meeting convened by the Collector.

The general awareness of the related organisations is far higher in the case of Korean functionaries, compared to some of their counterparts in Coastal Andhra. Enforcement of strict discipline for compliance, coupled with financial incentives like prizes and promotional opportunities, are often reported as factors contributing for better performance among the staff in Korea. In Andhra, while disciplinary action is reported for grave irregularity, and admonition for non-compliance of a directive from above, very few instances were reported about cash awards and promotional incentives. While a degree of oneness and intimacy manifest between staff of RDA and NACF in Korea, similar situation is not to be seen between Cooperatives and Agricultural Department in Coastal Andhra, though the former lend finance for agricultural inputs and the latter encourage appropriate use of fertilizers and pesticides.

In Korea with district branches of the NACF rendering integrated services leaves little scope for problems of coordination, among cooperatives. In Andhra, the federal character of the cooperatives and their organisation on functional basis adversely affect both vertical and horizontal coordination. For instance, the District Cooperative Marketing Societies (DCMS) are members of the State Cooperative Marketing Federation (MARKFED). However, an awkward situation of MARKFED opening district level branches, and DCMS not having any business transactions with MARKFED was noted with both the districts studied. This is also true of the links between State Consumers' Federation (FEDCON) and district wholesale stores or Cooperative Super Markets dealing in consumer goods. Contacts between District Cooperative Central Banks, which supply credit to the PACS and DCMS, which supply mostly fertilizer, are limited at best to finances and there is hardly any meeting point between the two organisations, let alone coordination at any level.

Myon/Mandal Level

In Korea, the structure of Myon administrative office, is similar to the district administrative office with about 20 officers, each one being in-charge of an activity. What is prevailing at district level also holds good at Myon level in Korea. As Myon office is also concerned with rural development work, it involves all the Ri-Chiefs under its control in these tasks, particularly to coordinate the village level institutions.

In Andhra, the administrative set-up at Mandal level consisted of Mandal Revenue Officer (MRO) incharge of general administration, Mandal Development Officer (MDO) for development administration assisted by extension staff of related development departments. But, in the two Mandals visited, many of the staff positions at the level of extension officer are looked after by the staff of the other Mandals for want of personnel. Further, though the area of operations of MRO and the MDO are made coterminous for the convenience of the public, formal linkages between the MRO and MDO are few if any.

Village Level

At the village level in Korea, the Ri-Chiefs coordinate the activities of village level voluntary associations. In Andhra, the Panchayats and Cooperatives function in water-tight compartments.

Thus, the relative integration of administrative and institutional structures, supported by village level organisations helped Korea effectively implement rural development activities. In Andhra, the multiplicity of administrative structures and the consequent problems of coordination and ineffectiveness of the existing village level rural organisations resulted in lopsided implementation of the rural development programmes.

SECTION–II

AGRARIAN STRUCTURE AND SUPPORTING INSTITUTIONAL AGENCIES

Discussion of development in agriculture is impossible without a consideration of institutional aspects, since changes in these aspects are primarily responsible for development (Race, 1976, p. 41).

Agrarian Structure

Structural aspects facilitated decline in the share of agricultural workers in Korea, while it resulted in near constancy in Andhra.

During the pre-colonial era, both in Korea and Andhra, social hierarchies and landed aristocracies were maintained, depriving the rural masses the right to ownership of property. When ownership rights were conferred, the peasants were subject to exploitative tax exactions either out of compulsions of meeting the expenditure on wars or to maintain a minority of the ruling elite in comfort even at the cost of starvation of the majority of the masses. A vast majority of the rural population in both the countries were deprived of right to ownership of land.

Agrarian Structure of Korea till 1948

However, the concept of 'public land policy' with equitable share for all peasants has been the guiding force governing land policies in Korea throughout its pre-colonial period. This policy, despite lapses in its effective implementation since fifteenth century, contributed to a more equitable agrarian structure within the given social setting, though denied ownership of land to those at the lowest rung of the social ladder like the serfs, public entertainers, butchers etc., (*see* Shin, 1970, 1971; Han, 1974; Henthorn, 1971 and Lee Ho-Chol, 1977).

In the colonial period, there persisted the Japanese greed to bring in arable land into the hands of Japanese settlers and the resultant land policies implemented in Korea. As a result, a relatively small percentage of peasant proprietors as well as a significant class of insecure and exploited tenants and a class of landless agricultural labour arose (Shin, 1971; Choo, 1979; and Lee, Man-Gap, 1984).

In respect of non-agricultural pursuits, while Korea never had a significant class of rural artisans, the limited few in the urban centres were discouraged by the State-controlled trade which had a monopoly, but during the colonial period, Japanese industrialisation facilitated absorption of agricultural population into industry which helped in to bring about structural transformation in the economy.

Agrarian Structure in the Post-Liberation Period in Korea

The land-reforms carried on through enactment of legislation in 1948 and especially the Land Reforms Act promulgated in 1950, imposing ceiling of 3 ha per farm-household, distribution of surplus land among tenants, transformed the tenant-dominated agrarian structure of colonial Korea into one of owner-proprietor status in the post-liberation period. The share of owner-farmers increased from mere 14.1 per cent in 1945 to 73.6 per cent by 1960 and share of tenants almost crashed from 45.8 per cent to mere 6.8 per cent during the same period (Kim, Woon-Keun, 1986, pp.17-8). Only a small segment (2.8 per cent owning less than 0.1 ha) could be considered as agricultural labour.

Even after the reform, many farm-labourers and tenants, who do not at all possess land still remained tenant-farmers-cum-labourers as the reforms could only help allot land to the registered tenants at the end of Japanese colonial rule (Lee, Man-Gap, 1984, p. 179).

Agricultural Conditions till 1965

Rural Korea had the advantage of an egalitarian agrarian structure, reformed tenancy and a very limited proportion of agricultural labour even by early fifties, The structural transformation Korea has undergone resulted in the decline in the percentage of work-force and agricultural labour in absolute terms since 1972.

Land-reforms meant for equitable distribution of land were not accompanied by agrarian reforms for about a 15-year period (Pak, 1983, p. 12). The absence of supporting programmes like credit, inputs and extension resulted in near stagnation of agricultural sector and pauperization of the small peasantry. The percentage of rural families owning less than one hectare increased from 68 per cent in 1945 to 78.9 per cent by 1957 (Cho, Dong-Pil, 1959, p. 118). The Korean agriculture features till mid-sixties were considered as one of (i) stagnation of productivity, (ii) pre-modernised family farming, (iii) narrowed arable land, (iv) mono-culture system concentrated on rice-farming and deficit management, (v) existence of large quantum of disguised unemployment, and (vi) prematurity of agro-processing industry. Also there was lack of organic inter-relation between agricultural and non-agricultural sectors. The data on crop yields during 1945 and from 1950 to 1965 also show that while there has been improvement compared to the 1945 position, the situation remained almost stable between 1950 and 1960 for most crops (Byun, Hyung-Yoon, 1967, pp. 56-7).

Agrarian Structure of Coastal Andhra, 1947-70

In the case of Andhra, extensive land grants by the rulers to those in their service and good looks on a hereditary basis (unlike in Korea where such grants were given in lieu of salary during the period of service) resulted in a comparatively more inegalitarian agrarian structure even within the given social structure which itself is highly inegalitarian (*see* Reddy, 1986; Ramana Rao, 1958; and Ramakrishna, 1983) . The British concern for augmenting revenue and self-perpetuation, through compromises with the powerful vested interests, contributed to the emergence of an agrarian structure, controlled by a class of intermediaries (Reddy, 1986; Ramakrishna, 1983; Lakshminarayana, 1958; Reddy and Raghunatha Rao 1975; Rao, G.N., 1985 and Slater, 1918).

However, in the case of Andhra, a significant class of rural artisans, particularly weavers, patronised by kings and encouraged by people were ruined and were converted into a class of agricultural labour by the colonial rulers out of greed for finding markets for their mill-made cloth. Thus, unlike in the case of Korea, colonial rule in Andhra contributed to structural retrogression and added a class of landless labour, in addition to the existing people (*see* Byun Hyung Yoon, 1967; for Korea and for Andhra *see*, Slater, 1918; Reddy and Raghunatha Rao, 1975 and Ramakrishna, 1983).

Land laws in Andhra were enacted during 1947-61 by the State Government with the objective of bringing about parity in the land rents in *Zamindari* areas on par with Ryotwari Areas through Andhra Pradesh (Andhra Area) Estates Land (Reduction of Rent) Act of 1947, Abolition of Zamindari and Inamdari (The Madras Estate Abolition and Conversion into Ryotwari) Act, 1948 and Andhra Inams (Abolition and Conversion into Ryotwari) Act, 1956. Laws were also enacted for fixation of fair rents and ensuring security of tenure (The Andhra Tenancy Act of 1956) and fixation of ceiling on agricultural land (The Andhra Pradesh Land Reforms Ceiling on Agricultural Holdings) Act of 1961.

It is of relevance to notice that Coastal Andhra accounts for a higher share of Zamindari and Inamdari lands, compared to other parts of the State. In 1940, these lands accounted for almost 1/3rd of the total assessed land in South Coastal Andhra (31 per cent), nearly one-half (49.5 per cent) in Coastal Andhra as against 26.56 per cent for the Andhra region. As such, abolition of these tenures should have an impact on the agrarian structure. However, the economic and social effects of Zamindari Abolition in Andhra has not changed significantly between 1946-47 and 1954-55 (Sarveswara Rao, 1963, p. 45).

The tenancy legislation which aimed at ensuring fair rents and security of tenure escalated the problem of tenancy. This is evident from the increase in the proportion of tenants from 16.08 per cent in 1951 to 28.01 per cent in 1961 and "continuing upward pressure on rent and insecure terms of tenancy despite legislation" (Parthasarathy and Prasada Rao, 1969, pp. 42, 48 and 329). The Village Survey Monograph of Unagatla indicates that the impact of tenancy reform in the village was one of absence of security to the tenant, which he used to enjoy for a period of 20 years under 'Registered Tenancy (Government of Andhra Pradesh, 1971, p. 83).

Another feature of agrarian structure of Coastal Andhra in the Post-Independent period is a growing class of agricultural labour. The proportion of agricultural labourers to total agricultural workers increased from 36.36 in 1961 to 41.69 by 1971.

In Andhra, neither the effective implementation of Zamindari/ Inamdari legislation, nor the scare of the tenancy and ceilings legislation with their legal loopholes, resultant time lag, and ineffective implementation, did not alter the basic features of the agrarian structure of Coastal Andhra. With inequitable land distribution there emerged a significant class of insecure tenants and a large and growing class of landless agricultural labour.

Agricultural Extension

In Korea

Korean agricultural extension started in 1904 with the establishment of first agricultural school in 1904 (Song, Hae-Kyun, 1979, p. 13). During the Japanese colonial period also, agricultural extension received emphasis, particularly during 1920-31, to overcome shortage of food production. During the Japanese regime, particularly during 1940-45, agricultural technicians in-charge of extension became the rulers of the farmers and farmers were forced to produce more food under coercive directions of agricultural technicians (Park and Hong, 1972, p. 41). In the post-colonial period, agricultural schools at secondary level devoted to vocational agricultural subjects were expanded till 1972.

Further, not only research and extension were integrated into one single organisation, but these also were entrusted with the responsibility of training farmers, rural youth, students and teachers in agriculture high schools. They disseminated scientific technique and knowledge for improvement of agricultural and rural life through fostering rural people's organisations. The Rural Development Law of 1962 has delegated such responsibilities to the Rural Development Administration (RDA). Moreover, the limited area for each extension worker also facilitated effective interaction with farmer members. For example, in 1985, at the local level, one extension worker was responsible for five Saemaul villages, 273 farm-households and 296 hectares of farm land (RDA, 1986, p. 23).

In Andhra

In India, though agricultural departments at the provincial level originated in the last half of the nineteenth century itself, establishment of farms to study crop diseases began in Madras Province only in 1904. The Indian Council of Agricultural Research (ICAR) could not undertake agricultural education in the country till mid-sixties as it had neither the financial resources nor the statutory authority to discharge this responsibility (Randhava, 1979, p. 222). Though plant-breeding research stations were started from around twenties, extension was not part of their functions till 1949. In Andhra Pradesh, Maruteru Rice Research Station, the oldest one in the State which was established in 1925, introduced extension only on 20.10.1974, with the objective of identifying the problems of cultivators in the coastal districts of the State (APAU, 1986, p. 75).

At the State and national levels in India, lack of integration of research and extension has been the characteristic feature of agricultural research organisation. Extension was never an objective of the National Agricultural Research Institute, *i.e.*, ICAR (*see* Balaguru and Raman, 1988, p. 103). At the State level also, this dichotomy persisted. While research centres have gone under the control of the Agricultural Universities, extension has been under the control of the Director of Agriculture. Under the Training and Visit System (TVS), which was initiated in Andhra Pradesh since 31st July 1982, there is provision for linking research with extension, through conducting monthly workshops at the 17 agricultural research stations for imparting training to all the departmental officers of 22 districts. Despite TVS, the objective of establishing a single line of command in agricultural extension could not materialise. As a result, in all the districts, there are agricultural extension staff working under Panchayat Raj department, and TVS. Command Area Development Agency (CADA) has its own extension staff without any known mechanism for coordination. Even under the TVS, the number of families to be covered by a Village Extension Officer in Andhra Pradesh is three times more than that of his Korean counterpart. Under the TVS in Andhra, one Village Extension Officer has to cover 800 operating holdings. However, in parctice till 1983-84, 3000 village Development officers of Panchayat Raj Department were not deployed for this work. Hence, the remaining 3,524 Village Extension Officers were adjusted to cover all the districts. As a result, the quantum of work for each Village Extension Officer almost doubled.

Thus, there are significant differences between Korea and Andhra with respect to agricultural extension. Integration between research and extension was sought after by local organisations in Korea. While in India, these are almost missing both in the past and also at the present. Further, agricultural science never formed part of syllabi at secondary school level in Andhra, which was assiduously implemented in Korea.

Rural Delivery System : Cooperatives

Cooperatives enable the small and the weak to overcome the chain of constraints like lack of access to information, investible resources and inability to organise new production methods (Race, 1976, p. 50); as an organisational device, institution builds up the 'countervailing power' of the rural masses. It is also a technique of action based on the principle of mutual help, is also considered to be of great significance as a structural element for grouping of individuals in the rural transformation process for the spread of new methods and techniques and for the organisation of new systems of economic communication (Dulfer, 1974, p. 3). As an institutional device, cooperative societies were started both in Korea (1920) and India (1904).

During the colonial period, in both the cases, cooperatives have not struck roots. In India, while one-village one-society stalled their viability, in Korea, their organisation at the district (county) level stood in the way of their success. In the post colonial period, in both the countries, efforts were made to make them effective. Let us now explore for some landmarks in the development of operatives, alongwith their contribution to rural transformation.

Cooperatives in Korea

The post-colonial developmental process of Korean agricultural cooperatives (1945-80) could be divided into three stages (Park, Jin-Hwan, 1984, p. 5) : (1) During 1945-55, the activities of agricultural cooperatives virtually ceased without function for the primaries; (2) During 1955-70, primary cooperatives were organised almost at the rate of one society per one administrative village, and most of them became defunct for want of viability; (3) During the period from 1970 to 1984, primary cooperatives became effective units. The village cooperatives were merged to organise viable cooperatives, at the rate of one per one Myon, through implementation of a system of incentives like special loaning programmes, low interest rate policy, direct and indirect subsidy systems during the early 1970 (Kim, Young Chul, 1986, p. 12).

After this merger, all the functions, like supply of credit, marketing, supplies and member-farmer insurance were shifted from the middle tier (district) agricultural cooperatives to PACS (Kim, Young Chul, 1986, p. 13).

Establishment of a Single National level federation for agricultural cooperatives in 1971 *i.e.*, National Agricultural Co-operative Federation (NACF) by merging the Korean Agricultural Bank and the Farmers' Agricultural Cooperative is another land-mark in the history of Korean agricultural cooperatives. Since then cooperatives have played a significant and growing role in Korean rural transformation. Within a short span of time, PACS have not only handled diverse supporting services to farmers, but also built up creditable market standing in input supplies and marketing of cash crops (Table 4.1). Their share in farm credit also improved from mere 27.6 per cent to 70 per cent by 1982 (Table 4.2).

Since 1962, Korean cooperatives continued to be exclusive distributors of fertilizers and as such their market share continues to be 100 per cent. In addition to pesticides and seed, other farming inputs like polyethylene film for green-house farming, polypro-pylene bags for cereal packing, split bamboo for setting up of rice seed-beds are also handled by most of the PACSs. In 1984, about 98 per cent of the PACSs were distributing consumer goods like processed food, clothing, kitchenware, sanitaryware, housing materials, stationery and consumer durable goods through their chain stores.

Table 4.1 : Market Shares of Agricultural Cooperatives in Korea

(In percentage)

Sl. No.	*Item*	*1973*	*1974*	*1975*
1.	Farm Input Supply	56.8	61.0	75.6
2.	Fertilizer	100.0	100.0	100.0
3.	Farm Chemical (Pesticides)	40.0	40.8	73.5
4.	Feed Stuff (Cattle Feed)	30.4	31.4	39.8
5.	Cooperative Marketing	17.6	20.9	24.0
6.	Foodgrains	10.5	12.1	14.4
7.	Fruits	34.4	35.3	37.2
8.	Livestock Products	4.2	12.2	20.1
9.	Cash Crops	73.9	76.5	78.3

Source : NACF 1978, p. 93

Table 4.2 : Relative Share of Cooperatives in the Borrowings of Farm Families in Korea, 1971-1982

(Percentage)

Year	*Share of Institutional Credit (All Sources)*	*Share of PACS*	*Private Credit*
1971	31.0	27.6	69.0
1976	37.1	34.1	62.9
1978	61.4	58.5	38.6
1982	73.9	70.1	26.1

Source : Kim, Young Chul, 1986, p. 8.

Though cooperatives heavily depended on Government support during sixties for marketing business, since mid seventies, they initiated marketing of farm products on their own through establishment of marketing centres. These centres were operated by NACF and its member-cooperatives for sale of agricultural raw materials to processors on contractual basis, and supply of vegetables and vegetable products to Korean Armed Forces, retailing of farm products and processed foods at large-scale super markets operated by NACF, and export of commodities like processed mushrooms etc.

The cooperative marketing centres have also contributed to improvement of the wholesale market in fruits and vegetables in Korea. Farmers are provided daily with up-to-date marketing information on supply and demand situation and prices at different markets, through automatic telephone answering devices, mass media and other publications since 1984. PACSs have also entered processing. During 1984, as many as 125 of PACSs operated 144 mills for processing of rice, barley and other grains.

Since 1977, NACF and its affiliated PACSs have taken over the business of Life Insurance and Damage Insurance from the Government. In addition, they provided farm guidance work through encouraging grassroots organizations.

Case Studies of Primary Agricultural Cooperatives in Korea

Let us now look at the working pattern of Backsan PACS and Hyondo PACS, which serve the villages, Keumpani Ri and Jukjeon Ri.

Baksan PACS

Backsan PACS was formed in 1970. It has a jurisdiction on 12 administrative villages, consisting of 53 natural villages. It has established a branch to serve 19 natural villages. Of the 1881 farm households in the area of operation of the society, 1,873 or 99 per cent were members as on 10.10.1985.

Since its inception, provision of credit, supply of inputs like fertilizer and pesticides, and marketing of produce and supply of consumers' goods were being handled by the society.

The society is managed by a Board, consisting of nine members which include: President, six Directors and two Auditors, all elected by the General Body. Its day-to-day management is run by an office with 32 staff members. The office-staff consists of a Manager, two Departmental Managers, assisted by six Class III and seven Class IV officials and eight technically qualified staff to extend farm guidance to members. Its infrastructure consists of two administrative offices, including the Branch Office, one Super Market, one selling point (branch level), 11 grain godowns, six fertilizer godowns, one pesticide godown, one farm machine workshop, and one gasoline station. As on 31.12.1984 the business turnover of the society was 336 million Won; 70 per cent of this was disbursement of credit, while 30 per cent relates to Government business like handling of rice etc. Both in terms of deposit mobilisation and profits, it fared better compared to the district average. Its deposits were 788 million Won against the district average of 698 million Won per PACS. Its profits were nine million Won against the district average of six million Won per PACS. It has disbursed dividend at 3.2 per cent during 1984 and planned to raise it to six per cent in 1985.

At the village level, the society had the advantage of village level organisations in carrying out its activities. There were 53 Saemaul Farming Associations, 53 Saemaul Women's Associations, 48 Saemaul Young Boys and Girls Associations, 2 Agricultural Farm Machine-User Groups and 53 Joint Working Groups.

Hyon-do PACS

The Hyon-do PACS was established in 1969. As the society was established in an area classified as semi-mountainous, it had a wide area of operation covering 24 administrative and 96 natural villages.

As on 31.8.1985, of the 1,339 farm-households in its jurisdiction, 1, 218, *i.e.*, 90 per cent were members of the society. It is being managed by a Board of Directors, consisting of nine Members, a pattern common to all PACS in Korea. Its business activities are carried on by a team of 15 employees, headed by a Manager. The Society has a Departmental Stores adjacent to its banking section. It has two warehouses each of 100 tons capacity for storage of grain, three warehouses to store fertilizer with a total capacity of 122 tons, one pesticide warehouse with 32 tons capacity, four trucks and one car.

In the history of the society, its transactions during the decade 1976-85 show the diversity of services provided by the Society as well as gradual progress it made (*see* Appendices 4.1 and 4.2). As on 31.12.1984, it had a business turnover of 91 million Won, with a net profit of seven million Won. It has declared two per cent dividend. However, compared to the national averages, the percentage of overdues appear to be rather high.

At the village level, its supporting structures include 24 farming Associations, Saemaul Women's Associations, Saemaul Young Boys and Girls Associations and Joint Working Groups.

Common Features of Korean PACS

Management of both the societies Backson and Hyondo, have a thorough understanding of the people and economy in their area of operation and keep themselves abreast of the changes. In addition, they conduct an annual credit survey of rural households to obtain information on assets, production, sales, farm management, loan repayment, etc., for updating the credit status card of the member, which forms the basis for sanctioning loans by the screening committee.

Coordination among cooperatives and the Rural Development Office at the Myon level helps for their working together in solving problems of the farmers. For instance, the loan screening committee consists of the President of the PACS, Chief of Myon Rural Development Office and two leading farmers.

Both the societies, like most of the PACS in Korea, procure levy paddy for the Government and sell rice in addition to undertaking marketing on their own. Most of the supplies to PACS are channelled through Branch Offices of NACF at the district level. But, PACS are also free to buy on their own from the open market for sales through their Departmental Stores.

PACS in Korea prepare detailed perspective plans, for a three-year period, and strive hard to realise the planned targets through continuous monitoring. At the weekly meetings, the staff of the PACS, review the progress and discuss action plans. It means PACS have development oriented organisations, not simply rule regulating bureaucracies.

Factors Responsible for Korean Cooperative Success

The positive and supportive role of the Korean State, structural and functional integration with a strong unified federal body, effective people's participation in the working of Primaries are responsible for the success of Korean Agricultural Cooperatives.

Korean State has not fettered the cooperative with an elaborate legal framework or an army of bureaucracy to boss over. It extended aid without interfering in the day-to-day working of the Primaries. It used cooperatives as its agents to distribute fertilizer, procure, process and distribute foodgrains. It helped augmenting the deposits of Primaries by remitting levy payments of farmers to their deposit accounts with Primary Cooperatives. It never compelled Cooperatives to waive loan repayments and permitted high penal interests on loans overdue. Thus the Korean State has created a favourable environment for the Cooperatives to play a really effective role in the Korean rural transformation.

Establishment of a single national level federation of Agricultural Cooperatives (NACF) to support the Primaries and integration of diversified functions in a single organisation at the Primary level is a major factor for the success of Korean Agricultural Cooperatives. This facilitated functional integration of all the related services in the Rural Delivery System. The role played by the NACF and its branches in strengthening the Primary Cooperatives is another factor for the Korean success. The Apex body and its branches constantly guide, help and monitor Primaries without competing with Primaries in any business activity in their area of operations. Over time, the NACF also gave freedom to the Primaries to buy consumer goods either from its branches or on their own, if necessary. NACF also owned the responsibility for strengthening Primaries through management guidance. Towards this end, it classified Primaries into two categories: (1) self-supporting and (2) support-needed. Self-supporting Cooperatives are again divided into two (a) developed and (b) developing for purposes of extending assistance as well as management guidance. In 1988, of the 1,463 PACS, 760 were regarded as developed, 609 as developing and 94 as support-needed. The organisational chart of the NACF, as well as the chart of major facilities provided by the NACF and its member Cooperatives clearly reflect on the integrated and diversified services rendered by these institutions in response to the fast-changing commercialized character of the Korean rural economy.

Enlightened and active participation and effective use of the diversified services by the members also greatly contributed for the success of the Cooperatives.

Cooperatives in Andhra

In India, Cooperatives are integrated mostly with the credit structure. Functional Cooperatives with accent on marketing, processing and consumers goods have their own structures at the taluk/block, district, State and National level. There are hardly any known linkages among different types of functional Cooperatives, either structurally or functionally. The National Cooperative Development Corporation (NCDC) which extends assistance and guidance to functional Cooperatives has no role in coordinating their activities. The absence of linkages among functional Cooperatives weakened the Rural Delivery System in Andhra.

In India, as also in Andhra, PACS constitute the single largest group. In view of the significance of PACS in the Rural Credit Delivery System, attempts have been made, time and again, to transform them into viable multi-purpose Cooperatives. In this during 1956-75, most of the State Governments in India resorted to compulsory amalgamation of PACSs to make them viable.

However, they continue to be weak. The national level committee which has gone into these aspects in 1981 observed the PACS, "are not competent enough to handle multi-term and multi-purpose credit" (RBI, 1981, p. 80).

Credit, particularly working capital has been continuing to be the major portfolio of PACS in India.

In credit, the share of institutional agencies had almost doubled during 1971-82 as a result of the entry of commercial banks into the agricultural finance. But, the role played by Cooperatives is not commensurate with their largest network in the countryside (Table 4.3).

Their performance in non-credit services is much poorer. In 1981-82, of the 64 per cent of viable PACS in the country, only 49

Table 4.3 : Share of Cooperative Finance in the Outstanding Debt of Farm Households in India during 1951-52 to 1981-82

(Percentage)

Year	*Institutional*	*Cooperative*	*Non-Institutional*
1951-52	9.10	3.10	90.90
1961-62	18.40	11.40	81.60
1971-72	31.70	22.00	68.30
1981-82	61.00	29.00	39.00

Source : 1. Shivamaggi, 1986, p. 277.
2. Reserve Bank of India, 1986, p. 445.

per cent were supplying inputs. Their performance had worsened during the closing period of eighties. In 1989, that out of the 94,000 PACS in the country, only 40,000 dealt in fertilizers and had not involved themselves in the distribution of other inputs like seeds and pesticides (Ardhanareswaran, 1989, p. 5). Further, there are wide inter-State variations in their working. For instance, in 1981-82, only eight per cent of the PACS in Andhra Pradesh and 20 per cent in West Bengal were supplying inputs, though more than 80 per cent of PACS in these States were classified as viable. Marketing is an area almost untouched by PACS with only two per cent of the societies in the country undertaking this task. Only 50 per cent are distributing consumer articles. However, in Andhra, during 1981-82, only 0.29 per cent and 15.17 per cent of PACS were handling marketing and consumer business (Mohan Rao, 1988).

In addition to PACS, other functional Cooperatives like marketing societies also supply inputs like fertilizers, etc. With respect to supply of fertilizer, the market share of Cooperatives declined from 59 per cent in 1970-71 to 46 per cent by 1980-81. Cooperatives accounted for 52 per cent of the total fertilizer sales points in the country in 1982-83. In Andhra, Cooperative fertilizer sales points formed only 25.7 per cent in 1980 (Chauhan, 1984, p. 12).

Even though marketing Cooperatives covered all the secondary and wholesale assembling markets, with their network at the district, State and National level, their market share in sale of marketable surplus is very limited. It is estimated to be 8 per cent in 1985-86. With the exception of sugarcane Cooperatives in Maharashtra and Dairy Cooperatives in Gujarat where integration of all stages of marketing was brought about, their contribution to strengthen the growers is rather limited (Pavaskar, 1986, p. 341). Studies on groundnut marketing in Kurnool and Anantapur districts of Andhra Pradesh show that the net returns to farmers, in both absolute and relative terms, were higher for the private channels than for the Cooperatives.

It is contextual that Cooperatives played limited role in the distribution of consumers goods in the rural areas as they are conditioned by the Government policies with regard to distribution of ration and other controlled commodities.

Case Studies of PACS in Andhra

In Andhra, the PACS in the developing village is ineffective and the farmers rely on commercial banking for credit needs. However, a Milk Supply Cooperative was established in the village in 1982, as part of an integrated dairy located at Sangam in the district. All the farm-households supplying milk to the dairy were enrolled as members. Inputs like cattle-feed were supplied to the society by the dairy, which owns a 100-tonne capacity plant from which the farmers were supplied cattle-feed. The veterinary doctor appointed by the dairy visits the village once in a week to check up the cattle's health and doctor's services also available on request within 24 hours at a nominal payment. While the milk Cooperative is doing a good job for the villagers, the PACS was almost dormant.

In the developed village, there was PACS since 1919 itself. However, its activities were limited to supply of short-term credit. As part of the viability programme, four neighbouring PACS were also merged into this society in 1975. It had an elected Board, consisting of nine members headed by the President. It had one Secretary, a Clerk, a Sweeper and a Night Watchman. In 1985, it had a share capital of Rs. 1.50 lakhs, including Government share of Rs. 30,000. The society constructed its own building and a 100-tonne capacity multi-purpose godown in 1986, under the World Bank-aided Rural Godown Project, sponsored by the National Cooperative Development Corporation.

The Society incurred a loss of Rs. 13,251 during 1983-84, and was classified as 'C' class. Its activities are limited to short-term credit advances and limited sales of fertilizers *i.e.*, Rs. 15,000 per annum. However, in 1986, it sold fertilizers worth of Rs. 1.00 lakh in Kharif season and also started sale of Government subsidised note-books worth Rs. 20,000 in 1986. It is also handling cloth business in a nominal way.

Poor management with low paid staff, absence of integrated supply channels, absence of any planning and desire to improve and diversify business are the characteristic features of PACS in general in Andhra.

Factors Contributing to Poor Performance of Cooperatives in India

The unimpressive performance of the Cooperatives in extending diversified services to the farmers, despite their wide network, federal structures and State aid could be traced to lack of vertical as well as horizontal linkages. Also federal bodies competed with member-units for their survival and there arose a pre-occupation with controlling and regulatory functions by the higher level structures, rather than developmental and promotional functions.

Schemes of reorganization and re-vitalization of these institutions have by and large tinkered with the area of operations of PACSs so as to make them viable and ended up with different degrees of success. No serious and lasting effort has ever been attempted in practice, despite the rhetoric to equip them for diversified business with the requisite guidance and support (Mohan Rao and Prasad, 1985, p. 179).

To sum up, while Korean Cooperatives responded to the challenge of providing diversified and integrated services to a modernizing agriculture, since seventies by forging effective linkages between primaries and higher level bodies, in Andhra, their operations are mostly limited to credit, due to lack of functional integration, weakness of institutions at all levels and higher level structures competing with primaries.

SECTION–III

PEOPLE'S PARTICIPATION IN RURAL INSTITUTIONS IN KOREA AND ANDHRA

Let us now find out about the people's involvement in rural institutions with reference to: (i) membership in rural institutions; (ii) use of institutional sources for various services; and (iii) the level of use of institutional channels in the services offered.

Membership in Rural Institutions

Membership includes membership in formal organisations like Cooperatives, youth clubs and women's clubs and in informal groups like 'Kye's of various types found in Korean villages. For analytical purpose, households are classified into three groups: (i) those which are not members of any institution; (ii) those with membership in one institution; (iii) those with membership in more than one institution. In Korean villages, membership largely refers to Cooperatives, Saemaul Women's Clubs and 'Kye', while in Andhra, it is limited to Cooperatives only.

Table 4.4 : Distribution of Rural Households with Membership in Rural Institutions

(Percentage)

Category	No membership in any institution		Membership in one institution		Membership in more than one institution		Total	
	Korea	*Andhra*	*Korea*	*Andhra*	*Korea*	*Andhra*	*Korea*	*Andhra*
I.	15.38	82.68	42.31	16.53	42.31	0.79	100 (26)	100 (127)
II.	6.98	70.97	37.21	24.73	55.81	4.30	100 (43)	100 (93)
III.	.0.00	47.13	20.83	49.42	79.17	3.45	100 (24)	100 (87)
IV.	0.00	44.65	19.05	51.78	80.95	3.57	100 (21)	100 (56)
V.	0.00	46.15	19.64	46.92	80.36	6.93	100 (56)	100 (130)
I - V.	4.12	60.24	27.65	35.90	68.23	3.86	100 (170)	100 (493)
VI.	33.33	89.19	50.00	10.81	16.67	0.00	100 (12)	100 (37)
VII.	44.44	94.67	44.44	5.33	11.12	0.00	100 (18)	100 (169)
VIII.	70.84	90.00	16.66	5.88	12.50	4.12	100 (24)	100 (170)
Total	16.07	73.99	29.02	23.01	54.91	3.00	100 (224)	100 (869)

Note : Figures in brackets indicate total number of households.
I. Ha. 0.01-0.50; II. Ha. 0.50-1.00; III. Ha. 1.00-1.50; IV. Ha. 1.50-2.00; V. Ha. 2.00 and above; V1. Rentiers; VII. Agricultural I Labour, VIII. Others.

Sharp differences could be observed between Korea and Andhra in respect of the number of households with membership in rural institutions (Table 4.4). In Korea, a high percentage of households are members in more than one institution, while in Andhra, a large percentage of households are not members in any institution. This difference is largely due to the multiplicity of institutions even at the natural village level in Korea and their relative usefulness, as against the weakness of the institutions and absence of institutionalised group activity in Andhra. Further, the limited services provided by the PACS also account for the low percentage of membership in institutions in Andhra. Membership in more than one institution among a few in Andhra because of separate organisations for working capital and term credit.

As about institutional membership of households, a relatively low percentage of marginal farmers and agricultural labour households are members in rural institutions both in Korea and Andhra. There is awareness that there is limited usefulness of these in enriching their life-styles and also limited decision-making role they themselves have in these bodies. As far as cooperatives are concerned, there is a prevalent thinking that their problems cannot be tackled by cooperatives alone.

In Andhra, despite an avowed policy in favour of admission of marginal and small farmers into cooperatives and allocation of a fixed share in the total credit, their membership in cooperatives continue to be at a low level. Low level of literacy that limits needy people's awareness as well as options, the non-viable nature of their household in addition to discriminatory attitudes that manifest in a stratified society keep local institutions in the grip of dominant social groups.

Level of Use of Institutional Channels

Activity Status of Households in Rural Institutions

The marked differences between Korea and Andhra, in terms of number of rural institutions, and differential participation in the conduct of these institutions, called for a common measure to capture these differences. For this purpose, activity status of each rural household was computed (Table 4.5).

As in the case of membership, a majority of the households in Andhra are clustered in the low activity status reflecting upon the nominal nature of membership. Only a small percentage of the rural households are in the medium and high status category. The homogeneous nature of Korean natural villages, clustered with kin networks, high level of literacy, traditions of participation in group activity, and the relevance of those institutions to their immediate needs account for high activity status of rural households in Korea. In Andhra, limited institutional structures, high level of illiteracy, limited role of the institutions in relation to one's well-being, the heterogeneous nature of stratified rural system with inegalitarian ethos and the general apathy of the people towards rural institutions explains the low activity status of various households.

A glance at the activity status of rural households in rural institutions across size-groups shows relatively poor activity status among marginal farmers, agricultural labour and rentier class households in Korea and Andhra (Table 4.5).

Significance of Institutional Agencies in the Farm Economy of Rural Households

Apart from membership and patronage of institutions for services, what is of significance is the extent to which farm-households are integrated with institutional channels in their transactions. This was examined by considering the share of farm-households in credit purchases from Government and Cooperatives in the total purchases of farm inputs, consumer goods and sale of farm output of sample households.

Credit

The share of institutional borrowings in the total borrowings of sample farm households during 1985-86 in Korea and Andhra villages are shown in Table 4.6.

Table 4.5 : Distribution of Rural Households by Level of Activity Status in the Institutions (Census Data)

(In Percentages)

Category	Low		Medium		High		Total	
	Korea	*Andhra*	*Korea*	*Andhra*	*Korea*	*Andhra*	*Korea*	*Andhra*
(1)	(2)	(3)	(4)	(5)	(6)	(7)	(8)	(9)
I.	50.00	95.45	45.45	0.00	4.55	4.55	100 (22)	100 (22)
II.	40.00	85.18	50.00	14.82	10.00	0.00	100 (40)	100 (27)
III.	20.83	93.48	66.67	4.35	12.50	2.17	100 (24)	100 (46)
IV.	19.05	93.56	76.19	3.22	4.76	3.22	100 (21)	100 (31)
V.	19.64	87.14	69.64	11.43	10.72	1.43	100 (56)	100 (70)
I-V Total	28.83	90.31	61.96	7.65	9.21	2.04	100 (163)	100 (196)
VI.	75.00	100.00	25.00	0.00	0.00	0.00	100 (8)	100 (4)
VII.	80.00	100. 00	10.00	0.00	10.00	0.00	100 (10)	100 (9)
VIII.	57.14	58.82	42.86	29.41	0.00	11.77	100 (7)	100 (17)
Total	34.57	88.49	56.91	8.85	8.52	2.66	100 (188)	100 (226)

Note : 1. Column 1: as noted ante.

2. Activity score of the household is computed by adopting the following procedures: (i) Score is given for nominal membership; (ii) Score for members attending the G.B. meeting at least once in the preceding three years; (iii) Scores for office bearership for every adult member in the households.

3. Figures in the brackets indicate total number of households.

Table 4.6 : Share of Institutional Borrowings in the Total Farm Borrowings by the Sample Farm-Households during 1985-1986

(In Percentage)

Size Group	*Share of Institutional Borrowings*	
	Korea	*Andhra*
I.	66.86	14.10
II.	89.31	40.48
III.	85.65	32.42
IV.	98.72	69.36
V.	100.00	61.64
Total	92.88	54.11

In Korea, 93 per cent of the total borrowings are from Co-operatives as against 54 per cent in Andhra. Discipline imposed by institutions in ensuring repayment as well as repayment ethic on the part of the borrower's account for the differences. As mentioned earlier, Korean PACS do lot of follow up on utilisation of loan through its extension staff, in addition to imposing high penal interest rates. In Korea, one employee will be in-charge of a group of borrowers and he has special responsibility to ensure repayment by these households. In Andhra, post-loan follow-up on utilisation is almost nil, both in case of Cooperatives as well as in commercial banks, nor they remind borrowers about repayment as often as Korean PACS do. The low-key repayment ethic is further waning away under the impact of populist preachings of politicians. Above all, the coverage of households in terms of mere membership is also low in Andhra.

Though the significance of Cooperatives in the total borrowings of the first group are lower compared to other groups in Korea, in Andhra it is the lowest. The relatively low significance of Cooperative finance in the total borrowings of the first size group can be seen in the Korean Cooperatives' awareness that their problem is one of poverty and they also cannot take care of their needs. In Andhra, the share of the first group is far lower because their access to Cooperatives and commercial banks depends on the coverage of these households under IRDP by DRDA.

Farm Inputs

As none of the sample households in Andhra purchased farm inputs from institutional sources, analysis is limited to Korean households only (Table 4.7).

In Korea, nearly two-thirds of requirements of seed, around 4/5th of pesticides and 100 per cent of the fertilizers are met by institutional sources, mostly by PACS. There is near total reliance on cooperatives for pesticides and comparatively greater reliance for seed by marginal farm-households in Korea. In spite of monopoly of Korean Cooperatives in distribution of chemical fertilizers, there is equitable access to these groups into institutional channels made possible by an egalitarian socio-economic structure.

Table 4.7 : Distribution and Share of Value of Farm Inputs Purchased from Cooperative in Korea (Sample Households Data)

(In Percentage)

Size Group	*Seed*	*Fertilizers*	*Pesticides*
I.	76.40	100	98.73
II.	56.68	100	99.18
III.	42.82	100	86.44
IV.	46.35	100	100.00
V.	73.95	100	69.26
Total	69.45	100	78.35

Note : No sample farm-household lifted these inputs from the Cooperatives in Andhra.

Consumer Goods

As mentioned earlier, PACS in both the Korean villages maintain Departmental Stores, wherein Government subsidised rice is also sold in addition to many consumer goods. In Andhra, in the sample villages, the Cooperatives are not involved in the distribution of ration articles like rice, wheat, sugar and oil, as these depots are in the hands of private sources. As such, the analysis is limited to Korean households only (Table 4.8).

Barley is the major item purchased by farm households, as most of them have given up cultivation of Barley as there was slackening demand with increase in incomes. There is a relatively low share of Cooperatives in the consumer goods purchased by farm-households as there are periodical weekly markets (a feature

Table 4.8 : Values of Barley, Sugar and Condiments and Spices purchased from Cooperatives in relation to the Total Monthly Requirements by the Sample Farm Households in Korea

(In Percentages)

Size Group	*Barley*	*Sugar and Condiments and Spices*	*Total*
I.	16.42	0.00	11.09
II.	26.25	9.57	23.52
III.	16.42	3.46	8.54
IV.	71.72	3.20	31.50
V.	0.00	9.29	9.29
Total	25.93	4.89	16.92

continuing from ancient times) much nearer to their native villages, wherein daily necessities are purchased once a week. Primary Cooperatives also do not deal in consumer durables, as people prefer to buy the same from big Departmental Stores in cities.

Marketing

In Korea, NACF and PACS together, procure levy paddy on behalf of Government, process and sell the same through their distributive channels both in the urban and rural areas. In addition to Government levy paddy, they also buy paddy and other commodities on their own for distribution through their networks. Though during 1985-86 the Government purchases accounted for only 11 per cent of the total paddy, the PACS under study handled nearly 1/3rd of the HYV paddy marketed by the farm-households (Table 4.9).

In one of the Andhra villages, Gollapadu, the milk supply cooperative purchased all the marketed milk by the member producers. However, there is total non-involvement of Cooperatives, *i.e.*, PACS and DCMS, in marketing activity as there is lack of assured business as well as lack of coordination between the consumer wing and marketing wing of the Cooperatives, which almost act as separate entities without any involvement. Added to this, there is the reluctance of Government agencies like Food Corporation of India to use Cooperatives as their agents.

Table 4.9 : Share of HYV Paddy Marketed Through PACS in the Gross Value of Product of Paddy in Korea

(In thousand Won)

Size Group	*Total Value of paddy produced*	*Value of HYV paddy marketed by PACS*	*Share of (2/1)*
	(1)	(2)	(3)
I.	8,720	4,882	55.99
II.	35,757	19,974	55.86
III.	34,009	12,491	36.73
IV.	27,045	20,250	74.83*
V.	218,431	52,794	24.17
Total	323,962	110,391	34.08

Note : * Proportion of HYV paddy in the total cropped area is as high as 75.00 per cent in this group as compared to the overall of 37.00 per cent.

U.S. Dollar is equal to 881.45 Won at 1986 exchange rate.

The preceding analysis reveals that there is integration of various administrative agencies connected with rural development at the local level also under the stewardship of a single ministry in Korea resulting in better coordination, in contrast to the multiplicity of independent and autonomous bodies in India. Similarly, in Korea, integration of agricultural research and education in a single agency facilitated effective extension of agricultural knowledge to the farmers. The establishment of a single national federation of agricultural cooperatives to guide, support and monitor the functioning of Primary Agricultural Cooperatives enabled them to effectively render diversified services to the rural households. The absence of such effective integration between agricultural research and extension in Andhra, higher volume of work-load per extension worker stood in the way of effective agricultural extension. The absence of a single federation for agricultural cooperatives, lack of a strong body to coordinate various federations, the weakness of federations and primaries hindered diversified services to the farmers in Andhra. The case studies of cooperatives in the sample villages in Korea and Andhra, the census and sample study data also testify the relatively dismal picture of cooperatives in Andhra when compared with Korea.

The census and sample study data indicate that peoples' participation and use of cooperatives in Korea was higher. There is equitable access for the Korean households to these structures, in contrast to the differential and inequitable access to the services rendered by them in Andhra. May be the egalitarian social and agrarian structures in Korea are more responsive than the obstructive socio-economic structures in Andhra.

ANNEXURE 4.1

MAJOR LANDMARKS IN THE HISTORY OF HYON–DO PACS —1970-1986

S. No.	*Activity*	*Year of establishment*
1.	Merger of Non-viable PACS, Construction of Seondong Pesticide Warehouse, Simok Fertilizer Warehouse.	01.01.1970
2.	Merger of Seondong Primary Cooperative Society and Construction of Seondong Grain Warehouse.	25.12.1970
3.	Construction of Office and Market.	28.10.1971
4.	Construction of Maebong Fertilizer Warehouse.	30.12.1972
5.	Construction of Jook Jeon Grain Warehouse.	30.09.1977
6.	Construction of Seondong Fertilizer Warehouse and Purchase of Warehouse of Gun Administrative Office.	25.08.1982
7.	Addition to Seondong Fertilizer Warehouse.	29.07.1983
8.	Purchase of Trucks for Transport of Goods and Opening of Consumer Goods Sales Counter.	01.02.1985
9.	Purchase of Office Car.	07.04.1986

ANNEXURE 4.2

BUSINESS TRANSACTIONS OF HYONDO PACS— 1976-85

(Unit: 1000 Won)

Year	No. of members	Deposits	Loans advanced	Loans Recovered	Marketing of Paddy, fruit, vegetables etc.	Sale of Fertilizer, pesticides, HYV of Seed etc.	Sale of Consumer goods	Total Revenue	Net Profit	No. of Staff
1976	1110	77.885	115.133	73.710	52.452	63.051	18.674	15.990	96	12
1977	1110	111.796	116.299	60.077	30.531	79.188	25.169	24.096	2620	12
1978	1110	167.139	176.964	84.651	77.456	89.420	34.038	37.508	5067	12
1979	1168	194.000	285.186	106.936	134.000	94.000	40.000	44.451	2465	13
1980	1168	310.000	329.182	156.793	350.000	97.000	55.000	44.529	3452	12
1981	1160	350.000	387.246	243.721	124.000	180.000	62.000	66.375	4112	12
1982	1160	413.564	542.061	271.869	89.563	143.871	79.215	75.491	6425	12
1983	1227	371.630	551.973	312.531	50.342	182.961	182.709	83.642	6598	12
1984	1218	558.735	695.570	367.140	253.232	208.391	275.820	90.957	7243	14
1985	1207	613.084	961.189	548.460	329.315	217.908	335.021	114.971	14063	15

Note : US$ = 881.45 Won in 1986.

Source : Information provided by the Manager of the Hyondo PACS, 1986.

5

ECONOMY AND LIFE IN RURAL KOREA AND COASTAL ANDHRA

A Socio-Economic Profile of the Korean and Andhra Villages

Based on census data, this Chapter presents a comparative picture of the socio-economic characteristics of rural households, agrarian structure, extension services, the nature of factor markets, the status of rural households in factor markets and access to various segments of the rural delivery system. The impact of the transformation the two societies experienced during 1970-86 on the socio-economic status and quality of life of the rural households are also examined.

Geographical Description of the Field Work Area

Of the two Korean villages, Keumpani Ri is in Baekson Myon, Buan Gun (district) of North Cholla Province. It is 262 km. away from Seoul, the Capital city, 50 km. from Chonju, the provincial city and 20 km. from the district headquarters. It is located within 2 km. distance on the Kimje-Baeksan local highway. Juk jeon Ri, the semi-mountainous village is in Hyondo Myon, Chungchong Gun of North Chungchong province. It is located within 2 km. distance from Chongju-Shintanjin Road. It is at a distance of 150 km. from Seoul and 22 km. from Chongju, the provincial capital (*see* Map 5.1).

In Coastal Andhra, Eletipadu village in Iragavaram Mandal (Tanuku Taluk), West Godavari district is located on the Tanuku Amalapuram Road at a distance of 10 km. from Tanuku. It is at a distance of 45 km. from Eluru, the district headquarters and 450

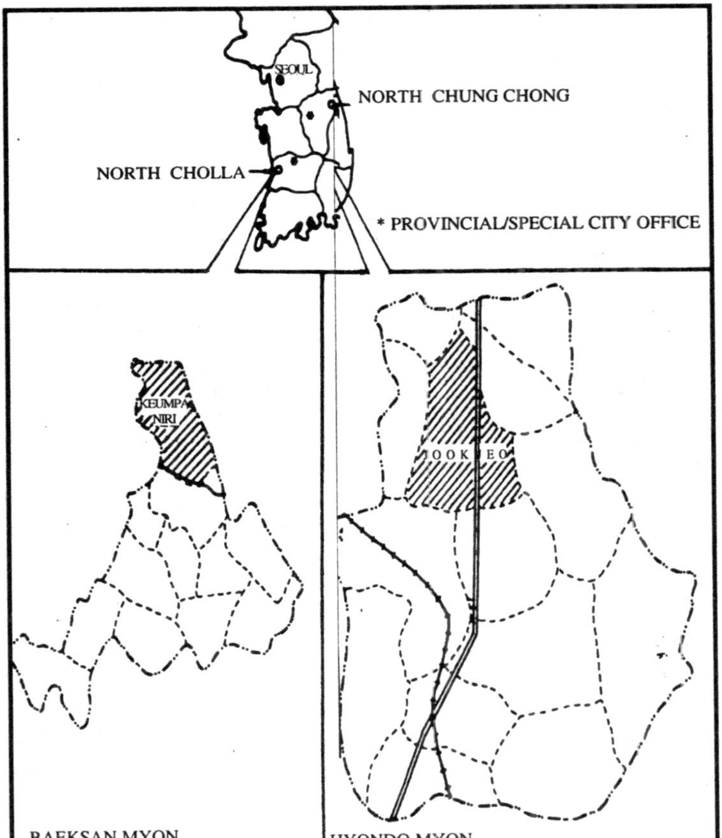

MAP 5.1 : Showing the Location of the Villages Selected in Korea for the Field Study

km. from Hyderabad, the State capital. The other village Gollapadu is in Muppala Mandal (Sattenapalli Taluk) of Guntur district. It is located at a distance of 5 km. from Narasaraopet on the Narasaraopeta-Sattenapalli Bus route. It is 65 km. from Guntur, the district centre and 335 km. from Hyderabad (Map 5.2).

Climate

Korea has cold winters and hot summers. The monthly temperature falls below freezing point in winter and raises to 78°F (25°C) in summer. The annual rainfall is about 1200 to 1300 mm and about 70 per cent of it falls in summer. Of the two villages, Juk-jeon Ri has relatively low temperature and cold winter due to its geographical location and semi-mountainous character.

Coastal Andhra region receives a normal annual rainfall of about 988 mm but varies from 692 mm to 1130 mm across districts. The temperature raises to more than 100°F. Of the two villages, Eletipadu had a rainfall of 1124 mm with relatively low temperature compared to Gollapadu which has a rainfall of about 800 mm and high temperature zone of more than 100°F.

Transport and Communication Facilities

The two Korean villages are well connected with Express Highways and connecting local road network. The nearest rail link for the two villages are their provincial cities *i.e.*, Chonju for Keumpani Ri and Chongju for Juk-jeon Ri. Roadways are the preferred and intensely used means of transport in Korea and in the villages under study as they are cheaper and time saving compared to rail-road facility. The local transport facilities are also well developed for both the villages because of developed network of all-weather roads to these villages. Taxi and truck facilities are abundant to carry men and material to these villages from the nearby Myon head-quarters.

Nearly 65 per cent of the Korean households had their personal transport facilities. Around 1/4th of the households had more than one type of personal transport. Cycles are used by around 30 per

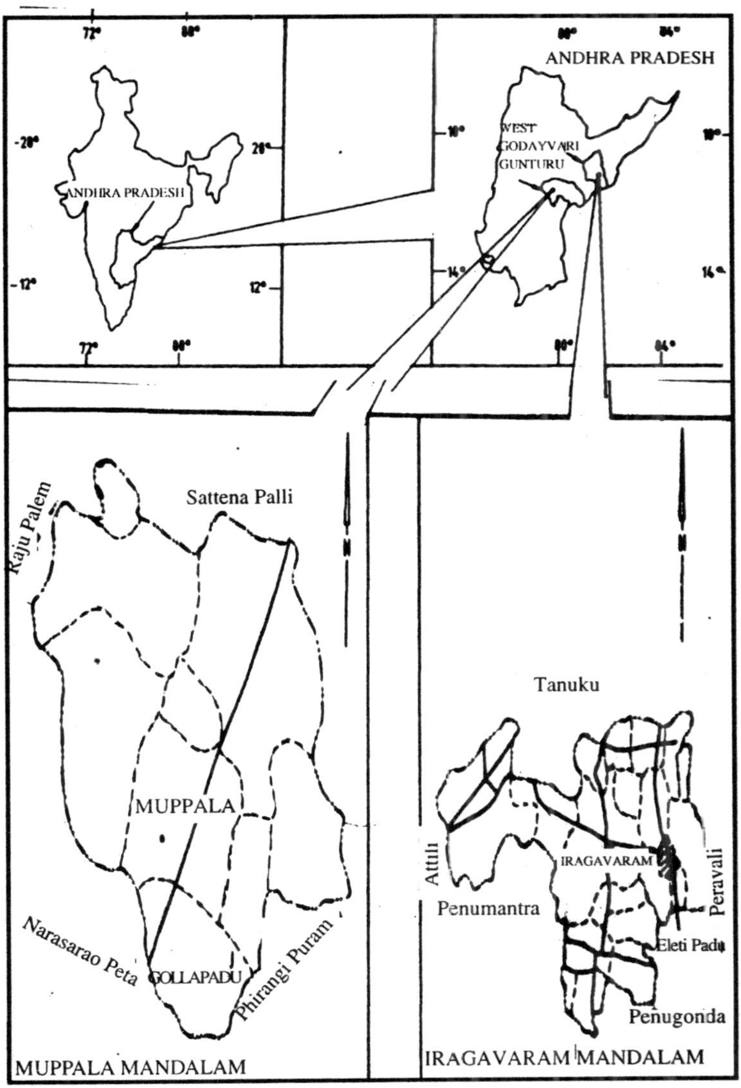

MAP 5.2 : Showing the Location of the Villages Selected in India for the Field Study

cent and power tillers by about nine per cent of the rural households. Trucks and power tillers are widely used for transporting goods to and from the villages to nearby market centres.

The Andhra villages, Eletipadu and Gollapadu are located much closer to the rail-road points *i.e.*, within 10 and 5 km. from the nearest railway stations, Tanuku and Narasaraopet respectively. They are also located on the local highways. However, the frequency of the public transport facilities are limited and time consuming compared to Korea.

Only 1/3rd of the Andhra villagers had their own means of personal transport. Cycle is the means for around 29 per cent. Bullock carts are the major means of local transport for goods though occasionally trucks and tractors are hired in peak agricultural and marketing seasons.

In addition to better transport facilities, Korean villages are served with better communication facilities. All the Korean natural villages had public address system from early 1970 for communication of messages to the villages. Korean villages are also served by efficient rural telephone system by 1984 while some from 1970 onwards. Korean farmers can make free calls to know the ruling prices in the market. In contrast, none of the two Andhra villages had telephones till 1986, while in others where they exist, their maintenance is rather poor.

Demographic Characteristics

Number of households as well as population is small in Korean villages (Annexure 5.1). As per the 1985 census, the two Korean villages have only 358 households with a population of only 1,603, while comparable figures are 901 and 4,233 respectively for the Andhra villages as per 1981 census. In both cases, females out-number males though their proportion is slightly higher in Korea.

Nuclear families predominate Korean villages. In Andhra, one-fifth are joint families. Age distribution of heads of sample households shows that Korean farmers are aged compared to Andhra farmers.

With respect to size, though the traditional Korean farm family size is as high as 6.2 in sixties, since seventies, there has been a gradual decline from 5.57 in 1975 to 4.42 by 1985. The average size of rural household in the Korean villages is 3.38 as against 4.89 in Andhra. This can be traced to the difference in the adoption of family planning practices in Korea (65 per cent) and Andhra (49 per cent).

Though there are less number of workers per household in Korea (1.84) the proportion of workers to population (54.55) is comparatively high. In Andhra, while the number of workers per household is 2.58, their share in population (52.76) is less than that of Korea. The proportion of females in the work-force is also higher in Korea, that is, 43.47 per cent as against 36.82 in Andhra.

Literacy and Education

In terms of literacy and access to technical education, Korean and Andhra villages are poles apart. While only 5.83 per cent of heads of farm-households are illiterates in Korea; in Andhra, their proportion is as high as 51.09 per cent. Similarly while 17.42 per cent of the heads of Korean rural households had technical education; the proportion of such households in Andhra is only 0.45 per cent. Though not so sharp, similar differences are manifested in the proportion of those with primary and secondary education. These differences are largely attributable to relative developments in education in the pre-colonial, colonial and post-Independence periods in the two countries.

Levels of literacy among children and adults of the sample villages provide a better perspective on the state of things at present (Table 5.1).

The low percentage of children attending schools in Andhra is largely attributable to apathy towards children's education, particularly among the poorer strata. The children of the poor assist their parents through taking care of their siblings and by joining the work-force. The adult education programme is also not very effective. In collegiate education, the developed villages in Korea and Andhra stand on the same footing.

Table 5.1 : Select Aspects of Education in Korean and Andhra Villages (Census Data)

(In Percentage)

S. No.	Item	Korea		Andhra	
		Keumpan Ri	*Juk-Jeon Ri*	*Eletipadu*	*Gollapadu*
I.	Percentage of children in the age group 5-15 attending schools	93.16	93.48	62.42	49.10
II.	Percentage of literates in the age group of 16 and above	98.10	93.10	59.10	28.02
III.	Percentage of collegiates in the age group of 16 and above	9.78	7.54	8.14	2.50

A relatively low percentage of Andhra children are attending school. There are also wide variations in this respect between the two Andhra villages. The sharp difference among the two Andhra villages reflects on their level of development. The developed Andhra village had two primary schools, one middle school and a high school, whereas the other village (which is relatively populated) has only one primary school.

Occupation

Korean census classifies farm-households into three categories, full-time, part-time class-I (whose agricultural income is more than 50 per cent of total annual income) and part-time class-II (whose agricultural income is less than 50 per cent of total income). The category whose main occupation is not farming formed 11.13 per cent of the farm households; non-farm households formed 6.8 per cent in North Cheongwon, and 8.4 per cent in North Cholla province. However, the village level data obtained from each of the natural villages (Annexure 5.1) show that 79 of the 358 Korean households *i.e.*, 22 per cent are non-farm-households in 1985.

Census data of Andhra Pradesh provide details of population by broad occupation groups based on work status but not on income criteria. In Andhra Pradesh cultivators formed 32.7 per cent in the total main workers as per 1981 census. The estimates of rural households in Andhra for 1977-78 show that cultivating households are less than 45 per cent of rural households in all the Coastal Andhra districts (Parthasarathy, G., 1989, p. 53). The results of the census data on the occupation of rural households based on occupational criterion showed that there are relatively small percentage of cultivating households in Andhra (56.73) compared to Korea (76.34). The percentage of agricultural labour households is higher in Andhra (20.00) while it is 9 per cent in Korea.

Households with secondary occupation formed around 8.5 per cent in Korea in contrast to 24 per cent in Andhra, but this has to be viewed cautiously. The major source of secondary occupation reported in Korea and in Andhra is agricultural labour, though proportions vary. In Korea, the low percentage of those reporting agricultural labour as secondary occupation is due to the practice of exchange labour. In Andhra, a large percentage of marginal and small households also depend on wage labour.

The relative difference in self-employment in the two cases is due to the predominance of service castes in Andhra while such services are non-existent in Korea.

Employment of Children Outside the Village

As the rural societies get increasingly integrated with urban, it is necessary to assess the number of households with employment of children outside the village and the nature of jobs held by them. The single digit figure for Andhra is in sharp contrast to Korea, where in more than 50 per cent of the rural households, children are employed outside the village (*see* Table 5.2). It reflects upon the see-saw transformation rural Korea has undergone due to growth of employment in the urban industrial sector and on account of the labour-intensive methods adopted in the first phase of its industrial development. In contrast, the capital-intensive industrialization in the midst of unlimited supply of labour in rural and urban areas resulted in slower rate of growth in Indian economy without any perceptible impact on rural areas. The percolation of benefits of industrial growth across different strata of rural households in Korea as against the static pattern in Andhra also account for this phenomenon.

In Korea and Andhra, children of the rentier classes and non-agricultural households benefited more compared to those of agricultural households. Among agricultural households, those with land benefited more compared to the agricultural labour households. However, in Andhra such benefits accrued mostly to the rentier and business households while artisan/self-employed groups lagged behind even agricultural labour households.

Table 5.2 : Percentage of Rural Households with Children Employed outside the Village in Korea and Andhra in 1986 (Census Data)

S. No.	Size-Group	Percentage of Rural Households with children employed		Total Households	
		Korea	Andhra	Korea	Andhra
1.	Ha. Below 1.25	50.00	7.09	26	127
2.	Ha. 1.26-2.50	48.84	4.30	43	93
3.	Ha. 2.51-3.75	58.33	3.45	24	87
4.	Ha. 3.76-5.00	52.38	14.28	21	56
5.	Above 5.01	51.79	7.69	56	130
	Total cultivating households	51.76	6.90	170	493
6.	Rentiers	91.67	40.54	12	337
7.	Agricultural Labour	44.44	3.55	18	169
	Total Agricultural households	53.50	7.87	200	699
8.	Business	75.00	14.75	4	61
9.	Employees	—	5.40	10	37
10.	Artisan/Self-employed	100.00	1.59	1	63
11.	Others	88.89	66.67	9	9
	Total Non-Agricultural households	66.66	10.58	24	170
	Total Rural households	53.12	8.40	224	869

Difference in opportunities accounts for relative differences in the percolation of benefits of growth among different strata of rural households. The absence of sharp inter-group differences in Korea may be because of absence of social inhibitions to seize opportunities. However, in Andhra the limited opportunities and reluctance to move out is because of incompatability between opportunities *vis-a-vis* one's position in the social hierarchy. This explains for unequal percolation of limited benefits of growth.

The nature of jobs held by children of rural households also reflects on the differential transformation (Annexure 5.3). While 60 per cent are in skilled jobs and in 1/5th of cases, more than one child is employed in Korea, in Andhra nearly 40 per cent are in unskilled jobs and only in one household out of a sample of 869 more than one child is employed outside the village.

In Korea, children of the marginal and small farmers and agricultural labour households, alone opted for unskilled jobs, whereas in Andhra, it is common to all rural households except in the case of those in business. This shows the vulnerable status of rural households of Andhra, with low level of literacy and demographic pressure, while in Korea, a high rate of literacy, vocational education and a developed industrial sector, gave fillip to the farm sector in many ways. However, in Korea children of only a small percentage of the better-off strata of rural households are in salaried jobs. In contrast, in Andhra, in all except in one sizegroup, the percentage of such households is higher compared to Korea.

Land Utilisation and Cropping Pattern

Classification of land utilisation is different in Korea and Andhra. In Korea, it is classified into paddy area, up-land (unirrigated), orchards, grass-land and forests; while in Andhra, it is classified into various categories *viz*., forests, barren and uncultivable land, cultivable waste, current fallows and net area sown.

In Korean villages there is hardly any area under grass or forest lands as against 43 per cent of cultivable waste in the developing Andhra village. The intensity of land-use in Korea is 130.9 per cent in 1979, but declined to 120.4 per cent by 1985. In the sample villages it was around 114.75 in 1985. The intensity of cultivation is much higher in the Andhra villages with 98 per cent and 60 per cent of area under double crop paddy in the developed and developing villages respectively. In addition, 37 per cent of the area is under third crop in the developed village. In Korean villages, only 2.72 per cent of the area is under vinyl farming, which is highly capital intensive.

Irrigation

Both Korean and Andhra villages are intensively irrigated with canals. Unirrigated area forms 11.88 per cent in Korea and only 7.62 per cent in Andhra. However, in Korea, around 1.75 per cent of irrigated area is under pump system or lift irrigation as one village is located in a semi-mountainous region.

Crop Pattern

Paddy accounted for more than 80 per cent of the cropped area in both. Next to paddy, vegetables (seven per cent) and gram and fodder (nine per cent) are grown in Korean and Andhra villages respectively.

Extension

Korean villages had the advantage of relatively better extension services as exclusive attention is paid to extension activity by field level extension staff and supplementary role played by cooperatives. In Andhra, the village level extension staff are multi-purpose workers and cooperatives do not purposefully undertake any extension work. Even the Training and Visit (TV) System is not effective in Andhra for want of adequate number of personnel.

Differential Access to Extension

Public services like extension tend to gravitate towards better- off strata of rural society, bypassing the marginal and small. This is all the more in stratified societies. In Andhra, only fraction of farm-households had access to extension. There is also discrimination in coverage of different strata. Around 90 per cent of marginal farmers are left out untouched by the extension system in Andhra.These discrepancies in coverage are attributable either to relative shortage of personnel or to lack of their accountability. In Korea, 90 per cent of farm-households enjoy extension services. Adequate staff and greater accountability on their part made it possible in Korea.

Differential Pattern in the Use of Improved Seed

Differences in the exposure to extension media also get reflected in the use of improved seed. Prior to seventies a higher percentage of Andhra farm-households used improved seeds, as these are introduced much earlier than in Korea. Koreans strong preference for traditional glutinous rice resulted in lower adoption of HYV seed, especially in the higher size-groups. The positive association between percentage of users and size of operated area in Andhra is partly a result of the low risk-taking capacity and limited access to extension for marginal and small farmers.

With favourable price and assured procurement up to 40 per cent of the HYV product, and pressures from above, majority of Korean farmers adopted HYV paddy since 1970s. In Andhra, low adoption after nearly a decade of time lag for the marginal farm households to shift to HYV seed cannot be traced alone to extension lapses as financial constraints also account for this.

Agrarian Structure and Tenancy

The agrarian structure and nature of tenancy in an economy which has witnessed significant transfers of labour out of agriculture to industry and undergone successful implementation of land reforms is likely to be different from the one with growing numbers in agriculture and without effective land reforms. The former is supposed to have a more egalitarian agrarian structure with increase in average size of holdings while in the latter inegalitarian structure persists with marked decline in average size of holdings. While tenancy of a higher order may persist in both, the nature of tenancy is likely to be different *i.e.*, less oppressive in the former compared to the latter.

The micro level data on owner and operational holdings in the

Korean and Andhra villages substantiate the above observations. This is evident from relative differences in the land concentration ratios and average size of both owner and operational holdings (*see* Table 5.3). For all rural households, the value of Gini Coefficients are very low in Korea *i.e.*, 0.009 as against 0.51 in Andhra. The apparent similarities in the coefficients for landed groups have to be viewed in the context of absolute decline in farm population of Korea since 1970, reluctance of youth to pursue farming and the Korean Government's policy (1986) of upward revision of ceiling limits for ensuring Korean farmers' comparable living standards of urbanites. In contrast, Andhra now exhibits the agrarian structure of 1950s in Korea, with relatively lower size of owner holdings.

Data on operational holdings also presents a similar picture, on account of greater out-migration of better-off farm-households with children employed in cities and their inability to cope up with farming in a situation of growing labour scarcity. In Andhra, the limited scope for out-migration and the labour surplus village environment accounts for their continuation in farming without any positive impact on the distribution of operation holdings and declining average size. Though marginal holdings accounted for higher proportion (40 per cent) with only 14 per cent of operated area in both, the nature and problems are different. In Korea these are operated mostly by the aged, with substantial remittances from the children employed in non-farm sector whereas in Andhra it is struggle for survival without opportunities for off-farm earnings.

Tenancy

Both Korea and Andhra attempted tenancy reforms. The Korean Land Reforms Act of 1950 legally abolished and prohibited tenancy. But it was never implemented. The Andhra Tenancy Act of 1956 enacted to provide security of tenure and fair rents remained a dead letter. Tenancy is expected to be higher in both though the nature and causes differ. In Korea it is the result of large scale out-migration to seize growing non-farm employment opportunities. In Andhra the struggle for existence by a vast majority of landless,

Table 5.3 : Distribution of Farm-Households in Korea and Andhra by Owned Area and Operated Area : Size-wise during 1985-86 (Census Data)

(In Percent)

Size-Group	Korea						Andhra					
	Owned Holdings			Operational Holdings			Owned holdings			Operational holdings		
	House-holds	Owned Area	Average size	House-holds	Opera-tional area	Average size	House-holds	Owned Area	Average size	House-holds	Opera-tional area	Average size
(1)	(2)	(3)	(4)	(5)	(6)	(7)	(8)	(9)	(10)	(11)	(12)	(13)
0.01 -0.50	24.03	3.80	0.27	15.29	2.37	0.31	33.27	6.90	0.29	25.76	5.07	0.30
0.50 -1.00	29.87	12.54	0.70	25.29	9.80	0.78	23.45	12.88	0.78	18.86	8.76	0.72
1.00 -1.50	15.58	11.37	1.21	14.12	8.85	1.27	9.42	8.23	1.23	17.65	13.57	1.19
1.50 -2.00	8.44	9.04	1.77	12.35	11.04	1.81	16.43	20.52	1.76	11.36	12.13	1.65
2.00-4.00	11.69	21.28	3.01	21.18	28.93	2.77	11.22	22.99	2.89	20.89	37.76	2.79
4.00-8.00	8.44	29.05	5.69	8.24	23.46	5.77	5.61	23.94	6.02	4.87	18.62	5.90
8.00 and above	1.95	12.92	10.96	3.53	15.55	8.93	0.60	4.54	10.66	0.61	4.09	10.38
	100.00 (154)	100.00 (254.36)	1.66	100.00 (170)	100.00 (344.56)	2.02	100.00 (499)	100.00 (704.11)	1.41	100.00 (493)	100.00 (760.78)	1.54

Gini Coefficients : Korea = 0.465176; Andhra = 0.487783

marginal and small farmers with limited farm and off-farm employment account for tenancy.

As a result in both, pure owners formed a little more than 40 per cent of cultivating households operating around 40 per cent of area. The proportion of owner rentiers and the area leased out by them in Andhra is more than twice that of Korea reflecting on the pressure for leased in land in Andhra with consequent adverse effects on lease market. With more or less equal proportion of pure tenants in both but with a relatively low proportion of leased in area in Andhra also reflects on its tenurial situation. Comparatively higher proportion of owner tenants and area under owner tenancy in Korea is indicative of the compulsions for economies of scale with growing mechanization and a growing desire for higher standards of living (Table 5.4 and 5.4.1). This also explains for higher proportion of tenants and leased in area in the higher size groups in Korea. In Korea though around 40 per cent of marginal farmers lease in equal percentage of area (as against 50 per cent in Andhra) this is mostly accounted for by the aged surviving on remittances while it is otherwise in Andhra.

Another feature of lease markets is in Korea, almost all classes of lessors, except the small, leased out mostly to the marginal farmers (Table 5.5). In Andhra, all classes of lessors, including marginal farmers, leased out mostly to small farmers. However, agricultural labourers mostly leased out to marginal farmers and other farmers. Further, there are no lessors among agricultural labour households in Korea. Another difference is, while in Korea only rentiers leased-out to agricultural labour households, in Andhra, about one-third of the big farmer lessors leased-out to agricultural labour to ensure labour supply for farm operations. In Andhra land is leased out to more than one class of lessees by most of the lessor classes. Perhaps this practice is to play safe apprehensive of possible risks in leasing-out to one lessor in view of the tenancy laws. In Andhra the low preference to lease-out to marginal households in contrast to Korea also reflects upon the relative viability of Korean marginal farm households. Korean transformation facilitated greater access to leased land to the marginal groups. In Andhra, the transformation that has taken place

Table 5.4 : Percentage Distribution of Cultivating Households and Area Held by Nature of Tenancy in Korea —1985-86

(*Census Data*)

Size-group (Ha.)	*Pure owners*		*Owner rentiers*		*Pure tenants*		*Owner tenants*		*Total*	
	No.	*Area (Ha.)*	*No.*	*Area (Ha.)*	*No.*	*Area (Ha.)*	*No.*	*Area (Ha.)*	*No.*	*Area (Ha.)*
0.01-0.50	53.85	60.34	19.23	11.75	19.23	19.83	7.69	8.08	26	8.17
0.50-1.00	48.84	45.48	9.30	11.79	20.93	21.53	20.93	21.20	43	33.77
1.00-1.50	54.17	53.46	4.16	4.72	16.67	17.72	25.00	24.10	24	29.46
1.50-2.00	28.57	28.86	—	—	19.05	18.75	52.38	52.39	21	38.04
2.00-4.00	36.11	34.19	2.78	3.94	13.89	13.80	47.22	48.07	36	99.68
4.00-8.00	50.00	46.10	14.29	18.14	7.14	6.53	28.57	29.23	14	80.83
8.00 and above	33.33	38.03	—	—	—	—	66.67	61.97	6	54.61
Total	44.70	40.38	7.65	7.23	16.47	11.89	31.18	40.70	170	344.56

Table 5.4.1: Percentage Distribution of Cultivating Households and Area by Nature of Tenancy in Andhra—1985-86

(Census Data)

Size-group Total (Ha.)	*Pure owners*		*Owner rentiers*		*Pure tenants*				*Owner tenants*	
	No.	*Area (Ha.)*	*No.*	*Area (Ha.)*	*No.*	*Area (Ha.)*	*No.*	*Area (Ha.)*	*No.*	*Area (Ha.)*
0.01-0.50	74.01	66.79	5.51	11.54	18.90	19.78	1.58	1.89	127	38.57
0.50-1.00	37.63	42.16	8.61	9.72	37.63	30.38	16.13	17.74	93	66.65
1.00-1.50	24.14	23.60	24.14	21.66	9.20	9.29	42.52	45.45	87	103.23
1.50-2.00	16.07	15.33	25.00	23.41	3.57	3.94	55.36	57.32	56	92.28
2.00-4.00	33.01	36.52	27.18	23.16	1.94	1.83	37.87	38.49	103	287.27
4.00-8.00	62.50	62.42	8.33	11.20	—	—	29.17	26.38	24	141.68
8.00 and above	66.67	55.73	—	—	33.33	44.27	—	—	3	31.13
Total	42.60	39.83	16.23	18.05	14.60	7.91	26.57	34.21	493	760.79

Table 5.5 : Percentage of Households by Status of the Lessee and Lessor in Korea and Andhra in 1986 *(Census Data)*

Status of Lessee / *Status of Lessor*	*Korea*						*Andhra*					
	Marginal farmers	*Small farmers*	*Other farmers*	*Agrl. Labour*	*More than one*	*Total No. of Lessors*	*Marginal farmers*	*Small farmers*	*Other farmers*	*Agrl. labour*	*More than one*	*Total No. of Lessors*
Marginal Farmers	25.00	50.00	—	25.00	—	100.00 (4)	—	80.00	10.00	10.00	—	100.00 (10)
Small Farmers	100.00	—	—	—	—	100.00 (1)	16.67	66.66	—	—	16.67	100.00 (6)
Other Farmers	50.00	—	50.00	—	—	100.00 (2)	—	50.00	—	33.33	16.67	100.00 (6)
Rentiers	33.33	16.67	16.67	8.33	25.00	100.00 (12)	14.70	38.24	17.65	11.76	17.65	100.00 (34)
Agrl. Labour	—	—	—	—	—	—	60.00	—	40.00	—	—	100.00 (5)
Non-Agrl. Rentiers	100.00	—	—	—	—	100.00 (3)	27.03	40.54	8.11	5.40	18.92	100.00 (37)
Total No.of Lessees	45.45 (10)	18.18 (4)	13.64 (3)	9.09 (2)	13.64 (3)	100.00 (22)	19.39 (19)	43.88 (43)	12.24 (12)	9.18 (9)	15.31 (15)	100.00 (98)

is in the direction of proletarianisation of the marginal and marginalisation of the small.

Land Market

The nature and character of the land market and the relative status of the rural households in this market largely depends on the stage of the economy. In an economy where majority are dependent on agriculture with limited non-farm avenues, the land market will be a sellers market with few sellers and all classes craving to acquire land. On the contrary in a situation of limited numbers in agriculture with non-farm avenues, the land market is mostly a buyers market with many sellers among all classes. However, Government interventions in the form of putting a limit on the ownership will influence the land market in favour of the non-rich irrespective of the stage of development. But its impact again depends on the efficacy of intervention.

In the pre-green revolution period *i.e.*, prior to 1970, land transactions both in Korea and Andhra are almost similar with sellers and buyers forming two and six per cent of the rural households and sales and purchases forming one and nine per cent of owned land in both. However in Korea, the percentage of sellers and area sold will be higher than what the data shows if allowance is made for out-migration (Table 5.6).

Though the pre-1970 land market helped augmenting the land base of the villages in both, there are differences with respect to gains across groups. In Korea big farmers, pure and non-agricultural rentiers did not figure in the land market while the middle group lost three per cent of land. In contrast in Andhra the big farmer and rentier classes entered the market as buyers only and improved their land base. Gains in land by marginal and small farmers are more in Korea, while marginalisation of the marginal farmers is more in Andhra. Further, in Korea the percentage of buyers among agricultural labour households is also higher though in terms of area it is more in Andhra (*see* Table 5.6).

With sellers out-numbering buyers and disposal of land by all groups, rural Korea of post-1970s is different from Andhra, with

Table 5.6 : Inter-Group Land Transactions in Korea and Andhra Before 1970 *(Area in Hectares)*

Category of Rural Households	Korea						Andhra					
	Buyers		Sellers		Total Rural House-holds	Total Area owned	Buyers		Sellers		Total Rural House-holds	Total Area owned
	Number	Area pur-chased	Number	Area sold			Number	Area pur-chased	Number	Area sold		
Marginal Farmers	4 (5.63)	9.54 (26.68)	1 (1.41)	0.09 (0.25)	71 (100)	35.76 (100)	11 (5.14)	13.55 (13.14)	3 (1.40)	1.37 (1.33)	214 (100)	103.09 (100)
Small Farmers	4 (11.43)	11.07 (22.39)	1 (2.86)	1.05 (2.12)	35 (100)	49.45 (100)	5 (5.56)	10.42 (6.89)	3 (3.33)	1.33 (0.88)	90 (100)	151.34 (100)
Medium Farmers	—	—	1 (4.55)	1.86 (2.96)	22 (100)	62.84 (100)	5 (12.50)	7.73 (6.09)	1 (2.50)	2.02 (1.59)	40 (100)	126.96 (100)
Big Farmers	—	—	—	—	15	106.26	1 (3.03)	2.02 (0.99)	—	—	33 (100)	203.86 (100)
Pure Farmers	—	—	—	—	4	22.10	3 (6.82)	2.02 (4.87)	—	—	44 (100)	41.49 (100)
Non-Agri. Rentiers	—	—	—	—	—	—	1 (33.33)	0.16 (4.40)	—	—	3 (100)	3.69 (100)
Others with land	2 (50.00)	0.36 (7.58)	1 (25.00)	0.22 (4.63)	4 (100)	4.75 (100)	3 (6.82)	4.45 (7.14)	4 (9.09)	4.04 (6.49)	44 (100)	62.29 (100)
Agri. Labour	4 (8.16)	2.40	—	—	49 (100)	—	20 (6.76)	19.29	—	—	296 (100)	—
Other landless	—	—	—	—	24	—	3 (2.86)	2.02	—	—	105 (100)	—
Total	14 (6.25)	23.41 (8.33)	4 (1.79)	3.22 (1.15)	224 (100)	281.16 (100)	52 (5.98)	61.66 (8.90)	11 (1.27)	8.76 (1.27)	869 (100)	692.72 (100)

Note :Figures. in brackets indicate percentages to total.

buyers out-numbering sellers and net gains in land. However, there are similarities and differences. In both, the percentage of sellers and area sold increased with size of holding, except in the case of big farmers in Korea. The structural transformation Korea experienced and the out-migration of youth from rural areas accounted for disposal of land by all cultivating groups. The scare of radical ceiling and tenancy laws enacted in post-1972 explains for the land sales by pure rentiers in Andhra (*see* Table 5.7).

The net loss of land by almost all strata of farm-households in Korea is mostly voluntary, *i.e.*, to shift away from agriculture and rural areas. But, in Andhra, the marginalisation of around five per cent of marginal and small farm-households is largely involuntary, *viz.*, high percentage of dependents, indebtedness to private sources, reluctance to hire-out labour on social considerations and old age. However, marginal and small groups particularly those with access to institutional credit improved their land-base.

Landless groups in both Korea and Andhra had a better access to ownership of land in post1970s. In Korea, the growing scarcity of labour and rising farm wages attracted a small percentage of the agricultural labour households to stay on in the rural areas. Wage incomes and remittances from children helped them to acquire land in Korea. In Andhra, around one-fourth of agricultural labour households, mostly belonging to weaker sections with relatively high ratio of workers to family size acquired land.

Dynamics of Land Transactions

Both in Korea and Andhra, prior to 1970, purchase and sale of land is from outside the group (Table 5.8). Group-wise, marginal farmers of Korea purchased more than 3/4ths from other groups, while in Andhra only 55 per cent of land is purchased from outside the group. This group sold limited land but to others only. In Korea, 75 per cent of small farmers purchased 95 per cent of land from others. Only 40 per cent of small farmers of Andhra purchased 46 per cent of land from others. While there are no sales by the Korean small farmers during this period, in Andhra, 2/3rds of sellers among small farmers, sold land to others. Korean big farmers and rentiers

Table 5.7 : Inter-Group Land Transactions in Korea and Andhra During 1971-1986 *(Area in Hectares)*

Category of Rural Households	*Korea*						*Andhra*					
	Buyers		*Sellers*		*Total Rural House-holds*	*Total Area owned*	*Buyers*		*Sellers*		*Total Rural House-holds*	*Total Area owned*
	Number	*Area pur-chased*	*Number*	*Area sold*			*Number*	*Area pur-chased*	*Number*	*Area sold*		
Marginal Farmers	4 (6.58)	1.81 (4.65)	6 (7.89)	1.87 (4.80)	76 (100)	38.96 (100)	40 (18.60)	27.71 (25.51)	9 (4.19)	2.89 (2.66)	215 (100)	108.61 (100)
Small Farmers	3 (8.57)	1.56 (3.16)	8 (22.86)	3.50 (7.08)	35 (100)	49.44 (100)	19 (20.88)	27.34 (18.98)	5 (5.49)	2.83 (1.96)	91 (100)	144.08 (100)
Medium Farmers	2 (14.29)	0.98 (2.37)	6 (42.86)	8.57 (20.72)	14 (100)	41.36 (100)	6 (15.38)	11.33 (9.43)	6 (15.38)	7.88 (6.56)	39 (100)	120.19 (100)
Big Farmers	—	—	3 (27.27)	11.16 (14.72)	11 (100)	75.80 (100)	3 (12.00)	4.45 (2.68)	9 (36.00)	23.97 (14.41)	25 (100)	166.32 (100)
Pure Rentiers	—	—	2 (14. 29)	0.98 (2.39)	14 (100)	40.94 (100)	1 (2.70)	0.40 (0.77)	5 (13.51)	5.87 (11.27)	37 (100)	52.09 (100)
Non-Agrl. Rentiers	—	—	—	—	—	—	—	—	—	—	45 (100)	57.75 (100)
Others with land	1 (25.00)	1.15 (14.63)	2 (50.00)	1.56 (19. 85)	4 (100)	7.86 (100)	9 (19.15)	10.01 (18.18)	16 (34.04)	25.98 (47.18)	47 (100)	55.07 (100)
Agri. labour	11 (23.40)	9.02	—	—	47 (100)	—	47 (23.15)	30.11	—	—	203 (100)	—
Other landless	1 (4.35)	3.13	—	—	23 (100)	—	14 (8.38)	11.74	—	—	167 (100)	—
Total	23 (10.27)	17,65 (6.94)	27 (12.05)	27.64 (10.87)	224 (100)	254.36 (100)	139 (15.99)	123.09 (17.48)	50 (5.75)	69.42 (9.86)	869 (100)	704.11 (100)

Note : Figures in brackets indicate percentages to the total.

Table 5.8 : Inter and Intra-Group Land Transactions in Korea and Andhra Before 1970

(Area in Hactares)

Category of Rural Households	Korea								Andhra							
	Purchases from				Sales to				Purchases from				Sales to			
	With in the group		Outside the group		Within the group		Outside the group		Within the group		Outside the group		Within the group		Outside the group	
	Number	Area	Number	Area	Number	Area	Number	Area	Number	Area	Number	Area	Number	Area	Number	Area
Marginal Farmers	1 (25.00)	1.59 (16.67)	3 (75.00)	7.95 (83.33)	—	—	1	0.09	1 (9.09)	6.07 (44.80)	10 (90.91)	7.48 (55.20)	—	—	3 (100)	1.37 (100)
Small Farmers	1 (25-00)	0.46 (4-16)	3 (75-00)	10.61 (95.84)	—	—	1	1.05	3 (60.00)	5.56 (53.36)	2 (40.00)	4.86 (46.64)	1 (33.33)	0.69 (51.88)	2 (66.67)	0.64 (48.12)
Medium Farmers	—	—	—	—	—	—	—	—	1 (20.00)	0.81 (10.48)	4 (80.00)	6.92 (89.52)	—	—	1 (100)	2.02 (100)
Big Farmers	—	—	—	—	—	—	—	—	—	—	1 (100)	2.02 (100)	—	—	—	—
Pure Rentiers	—	—	—	—	—	—	1	1.86	—	—	3 (100)	2.02 (100)	—	—	—	—
Non-Agrl. Rentiers	—	—	—	—	—	—	—	—	—	—	1 (100)	0.16 (100)	—	—	—	—
Others with land	—	—	2	0.36	—	—	1	0.22	—	—	3 (100)	4.45 (100)	—	—	4 (100)	4.04 (100)
Agrl. Labour	—	—	4	2.44	—	—	—	—	—	—	20 (100)	19.29 (100)	—	—	—	—
Other landless	—	—	—	—	—	—	—	—	—	—	3 (100)	2.02 (100)	—	—	—	—
Total	2 (14.29)	2.05 (8.76)	12 (85.71)	21.36 (91.24)	—	—	4	3.22	5 (9.62)	12.44 (20.18)	47 (90.38)	49.22 (79.82)	1 (9.09)	0.69 (7.88)	10 (90.91)	8.07 (92.12)

have not purchased any land, the limited purchases by these groups in Andhra is from outside their group. In the case of other groups, the sales transactions are not only limited but to outsiders only.

In the post-seventies inter-group land transactions are marked by predominance of purchases and sales from outside the groups in both Korea and Andhra (Table 5.9).

The comparative picture of land transactions during the pre- and post-green revolution periods in Korea shows that it is more or less the same with predominance of land transactions from outside the group and control over land shifting in favour of marginal and small groups. In Andhra, this trend is seen only in the post-green revolution period. The flow of land to small groups and landless labour is more in the post-green revolution period than in the pre-green revolution period in both Korea and Andhra.

Labour Market

Apart from supply and demand conditions the nature of the labour markets is also influenced by the cultural practices regarding use of labour, segmentation and substitution of machines for labour. Korean labour market is characterized by exchange labour and increase in use of machine power; while availability of plenty of labour and sparse use of machine power are manifest features of the Andhra villages.

Labour households formed eight per cent in Korea as against 25 per cent in Andhra. As a result, while there is one landless labour household in Korea for 20.00 ha. of operated area, in Andhra there is one labour household for 4.50 ha. in 1985-86. However, at the present stage of development in Korea, there is one powertiller for every 5.00 ha. of operated area. In Andhra there is one tractor for every 126 ha. of operated area. Organised groups for exchange of labour 'pumase' exist in one of the nine natural villages of Korea, eventhough this practice is on the decline.

In the developed Andhra village, women of traditionally land-owning agricultural castes do not work even on their own farms. Use of migrant labour for peak agricultural operations like transplanting and harvesting is in vogue in Andhra and these operations are getting mechanised in Korea because of absolute decline in farm population.

Table 5.9 : Inter- and Intra-Group Land Transactions in Korea and Andhra during 1971-1986

(Area in Hactares)

Category of Rural Households	Korea								Andhra							
	Purchases from				Sales to				Purchases from				Sales to			
	With in the group		Outside the group		Within the group		Outside the group		Within the group		Outside the group		Within the group		Outside the group	
	Number	Area	Number	Area	Number	Area	Number	Area	Number	Area	Number	Area	Number	Area	Number	Area
Marginal Farmers	1 (20.00)	0.48 (26.52)	4 (80.00)	1.33 (73.48)	1 (16.67)	0.55 (29.41)	5 (83.33)	1.32 (70.59)	10 (25.00)	13.06 (47.13)	30 (75.00)	14.65 (52.87)	1 (11.11)	0.51 (17.65)	8 (88.89)	2.38 (82.35)
Small Farmers	1 (33.33)	0.40 (25.64)	2 (66.67)	1.16 (74.36)	2 (25.00)	0.98 (28.00)	6 (75.00)	2.52 (72.00)	5 (26.32)	8.40 (36.72)	14 (73.68)	18.94 (69.28)	—	—	5 (100)	2.83 (100)
Medium Farmers	—	—	2 (100)	0.98 (100)	3 (50.00)	4.56 (53.21)	3 (50.00)	4.01 (46.79)	2 (33.33)	2.83 (24.98)	4 (66.67)	8.50 (75.02)	1 (16.67)	0.20 (2.54)	5 (83.33)	7.68 (97.46)
Big Farmers	—	—	—	—	—	—	3 (100)	11.16 (100)	—	—	3 (100)	4.45 (100)	—	—	9 (100)	23.97 (100)
Pure Rentiers	—	—	—	—	—	—	2 (100)	0.98 (100)	—	—	1 (100)	0.40 (100)	—	—	5 (100)	5.87 (100)
Non-Agrl. Rentiers	—	—	—	—	—	—	—	—	—	—	—	—	—	—	—	—
Others with land	—	—	1 (100)	1.15 (100)	—	—	2 (100)	1.56 (100)	—	—	9 (100)	10.01 (100)	—	—	16 (100)	25.98 (100)
Agrl. Labour	—	—	11 (100)	9.02 (100)	—	—	—	—	—	—	47 (100)	30.11 (100)	—	—	—	—
Other Landless	—	—	1 (100)	3.13 (100)	—	—	—	—	—	—	14 (100)	11.74 (100)	—	—	—	—
Total	2 (8.70)	0.88 (4.93)	21 (91.30)	16.77 (95.07)	6 (22.22)	6.09 (22.03)	21 (77.78)	21.55 (77.97)	17 (12.23)	24.29 (19.73)	122 87.77	98.80 (80.27)	2 (4.00)	0.71 1.02	48 (96.00)	68.71 (98.98)

Relative Status of Farm Households in the Labour Market

More than one-third of the farm households in Korea and Andhra hire-in and hire-out labour and there are no significant differences across size-groups. Nearly 50 per cent of Korean households report self-sufficiency of labour as against 3 per cent in Andhra (*see* Table 5.10).

The percentage of households usually hiring-in labour form 42 and 17 respectively in Andhra and Korea. While there is inverse relationship between farm-size and hiring-in labour in Andhra there is no such pattern in Korea. However, hiring in by nearly one-third of the Korean households operating 1.00 ha. and 1.50 ha. is rather unique. The trend of increased hiring-in with increase in size in Andhra is indicative of decline in the average number of workers per household in the developed village.

In Korea, only one per cent of the marginal farm households, eight per cent of agricultural labour households and a comparatively small percentage of small farm-households hire out labour. However, there is increased use of power-tillers consequent to subsidization and institutional financing for purchase of powertillers in Korea. In contrast, in Andhra nearly 1/5th of farm-households are hiring-out labour in addition to the 1/4th of rural households living on agricultural labour. In Andhra, hire market for tractor service developed in post-seventies as a result of liberal institutional funding for buying tractors. Increasing use of tractors in post-harvest operations has adversely affected employment in agriculture.

Credit Market

Efforts have been made to evolve efficient institutional framework for the supply of credit in both. Credit market is developed both in Korea and Andhra. However, while efficient cooperatives in Korea are able to provide credit to a large percentage of farm-households, in Andhra despite existence of cooperatives and commercial banks, the coverage is rather limited.

Relative Status of Farm Households in the Credit Market

More than 80 per cent of the rural households in Korea and Andhra

Table 5.10 : Distribution of Farm-Households by their Status in the Labour Market in 1985-86

(Census Data)

Size-group	*Usually Hires-out*		*Hires-in Hires-out*		*Self-sufficient*		*Usually Hires-in*		*Total Households*	
	Korea	*Andhra*	*Korea*	*Andhra*	*Korea*	*Andhra*	*Korea*	*Andhra*	*Korea*	*Andhra*
I. 0.01-0.50	3.85	47.24	34.61	34.65	57.69	5.51	3.85	12.60	100	100
II. 0.50-1.00	2.32	23.66	55.82	49.46	34.88	2.15	9.30	24.73	100	100
III. 1.00-1.50	0.00	5.75	33.33	56.32	37.50	3.45	29.17	34.48	100	100
IV. 1.50-2.00	4.76	1.79	19.05	41.07	66.67	3.57	9.52	53.57	100	100
V. 2.00 and above	0.00	2.31	28.57	16.15	44.64	0.00	26.79	81.54	100	100
Total	1.75	18.46	35.68	37.32	45.61	2.84	16.96	41.58	100 (170)	100 (493)

are borrowers. There are no observable differences across size groups in both. In both the percentage of non-borrowing households is less though comparatively higher in Andhra. None of the Korean households are in lender's status while in Andhra such households formed one per cent.

Around 12 per cent are self-sufficient in both. However, the percentage of marginal farm-households in this category is higher in Korea while it is far less in Andhra (Table 5.11).

Differential Access to Institutional Credit

A high percentage of Korean farm-households had equitable access to credit during all the three points of time (Table 5.12). The absence of inequities in the flow of credit to different strata in Korea pertains to relative absence of social differentiation, small size of natural village, credit dispensation within the village by the village chief as per sanctions of the PACS. In Andhra, the co-operatives are not active as there are management problems and high level of overdues. Though commercial banks are also dispensing credit to the villagers, because of the existence of PACS, bank activity is limited to select individuals who are not members of the cooperatives.

There was greater inequity in access to credit prior to 1970s in Andhra. Role of the cooperatives was limited and the available credit was cornered by the relatively better-off strata of the rural society to the exclusion of poor and marginal farmers from the membership of cooperatives themselves. This trend has been arrested since 1970 through appropriate credit policies. Exclusion of relatively high percentage of farmers with 0.50 ha. and below in Korea is based on their perception that the problems of tiny households is one of relative poverty which cooperatives cannot tackle. In Andhra, their exclusion, despite a fixed share is the result of bracketing of marginal and small farmers as a single group. The tendency of the institutions to cater to the small than to the marginal farmers for consideration of recovery and security worked to the disadvantage of the marginal farmers.

Table 5.11 : Distribution of Farm-Households by their Status in the Credit Market (*Census Data*)

(In Percentage)

Size-Group	*Non-Borrower*		*Borrower*		*Self-sufficient*		*Lender*		*Total Households*	
	Korea	*Andhra*	*Korea*	*Andhra*	*Korea*	*Andhra*	*Korea*	*Andhra*	*Korea*	*Andhra*
I.	11.54	7.09	69.23	74.02	19.23	16.53	0.00	2.36	100 (26)	100 (127)
II.	0.00	1.08	86.05	88.17	13.95	9.67	0.00	1.08	100 (43)	100 (93)
III.	0.00	4.60	75.00	83.91	25.00	10.34	0.00	1.15	100 (24)	100 (87)
IV.	0.00	0.00	100	89.29	0.00	10.71	0.00	0.00	100 (21)	100 (56)
V.	0.00	1.54	92.86	88.46	7.14	8.46	0.00	1.54	100 (56)	100 (130)
Total	1.76	3.24	85.88	83.98	12.35	11.36	0.00	1.42	100 (173)	100 (493)

Note : Figures in brackets as noted ante.

Table 5.12 : Percentage Distribution of Farm Households with Access to Institutional Credit in Korea and Andhra during 1970-86

(Census Data)

Size-Group	*Before 1970*		*1971-80*		*1981-86*		*Total Farm Households with Access to Institutional Credit*		*Total Farm Households without access to institutional Credit*		*Total Farm Households*	
	Korea	*Andhra*	*Korea*	*Andhra*	*Korea*	*Andhra*	*Korea*	*Andhra*	*Korea*	*Andhra*	*Korea*	*Andhra*
I.	19.23	0.78	34.61	3.14	11.54	3.14	65.38	7.08	34.62	92.92	100 (127)	100 (26)
II.	18.60	1.07	41.86	10.75	20.93	7.52	81.39	19.35	18.61	80.65	100 (93)	100 (43)
III.	29.16	5.74	25.00	13.79	12.50	4.59	66.67	24.13	33.33	75.87	100 (87)	100 (24)
IV.	19.05	3.57	38.10	16.07	19.05	5.36	76.19	25.00	23.81	75.00	100 (56)	100 (24)
V.	30.36	6.15	37.50	9.23	12.50	6.92	80.35	22.30	19.65	77.70	100 (130)	100 (56)
Total	24.12	3.44	36.47	9.53	15.29	5.47	75.88	18.46	24.12	75.88	100 (493)	100 (170)

Note : Figures in brackets as noted ante.

Relative Significance of Institutional Source of Credit

The data on source of borrowing of the sample households (Table 5.13) show that a large percentage of rural households in Andhra still continues to rely on private sources, despite multiplicity of credit institutions in the area, *viz.*, two PACS, two branches of commercial banks and a branch of regional rural bank. This is in sharp contrast to Korean situation.

Major reasons for difference in the working of credit institutions are two-fold. Firstly, the degree of integration of the farm-household in terms of the diversity of services rendered and the extent to which various needs are met by cooperatives is far higher in Korea. In Andhra, the services are limited mostly to provision of credit by cooperatives and banking agencies. Diversified services and efficient rendering of services helped promotion of greater loyalty to cooperative institution in Korea, while it is not the case in Andhra. Further, in Korea, credit institutions impose greater discipline on members to ensure timely repayment. The cooperative employees and the village chief constantly remind borrowers about timely repayment. High penal interests are also imposed on defaulters and they cannot borrow from any other institutional source. The credit status card annually updated by the cooperative through its credit servicing also helps to avoid over-financing. In Andhra, the options open to the borrowers are rather high on account of multiplicity of institutional agencies, and lack of effective coordination among them which results in over-borrowing and consequential repayment problems. This is particularly seen in the developing village of Andhra, where sample households borrowed loans in 1983 and 1984 from institutional sources. Being defaulters, they turned to private sources in 1985. In Andhra, repayment ethic was not only low, but also further worsened with politicians and even State Government urging financial institutions to be lenient in recovering loans under some pretext or other. The low level of penal interest compared to those prevailing in the unorganized money markets also encourages borrowers not to clear institutional loans. This coupled with relatively low coverage of poorer households by institutional sources accounts for the low percentage of institutional borrowers in Andhra.

Table 5.13 : Distribution of Borrower Households by Source of Borrowing—Korea and Coastal Andhra (*Census Data*)

(*In Percentage*)

Size-Group	*Private*		*Cooperatives*		*Banks*		*Coops. & Banks*		*All the Three*	
	Korea	*Andhra*	*Korea*	*Andhra*	*Korea*	*Andhra*	*Korea*	*Andhra*	*Korea*	*Andhra*
I.	11.11	65.96	88. 89	8.51	0.00	20.21	0.00	0.00	0.00	5.32
II.	5.40	59.76	94.60	4.87	0.00	30.49	0.00	1.22	0.00	3.66
III.	11.11	41.09	88.89	10.96	0.00	43.84	0.00	0.00	0.00	4.11
IV.	23.81	26.00	76.19	10.00	0.00	50.00	0.00	4.00	0.00	10.00
V.	15.38	15.65	82.70	11.30	1.92	60.00	0.00	3.48	0.00	9.57
I-V.	13.01	41.54	86.30	9.18	0.69	41.06	0.00	1.70	0.00	6.52
VI.	0.00	81.81	75.00	9.09	25.00	9.09	0.00	0.00	0.00	0.00
VII.	80.00	99.08	20.00	0.00	0.00	0.92	0.00	0.00	0.00	0.00
VIII.	16.67	78.48	66.66	6.33	16.67	12.66	0.00	2.53	0.00	0.00
Total	16.47	57.27	81.19	7.17	2.35	29.69	0.00	1.47	0.00	4.40

I. 0.01-0.50 ha.; II. 0.50-1.00 ha.; III. 1.00-1.50 ha.; IV. 1.50-2.00 ha.; V. 2.00 ha. and above, VI. Rentiers; VII. Agricultural Labour; VIII. Others.

In Andhra comparatively high percentage of marginal farm households continue to depend on private sources whereas, in Korea, relatively higher percentage of marginal farm-households are borrowing from cooperatives. Further, low coverage of poor households at the membership stage by cooperatives and limiting credit to those sponsored by DRDA account for low percentage of institutional borrowers from this group. In Korea absence of discrimination helped many marginal and small farmers to borrow from cooperatives.

In both, non-farm-households mostly depend on private sources for their credit needs. But the percentage of such households is much higher in Andhra. Korean agricultural labour households, who join mutual financing scheme in cooperatives are eligible to borrow from them. Agricultural labour households are excluded from institutional sources of finance in India till mid-1970. This accounts for their poor coverage in Andhra. Also in Andhra villages not a single agricultural labour household reported borrowing from cooperatives. This is attributable to the financial weakness of cooperatives themselves in advancing consumption finance and legal hurdles in advancing term loans without mortgage or security. However, one per cent of these households secured loans from banks under IRDP.

Input Market

Developed markets for farm inputs *viz.*, fertilizer, pesticides and seed is common to the Korean and the Andhra villages. However, while institutional agencies control these markets and supply quality inputs at the door steps of the farmers in Korea, in Andhra these are flooded with private dealers supplying adulterated, spurious and sub-standard products. The share of various agencies in input supplies to farmers are given in Table 5.14.

Korean cooperatives enjoy monopoly distribution of fertilizers and supply it to members on credit. They do not enjoy such a monopoly in supplying improved seed and pesticides. In respect of improved seed nearly 42 per cent and in respect of pesticides around 2/3rds of Korean farm-households depended on

Table 5.14 : Share of Different Agencies in Input Supplies to Farm-Households—Korea-Andhra, 1985-86 *(Census Data)*

(In percentage)

	Big Farmer	*Private Dealer*	*Government*	*Coope-ratives*	*Total*
			Seed		
Korea	2.04	2.72	53.06	42.13	100.00
Andhra	79.55	11.50	8.31	0.84	100.00
			Fertilizers		
Korea	0.00	0.00	0.00	100.00	100.00
Andhra	1.64	93.65	0.41	4.30	100.00
			Pesticides		
Korea	0.00	25.15	0.60	74.25	100.00
Andhra	1.85	94.43	0.83	2.89	100.00

co-operatives. In contrast in the two Andhra villages, there is almost an exclusive reliance on private sources as cooperatives are not very active in supplying fertilizer and seed and do not handle fertilizers at all. Another notable feature is greater and equitable access to institutional sources of seed and pesticides to all strata of farmers and preferred use of these sources by the marginal farmers in Korea. In Andhra the limited supply of seed and fertilizers handled by cooperatives have not flown equitably with very limited access to marginal households.

The relative soundness of the Korean institutional agencies particularly cooperatives in providing diversified inputs of quality, the extension services offered by them to the farm-households, equitable access to information in Korea and weakness of the Primary Agricultural Cooperatives in Andhra and their inability to supply these inputs account for the differential picture in the input markets. In Andhra, absence of structural transformation, presence of a large class of landless labour with relatively higher size families has kept most of the marginal farm-households and a sizeable section of small farm-households to compete with the landless labour in the shrinking labour market with unprecedented shift towards the use of tractors for ploughing and other labour intensive operations. So much so, the transformation has adverse effect on the well-being of the poorer strata of rural society.

Ownership and Use of Tractors

Unlike biological and chemical innovations which can increase productivity and reduce losses, mechanical innovations like use of tractors have far reaching social implications depending upon the stage of development of the economy and resource structure. While the overall impact is likely to be positive in labour-scarce economies, the adverse effects are more likely to be felt in labour surplus economies. Trends in the ownership and use of tractors in Korea with decline in absolute numbers in the farm sector since 1970 and in Andhra with increase in numbers and with a sizeable class of landless wage labour show up the nature of transformation in the farm sector.

The use of tractors began on a limited scale in sixties in Andhra, during which period they were not in vogue in Korea. There is accelerated pace in the use of tractors by all strata of rural households in Andhra compared to Korea at all points of time (Table 5.15).

Product Market

The product market refers to paddy. In Korea as agents of Government, cooperatives purchase HYV paddy immediately after the harvest at procurement prices fixed by Government. They also purchase limited quantities on their own. However, millers are the major source of marketing in the villages. There is one ricemill in the developed Korean village. Small quantities are sold in periodical markets to meet urgent needs in both the Korean villages. In Andhra, millers and their agents are the major source of purchase. Though periodical markets operate in the developed Andhra village, paddy is rarely transacted.

Interlinked transactions are present in all the villages, though such transactions are limited in Korea. Marginal and small farm-households usually borrow money from the millers in advance and

Table 5.15 : Percentage Distribution of Farm-Households Owning and Using Power Tillers/Tractors for Farm Operations during 1960-86 in Korea and Andhra

(Census Data)

Size-Group	*Before 1960*		*1961-65*		*1966-70*		*1971-80*		*1981-86*		*Total Households owning and using Tractors*	
	Korea	*Andhra*	*Korea*	*Andhra*	*Korea*	*Andhra*	*Korea*	*Andhra*	*Korea*	*Andhra*	*Korea*	*Andhra*
I.	—	3.14	—	0.78	7.69	5.51	38.46	51.18	38.46	22.83	84.61	83.46
							(2)	(1)			(2)	(1)
II.	—	—	—	—	6.98	12.90	44.19	52.68	25.58	29.03	76.74	94.62
							(3)		(7)		(10)	
III.	—	2.29	4.76	2.29	4.17	13.79	54.17	65.52	25.00	16.09	87.50	100.00
							(6)		(4)		(10)	
IV.	—	—	9.52	1.78	9.52	10.71	47.62	62.50	28.57	16.07	95.23	91.07
							(4)	(2)	(4)	(1)	(9)	(3)
V.	—	0.76	1.78	1.54	12.50	24.61	58.92	54.61	25.00	8.46	98.21	90.00
			(1)		(3)		(24)	(2)	(11)		(39)	(2)
Total	—	1.42	2.35	1.22	8.82	14.00	50.00	56.19	27.65	18.26	88.82	91.07
			(2)		(3)		(39)	(5)	(26)	(1)	(70)	(6)

Note:Figures in brackets indicate households owining power tillers and tractors absolute figures.

thus are obliged to sell the product to them. While there is no price discrimination *per se*, because of interlinked transactions, the timing of sale will be such that works often to the disadvantage of the producer in both Korea and Andhra.

Relative Status of Farm-Households in the Product Market

Only six per cent of the farm households in Korea are buyers in the product market, as against nearly 20 per cent in Andhra (Table 5.16). The higher family size in Andhra and non-viable nature of marginal farms account for this phenomenon. Further, a small percentage of small and big farmers are in the buyers status, because of concentration in growing commercial crops for instance, in the developing village.

The percentage of farm-households who sell and buy is also high in Andhra. However, the percentage of marginal farms in this category is the same in both indicating thereby that compulsion for resources force these farms to sell and later buy to meet their cereal requirements. Nearly 1/3rd of the small households in Andhra are in this category, while there are none in Korea. A small percentage of big farmer households in Korea and a comparatively high percentage in Andhra are in buyers status as they produce the type of paddy they do not consume and also because of overselling for better prices before the harvest.

Around 20 per cent of the Korean and 10 per cent of Andhra farm-households are self-sufficient in paddy. These differences are much sharper in the case of marginal households with 50 per cent in Korea as against 13 per cent in Andhra being self-sufficient. However, a small percentage of Korean big farmers are also in this category as they are pure tenants paying kind rents.

The relatively low percentage of households in Andhra in 'sells only' category may be because of relatively weak status of marginal households in the product market.

Changes in the Occupational Structure of Rural Households during 1970-86

Based on the responses of the households on their principal source

Table 5.16 : Distribution of Farm-Households by their Status in the Product Market *(Census Data)*

(In Percentage)

Size-Group	Buys only		Sells and Buys		Self-sufficient		Sells only		Total Households	
	Korea	Andhra	Korea	Andhra	Korea	Andhra	Korea	Andhra	Korea	Andhra
I.	23.08	59.06	11.54	16.53	50.00	13.39	15.38	11.02	100 (26)	100 (127)
II.	9.30	20.43	18.60	26.88	21.91	17.21	44.19	35.48	100 (43)	100 (93)
III.	0.00	1.15	0.00	20.69	8.33	13.79	91.47	64.37	100 (24)	100 (87)
IV.	0.00	1.79	0.00	10.71	19.05	5.36	80.95	82.14	100 (21)	100 (56)
V.	0.00	0.77	1.78	6.15	5.36	1.54	92.86	91.54	100 (56)	100 (130)
Total	5.88	19.68	7.06	15.82	20.00	10.14	67.06	54.36	100 (170)	100 (493)

Note : Figures in brackets as noted ante.

of livelihood, the occupational structure of the rural households in 1970 and 1986 was worked out. These are shown in Table 5.17.

Table 5.17 : Occupational Structures of Rural Households in Korea and Andhra—1970 and 1986

Census Data (in percentages)

S. No.	Status	Korea		Andhra	
		1970	*1986*	*1970*	*1986*
1.	Marginal	31.25	16.52	18.30	10.70
2.	Small	15.63	11.16	12.08	9.90
3.	Medium	7.59	7.59	5.41	4.25*
4.	Big Cultivators	4.46	5.35	3.91	3.80
	Total Owner Cultivators	58.93	40.62	39.70	28.65
5.	Owner Tenants	—	17.41	0.92	10.70
6.	Pure Tenants	4.46	12.95	2.76	7.01
	Total Tenants	4.46	30.36	3.68	17.72
7.	Owner Rentiers	2.23	3.12	—	1.26
8.	Pure Rentiers	1.78	4.46	0.46	4.26
	Total Rentiers	4.01	7.58	0.46	5.52
9.	Permanent Farm Servants	—	—	5.18	0.23
10.	Agricultural Labour	21.88	8.93	29.92	23.13
	Total Agricultural Labour	21.88	8.93	35.10	23.36
	Total Agricultural Households	89.29	87.50	78.94	75.26
11.	Business	1.78	1.78	3.45	6.79
12.	Petty Trade	0.45	0.45	1.38	2.19
13.	Artisan/Self-Employed	1.34	0.89	8.64	6.79
14.	Employees	4.91	4.91	5.52	6.21
15.	Others/Non-Agricultural Labour	1.78/0.45	4.02/0.45	2.07	1.03/1.73
	Total Non-Agricultural Households	10.71	12.50	21.06	24.74
	Total Rural Households	100.00 (224)	100.00 (224)	100.00 (869)	100.00 (869)

Note: *includes fish farming (0.341).

Agriculture continues to be the mainstay of rural households both in Korea and Andhra, with only marginal decline during the 15-year period. However, significant changes have taken place within the agricultural sector in both cases *viz.*, decline in owner cultivators, tenant and rentier-households. But the rise and fall in various categories, except in the case of rentiers is rather low in Andhra compared to Korea.

Both in Korea and Andhra there has been marginal increase in the percentage of rural households in non-agricultural sector during 1971-86. In Korea the percentage of non-agricultural households is much lower compared to Andhra at both points of time. The small size of the Korean village communities, absence of a class of rural artisans and concentration of industry in urban areas accounts for this. In Andhra the shift of artisans, especially weavers, into agriculture and business pursuits resulted in the relative decline in the share of households engaged in self-employment.

Changes in the Relative Status of Rural Households Between 1970 and 1986

This aspect was examined with reference to the occupational position of the rural household in terms of major source of livelihood, as perceived by the head of the household*: To grasp the changes quickly, a criterion is followed to classify rural households into three types: (i) those whose occupational status remained unaltered, (ii) improved, and (iii) declined. The criterion used for this purpose is shown in Table 5.18.

The above criterion though appears to be arbitrary, particularly in respect of business and employee category, as neither the size of the business, nor nature of employment is taken into account. However, normally any shift from business to agriculture or otherwise may be viewed as an improvement in the status both in Korea and Andhra. This is also true of shift from employee's into business or *vice-versa*. As such cases are few, details on land ownership, nature of employment, or business of the households, educational level are taken note of in classifying business or employee households, the details of which are shown in Table 5.19.

During 1970-86, the percentage of households and the groups benefited by the transformation process show that Korea fared better

---

* Bi-variate distribution of rural households by their past and present status are shown in Annexure 5.3.

Table 5.18 Criterion for Classification of Rural Households based on their Relative Status : Korea and Andhra—1970-86

S. No.	*Class*	*No Change*	*Improvement in Status*	*Decline in Status*
1.	Owner Cultivators/Owner Tenants	Continuation in same class	Shift to higher size-group, Owner-Rentier, Rentier, Business or Employee.	Shift to lower size group, Pure Tenant, Agricultural Labour, Non-Agricultural Labour, Petty Trade, or Artisan/Self-employed.
2.	Owner Rentier/Rentier	"	Shift to Business or Employee	Shift to Pure Tenant, Agricultural Labour, Petty trade, or Artisan/Self-employed.
3.	Pure Tenants	"	Shift to cultivators, Owner-Tenants, Rentier, Business or employee	Shift to Agricultural/Non-Agricultural Labour, Petty Trade or Artisan.
4.	Permanent Farm Servants	"	Shift to any other class	—
5.	Agricultural Labour	"	Shift to any other class except permanent Farm Servant.	Shift to Permanent Farm Servant.
6.	Business	"	Shift to Medium/Big Farmer or Employees	Shift to Pure Tenant, Petty Trade or Agricultural Non-Agricultural Labour
7.	Petty Trade	"	Shift to Cultivating classes, Business or Employee	Shift to Agricultural/Non-Agricultural Labour
8.	Artisan/Self-Employed	"	Shift to owner Cultivation, Business or Employee	Shift to Agricultural/Non-Agricultural Labour
9.	Employee	"	Shift to Higher Cultivatings, Class, or Business.	Shift to Marginal/Small Cultivator Class/ Tenant, Artisan or Labour
10.	Other Non-agricultural Labour	"	Shift to any other class except Agricultural Labour	Shift to Agricultural Labour

Table 5.19 : Distribution of Rural Households by Changes in Status : Korea and Andhra—1970-1986 (*Census Data*)

(*In percentage*)

Class	*Korea*				*Andhra*			
	No Change	*Improvement*	*Decline*	*Total*	*No Change*	*Improvement*	*Decline*	*Total*
Marginal	40.00	57.14	2.86	100.00 (70)	40.25	55.98	3.77	100.00 (159)
Small	37.14	37.14	25.72	100.00 (35)	52.38	45.72	1.90	100.00 (105)
Medium	52.94	23.53	23.53	100.00 (17)	44.68	40.43	14.89	100.00 (47)
Big	80.00	10.00	10.00	100.00	64.71	29.41	5.88	100.00 (34)
Sub-total	43.94	43.94	12.12	100.00 (132)	46.96	48.12	4.92	100.00 (345)
Owner Tenants	—	—	—	—	100.00	0	0	100.00 (8)
Pure Tenants	70.00	30.00	—	100.00 (7)	29.17	62.50	8.33	100.00 (24)
Rentiers	100.00	0	0	100.00 (9)	66.67	33.33	0	100.00 (4)
Permanent Farm Servants	—	—	—	—	4.44	95.56	0	100.00 (45)
Agricultural labour	34.69	65.31	0	100.00 (49)	71.54	28.46	0	100.00 (260)
Total Agricultural Households	45.50	46.50	8.00	100.00 (200)	53.64	43.58	2.78	100.00 (686)

Contd..

Table 5.19 : (*Contd..*)

Class	*Korea*				*Andhra*			
	No Change	*Improvement*	*Decline*	*Total*	*No Change*	*Improvement*	*Decline*	*Total*
Business	100.00	0	0	100.00 (4)	90.00	6.67	3.33	100.00 (30)
Petty Trade	100.00	0	0	100.00 (1)	75.00	-	-	100.00 (12)
Artisan/ Self-employed	66.67	33.33	0	100.00 (3)	69.33	25.33	5.34	100.00 (75)
Employees	100.00	0	0	100.00 (11)	79.17	16.67	4.16	100.00 (48)
Other Non-Agricultural Labour	100.00	0	0	100.00 (5)	72.22	16.67	1.11	100.00 (18)
Total Non-Agri. Households	95.83	4.17	0	100.00 (139)	75.95	18.58	5.46	100.00 (183)
Total Rural Households	50.89	41.96	7.15	100.00 (224)	58.34	38.32	3.34	100.00 (869)

Note : Figures in parentheses are number of households.

than Andhra. In Korea a higher percentage of rural households including the poor improved their status. However, acute shortage of farm labour and employment of children in non-agricultural pursuits in towns and cities with the aged staying in the village pushed nearly one-fourth of small and medium farm-households to sell away land. The resultant decline in the status of these households in the rural setting is purely voluntary, as land base is not so important for these households to survive.

In Andhra, with limited off-farm employment and the consequent greed to acquire land, the downward shift of around five per cent of farm-households may be because of natural division of property and involuntary circumstances into which the households were trapped. High percentage of marginal farmers among the owner- cultivator households and agricultural labour households in Korea improved their status. In Andhra, a relatively high percentage of marginal farmers, permanent farm-servants and tenants improved their status over time. While there are no differences in the percentage of marginal farmers benefited in both Korea and Andhra a higher percentage of pure-tenants have become owner-tenants in Andhra. While there is no class of permanent farm servants (PFS) in Korea, in Andhra they formed a little more than five per cent of the total rural households. More than 95 per cent PFS have improved their status. If one excludes the 60 per cent who became casual labourers, only 35 per cent of PFS households really improved their lot. In the case of agricultural labour, while 65 per cent improved their status in Korea, there is hardly any change in 2/3rds of these households in Andhra. These variations are largely attributable to out-migration of youth of the relatively better-off farm-households in Korea resulting in greater degree of leasing-out and sale of land and the absence of such features on any significant scale in Andhra. Of the 65 per cent of agricultural labour households of Korea who improved their position in 1986, 43 per cent became pure tenants and 12 per cent as owner tenants. In Andhra, only 15 per cent became tenants and 5 per cent as owner-tenants during 1970-86.

Non-agricultural households represent the group which almost remained static compared to other rural households both in Korea and Andhra. This is due to the limited options in the Korean village-setting for shifts within the non-agricultural sector and general aversion to shift from non-agricultural to agricultural pursuits. In Andhra, the growing preference for urban manufactured goods and for urban-based skilled workers for non-agricultural services forced non-agricultural households to shift from non-agricultural pursuits into agriculture either as a tenant or owner-cultivator. These account for the near constancy in the share of non-agricultural households in Korea and Andhra.

Relative Differences in Living Conditions

Relative differences in the transformation and differential impact on the well-being of different strata of rural households gets reflected in the living conditions *i.e.*, housing, access to services like electricity, drinking water and possession of consumer durables.

Housing

In rural societies, surpluses usually find their way into housing, partly out of necessity and partly for considerations of status. Thus, housing reflects on the economic status of the rural households.

Both in terms of the percentage of rural households owning houses and the type of housing facilities, Korea presents a better picture (*see* Annexure 5.4). Two factors largely account for the Korean phenomenon. There was a tremendous coercion by the Government to dispense with huts in the early phase of Saemaul Undong. The roof-improvement project and Government fillip to rural housing projects with subsidies and easy repayable instalment schemes is a major contributing factor. The favourable terms of trade for agricultural products since 1970s and inflow of remittances from children employed in the modern industrial sector is another factor.

In Andhra, the weaker sections rural housing programme of the Government was limited to a fraction of the rural households. The higher family size, limited and shrinking opportunities for earning in the rural areas account for the poor housing conditions in Andhra, with more than one-half of the rural households (58 per cent) live in thatched houses. However Korean houses are much smaller compared to Andhra huts. Climatic compulsions of maintaining temperature for nearly six months requiring considerable expenditure and the desire to utilise limited land resources to the optimum is responsible for the small size of Korean rural houses.

Access to Domestic Power Supply

Both Korean and Andhra villages were electrified in late 1960s. However, time lags persist across different strata of rural households in acquiring this facility owing to difference in affordability and type of housing (Annexure 5.3).

In Andhra, many households do not have access to electricity even in 1986 and there are marked differences across size-groups. In Korea nearly one-fourth of the households are electrified before seventies, and there are no perceptible differences across size groups in availing this facility.

Access to Power, Water Supply and Cooking Gas

In economies experiencing high rates of growth, with wider non-farm employment opportunities, absence of marked differences in ownership of means of production, the development of public utilities and access of rural households to these facilities is likely to be earlier and relatively more equitable. In contrast, in economies with slower rates of growth such facilities are likely to come late and even where provided, marked time lags are likely to persist in availing these facilities by different strata of society. Such lags are likely to be much sharper if there is widespread social and economic differentiation within the rural communities.

To reflect on the above aspects the period of access of rural households to electricity, domestic water supply are considered. For analytical convenience access to cooking gas is also considered along with the above two. The details are shown in Table 5.20.

Table 5.20 : Percentage Distribution of Rural Households by Period of Access to Electricity, Domestic Water Supply and Cooking Gas—Korea and Andhra, 1970-86 *(Census Data)*

(In Percentage)

Period	*Electricity*		*Water Supply*		*Cooking/Gas*	
	Korea	*Andhra*	*Korea*	*Andhra*	*Korea*	*Andhra*
Before 1970	23.66	4.48	12.50	4.14	1.78	0.23
1971-80	69.20	10.82	62.05	7.82	11.61	0.34
1981-86	4.46	12.66	17.86	4.14	31.25	3.34
Total Rural Households with Access to the Facility by 1986.	97.32	27.96	92.41	16.10	44.64	3.91

Access to Electricity

The two Korean villages had electricity only in 1970s though one or two of the nine natural villages covered by the two villages had this facility in late sixties. In Andhra one was electrified in 1965 and the other in 1970. Though Andhra villages had edge over Korean villages with relatively earlier access to power supply, the percentage of households with access to power supply is far lower in Andhra at all the three points of time. In Korea even by 1980 more than 90 per cent had domestic power supply. In contrast even by 1986, Andhra presents a picture of Korea of 1970 with only 28 per cent of rural households availing domestic power supply (*see* Table 5.20). There are no perceptible differences in availing this facility among the Korean households since 1970s. One reason for the Andhra scenario is possibly because of the predominance of thatched roofs for nearly 60 per cent of rural households.

Access to Domestic Water Supply

Most of the Korean natural villages had public water supply schemes way back in 1970s under the Rural Saemaul undong. For this purpose, Government extended both material and technical assistance and villagers shared the burden through labour and monetary contributions. In Andhra, even though the developed village had protected water supply, in the other village only a few houses have hand-pumps. The Andhra villages are served by a network of irrigation canals and tanks and most of the households meet their drinking water needs from the public taps and supplement it with canal water for general use. The sense of hygiene appears to be far less in Andhra compared to Korea.

As in the case of electricity, there are perceptible differences between Korean and Andhra rural households in respect of access to drinking water during the three points of time with Andhra presenting a picture comparable to Korea of 1970s.

Access to Cooking Gas

Nearly one-half of the Korean households are using different combination of firewood/coal and hay while Andhra villagers totally depend on these sources along with dung. Kerosene is used by around six and two per cent of households in Korea and Andhra villages respectively.

The differences are much more sharper in respect of cooking gas. Though in both the use of gas as fuel for cooking started by 1970s, it is not widely used even in Korea till 1980. However, by 1986, nearly one-half of the rural households shifted to gas. In contrast, in Andhra even by mid-1980 only a privileged few had access to this. However in both, there is no relationship between size of holding and access to this fuel. It is largely influenced by factors like flow of remittances, family size and personal preferences. Very few Andhra households had gobar-gas facility, though such units are being encouraged and subsidized since 1950 as part of the Community Development Programme. Adequate non-availability of dung because of decline in the maintenance of cattle accounted for poor response to gobar-gas in Andhra.

Consumer Durables

The type of consumer durables possessed and the percentage of households who can afford these also vary depending upon the stage of economy and relative affluence or poverty of the rural households. Because of the sharp differences in the nature of the two societies under comparison uniform items for a meaningful comparison has become difficult. As such society specific items are considered (*see* Table 5.21).

Table 5.21 : Percentage of Rural Households Possessing Select Consumer Durables in Korea and Andhra—1985-86.

(Census Data)

	Korea		*Andhra*	
S. No.	*Item*	*Households owning the item*	*Item*	*Households owning the item*
1.	Cooker	31.25	Iron safe	2.87
2.	Rice warmer	49.55	Sofa	2.42
3.	Grinder/mixee	30.80	Double cot	3.57
4.	Refrigerator	79.90	Radio/Transistor	41.89
5.	Electric fans	49.10	T.V.	2.30
6.	Radio/Transistor	48.21		
7.	T.V. (Black & White)	48.21		
8.	T.V. (Colour)	38.64		
9.	VCP/VCR	51.78		
10.	Telephone	59.38		

Certain consumer durables like TV/VCP/VCR are totally alien to Andhra rural households. Further, while nearly one-half of the Korean households possessed many of the consumer durables, in Andhra, only a fraction of the rural households had. Only in respect of radio/transistor around 40 per cent of the Andhra rural households reported possession. The Korean picture is more equitable with almost all strata of rural households possessing all the consumer durables despite variation. In Andhra certain strata of rural households like agricultural labour and even marginal farm households do not possess these items at all. Purchasing power in Korean villages is on par with their urban-counterparts, while it is not so in Andhra. Items like Television are beyond the means of many households in Andhra.

The differential transformation could be seen from the fact that even during seventies immediately after the ushering in of the Green Revolution, a sizeable percentage of Korean rural households had access to colour TV/VCP/VCR, Refrigerator and Telephone

Table 5.22 : Percentage of Rural Households possessing consumer durables of various types in Korea, 1970-1986

(*Census Data*)

Category	*Colour TV*				*VCP/VCR*				*Refrigerator*			
	Before 1970	*1971-80*	*1981-86*	*Total*	*Before 1970*	*1971-80*	*1981-86*	*Total*	*Before 1970*	*1971-80*	*1981-86*	*Total*
I.	—	—	30.77	30.77	—	11.54	15.38	26.92	—	26.92	50.00	76.92
II.	—	4.65	39.53	44.18	—	11.62	18.60	30.22	—	11.62	55.81	67.43
III.	—	12.50	25.00	37.50	—	25.00	33.33	58.33	—	33.33	50.00	83.33
IV.	—	14.28	14.28	28.56	—	57.14	19.05	76.19	—	—	52.38	52.38
V.	—	21.42	21.42	41.42	—	35.71	53.57	89.28	3.57	41.07	44.64	89.28
VI.	—	25.00	33.33	58.33	—	58.33	16.66	74.99	25.00	33.33	41.67	100.00
VII.	—	—	16.66	16.66	—	—	22.22	22.22	—	11.11	27.77	38.88
VIII.	—	—	45.83	45.83	—	4.16	8.33	12.49	—	12.50	66.67	79.17
Total	—	10.27	28.57	38.84	—	24.10	27.68	51.78	10.27	23.21	46.42	79.90

Category	Telephone				Cooking-Gas			
	Before 1970	1971-80	1981-86	Total	Before 1970	1971-80	1981-86	Total
I.	—	11.54	38.46	50.00	—	—	42.31	42.31
II.	—	9.30	46.51	55.81	—	—	16.28	16.28
III.	—	29.17	20.83	50.00	—	—	33.33	33.33
IV	—	—	42.86	42.86	—	—	28.57	28.57
V.	7.14	26.78	28.57	62.49	—	3.57	55.36	58.93
VI.	8.33	66.67	8.33	83.33	—	—	58.33	58.33
VII.	—	11.11	11.11	22.22	—	—	22.22	22.22
VIII.	—	12.50	20.83	33.33	—	—	37.50	37.50
Total	10.27	18.75	30.36	59.38	—	0.89	36.16	37.05

(*see* Table 5.22). The growth of the non-agricultural sector, with stress on consumerism, coupled with the Government's concern to maintain parity in rural-urban living standards, facilitated a large percentage of rural households to possess these items. Consumer durables like Refrigerator and Telephone are considered almost as necessities. In Andhra, in the given stage of development these items are mostly luxuries even for the well-to-do.

Conclusion

Thus, it can be seen that in Korea the successful land-reforms implemented by 1950, the structural transformation it witnessed since 1970 and the positive steps taken to revitalize the institutional agencies serving farm-households resulted in the widespread and relatively equitable percolation of benefits of growth and improvement in the living standards of rural households.

In Andhra, the limited impact of land-reforms in altering the agrarian structure, absence of any notable structural transformation and weaknesses of the institutional structures evolved to support agriculture and rural development resulted in seizure of the benefits of limited growth by the better-off strata of rural society. This can be seen from the differential access to institutions and disparities in the living standards in Andhra. Though Andhra also 'witnessed' flow of land to landless labour, marginal and small farmers, its positive impact on the living conditions is limited as the lease market continues to be governed by interlinked land and labour markets.

The changes in the relative status of rural households are further confirmed by the higher percentage of rural households, including the poor improving their status during 1970-86 in Korea. The favourable impact of Korean transformation is also manifest in land-market with control over land shifting into the hands of marginal and small farmers and emergence of a developed lease market.

ANNEXURE 5.1

POPULATION, FARM AND NON-FARM-HOUSEHOLDS AND AREA OPERATED IN EACH OF THE NATURAL VILLAGES IN THE KOREAN ADMINISTRATIVE VILLAGES

Name of Ri or Administrative Village	*Name of Ku or Natural Villages*	*Total Population*	*No.of Households*			*Area operated in ha.*
			Farm	*Non-Farm*	*Total*	
I. Kumpan Ri	1. Joong geum	108	25	0	25	23.9
	2. Wang geum	171	42	0	42	51.3
	3. Wong geum	133	25	9	34	42.4
	4. Sin Seong	76	16	5	21	33.7
	5. Hyunho	131	29	0	29	48.1
	6. Sin geum	173	35	10	45	112.5
II. Juk-Jeon-Ri	1. Juk Jeon-I	268	39	20	54	54.5
	2. Juk Jeon-II	188	26	15	41	56.7
	3. Juk Jeon-III	355	42	20	62	59.3

Note: Non-farm households refer to non-cultivating households.

ANNEXURE 5.2

DISTRIBUTION OF RURAL HOUSEHOLDS BY NATURE OF EMPLOYMENT OF CHILDREN WORKING OUTSIDE THE VILLAGE : KOREA AND ANDHRA—1986

(Census Data)

S. No.	Size-Group of operational holdings (in ha.)	Percentage of H.H. with children employed as: Unskilled Labour		Skilled Labour		Employees		Business		More than one		Total No. of Households with Children employed outside the village	
		Korea	Andhra	Korea	Andhra	Korea	Andhra	Korea	Andhra	Korea	Andhra	Korea	Andhra
1.	Below 1.25	15.39	66.67	69.23	11.11	7.69	11.11	—	11.11	7.69	0	100.00 (13)	100.00 (9)
2.	1.26-2.50	9.52	50.00	61.90	25.00	14.29	25.00	—	—	14.29	0	100.00 (21)	100.00 (4)
3.	2.51-3.75	—	66.67	71.43	33.33	7.14	0	0	0	21.43	0	100.00 (14)	100.00 (3)
4.	3.76-5.00	—	75.00	54.55	0	27.27	12.50	—	12.50	18.18	—	100.00 (11)	100.00 (8)
5.	Above 5.01	—	30.00	44.83	30.00	20.69	30.00	—	—	34.48	10.00	100.00 (29)	100.00 (10)
	Total cultivator households	4.55	55.88	57.96	17.65	15.90	17.65	—	5.88	21.59	2.94	100.00 (88)	100.00 (34)
6.	Rentiers	—	26.67	54.55	40.00	—	33.33	—	—	45.45	—	100.00 (11)	100.00 (15)
7.	Agri. Labour	12.50	33.33	50.00	33.33	12.50	33.33	—	—	25.00	—	100.00 (8)	100.00 (6)
	All Agr. Households	4.67	45.45	57.01	25.45	14.02	23.64	—	3.64	24.30	1.82	100.00 (107)	100.00 (55)

ANNEXIRE 5.2 (*Contd.*)

8. Business	—	—	66.67	44.44	33.33	44.45	—	11.11	—	—	100.00 (3)	100.00 (9)
9. Employees	—	50.00	—	—	—	50.00	—	—	—	—	100.00 —	100.00 (2)
10. Artisan/self-employed	—	—	—	100.00	—	—	—	—	100.00	—	100.00 (1)	100.00 (1)
11. Others	12.50	16.67	50.00	50.00	12.50	33.33	—	—	25.00	—	100.00 (8)	100.00 (6)
Total Non-Agri. Households	8.33	11.11	50.00	44.44	16.67	38.89	—	5.56	25.00	—	100.00 (12)	100.00 (18)
All Rural House holds	5.04	36.98	56.30	30.14	14.29	27.40	—	4.11	24.37	1.37	100.00 (119)	100.00 (73)

ANNEXURE 5.3

CHANGES IN THE RELATIVE STATUS OF THE RURAL HOUSEHOLDS—KOREA 1970-86 (*CENSUS DATA*)

(In Percentage)

Past Status 1970 / *Present Status 1986*	*Marginal*	*Small*	*Medium*	*Big*	*Sub-Total*	*Tenants (pure-tenants*	*Rentiers (owner-rentiers*	*Agrl. Labour*	*Non-Agrl. House-holds*	*Total*	*Percentage of House-holds*
Ha. 0.01-1.00 (Marginal)	40.00	11.42	2.86	1.43	55.71	32.86	7.14 (1.43)	2.86	1.43	100.00	31.25
Ha. 1.00-2.00 (Small)	20.00	37.14	11.43	5.71	74.28	20.00 (2.86)	2.86 (2.86)	2.86	—	100.00	15.63
Ha. 2.00-4.00 (Medium)	—	23.53	52.94	5.88	82.35	5.88	11.77	—	—	100.00	7.59
Ha. 4.00 and above (Big)	10.00	—	—	80.00	90.00	10.00	—	—	—	100.00	4.46
Sub-Total	27.27	18.94	11.36	9.09	66.67	24.24 (0.76)	6.06 (1.51)	2.27	0.76	100.00	58.93
Tenants	—	—	10.00	—	10.00	90.00 (70.00)	—	—	—	100.00	4.46
Rentiers	—	—	—	—	—	—	100.00 (55.56)	—	—	100.00	4.02
Agrl. Labour	2.04	—	—	—	2.04	55.10 (42.86)	—	34.70	8.16	100.00	21.88
Non-Agri. Labour	—	—	4.17	—	4.17	—	—	—	95.83	100.00	10.71
Total	16.52	11.16	7.59	5.35	40.62	30.36 (12.95)	7.59 (3.12)	8.93	12.50	100.00	100.00

ANNEXURE 5.3 (*Contd.*)
ANDHRA 1970-86

(In Percentage)

Past Status 1970 / *Present Status 1986*	*Marginal*	*Small*	*Medium*	*above Big*	*Sub-Total*	*Tenants (pure-tenants*	*Rentiers (owner-rentiers)*	*Agrl. Labour*	*Non-Agrl. House-holds*	*Total*	*Percentage of House-holds*
Ha. 0.0-1.00 (Marginal)	40.25	8.80	2.52	—	51.57	32.07 (0.63)	6.92	3.15	6.29	100.00	18.30
Ha. 1.00-2.00 (Small)	0.95	52.38	7.62	3.81	64.76	8.57	16.19 (5.71)	0.95	9.53	100.00	12.08
Ha. 2.00-4.00 (Medium)	—	10.64	44.68	14.89	72.34*	8.51 (4.25)	14.89 (6.39)	—	4.26	100.00	5.41
Ha. 4.00 and above (Big)	2.94	—	2.94	64.71	70.59	2.94	11.76 (5.89)	—	14.71	100.00	3.91
Sub-Total	19.13	21.45	9.85	9.57	60.29	18.84 (0.87)	11.30 (3.19)	1.75	7.82	100.00	39.70
Tenants	9.37	12.50	—	—	21.87	62.50 (21.87)	3.13	6.25	6.25	100.00	3.68
Rentiers	—	—	—	—	—	—	75.00	—	25.00	100.00	0.46
Agrl. Labour	7.21	0.66	—	—	7.87	20.65 (15.41)	0.66	61.64	9.18	100.00	35.10
Non-Agrl. Labour	1.09	3.28	—	—	5.47*	3.28 (2.18)	1.63	3.83	85.79	100.00	21.06
Total	10.70	9.90	3.91	3.80	28.65	17.72 (7.01)	5.52	23.36	24.75	100.00	100.00

Note : * includes households engaged in fish farming.

ANNEXURE 5.4.

PERCENTAGE DISTRIBUTION OF RURAL HOUSEHOLDS BY TYPE OF HOUSING KOREA—ANDHRA : 1985-86

(Census Data)

Category	Rented		Owned								Total No. of Households	
			Hut		Tiled House		Terraced Building		Two-storied Building			
	Korea	Andhra	Korea	Andhra	Korea	Andhra	Korea	Andhra	Korea	Andhra	Korea	Andhra
I.	—	3.15	—	74.02	57.69	20.47	26.93	1.57	15.38	0.79	100 (26)	100 (127)
II.	—	8.60	2.33	64.52	60.47	24.73	34.87	2.15	2.33	—	100 (43)	100 (93)
III.	—	2.30	—	60.92	50.00	31.03	37.50	5.75	12.50	—	100 (24)	100 (87)
IV.	4.76	—	—	48.21	38.10	37.50	47.62	14.29	9.52	—	100 (21)	100 (56)
V.	—	0.77	—	34.62	50.00	44.62	48.21	19.22	1.79	0.77	100 (56)	100 (130)
VI.	—	5.41	—	32.43	50.00	48.65	41.67	13.15	8.33	—	100 (12)	100 (37)
VII.	5.56	13.02	5.56	80.47	44.44	6.51	44.44	—	—	—	100 (18)	100 (169)
VIII.	—	20.59	—	47.65	54.17	21.18	41.67	10.00	4.16	0.58	100 (24)	100 (170)
Total	0.89	8.52	0.89	58.46	51.79	25.32	40.63	7.36	5.80	0.34	100 (224)	100 (869)

Note :Figures in brackets are absolute numbers.

6

SMALL FARM RICE ECONOMY
Korea and Andhra

This chapter is aimed to discern a comparative picture of small farm rice economy of Korea and Andhra with focus on physical inputs, yields and farm and off-farm incomes. However this does not purport to be a farm management study *per se*. This is based on the sample study of 120 farm households, 60 each from both Ko[illegible] and Coastal Andhra, juxtaposed against the backdrop of the mac[illegible] picture obtaining in the two societies, wherever possible for a meaningful understanding of the micro level situation.

Average Size of Farm

This average size of the farm of sample households is likely to be different from the one observed in the census, as the number of households in each strata is kept constant in both cases for purpose of comparison (Table 6.1).

Table 6.1: Average Size of Farm (in ha) of the Sample Households : Korea and Andhra

Size-Group	*Korea*	*Andhra*
I.	0.38	0.37
II.	0.79	0.88
III.	1.26	1.25
IV.	1.80	1.81
V.	4.23	3.78
Total	1.95	1.60

Across size-groups, there are no observable differences except in the case of last size-group. However, the size of farm is relatively higher in Korea compared to Andhra. But the average size of the sample households is relatively lower than the census data has shown *i.e.*, 2.02 ha. for Korea and 1.54 ha. for Andhra.

The percentage of owned land in operated area is higher in Andhra (74.56) compared to Korea (69.13). The percentage of net irrigated to net sown area is also higher in Andhra (94.00) as against 88.40 in Korea. In both, paddy is the single largest crop grown accounting for nearly 90 per cent of the cropped area. The intensity of cropping is higher in Andhra (143.17) compared to Korea (111.52) largely because of differences in agro-climatic conditions. In Korea there is positive relationship between size of holding and intensity of cropping on account of the expensive nature of vinyl farming. No such clear-cut relationship is to be found in Andhra.

Relative Significance of Traditional and HYV Paddy

In Korea and Andhra, high yielding varieties of paddy (HYV paddy) were introduced in late sixties, to augment food production. The Korean Government pressurized and induced farmers through price-support policies to increase area under HYV paddy till mid-seventies to attain self-sufficiency. However, the market-oriented Korean farmers swiftly went against Government policy and shifted from HYV to traditional paddy (TV paddy), taking cue from the Korean preference for glutinous rice, which fetched them a relatively higher price. They also successfully bridged the yield gap between TV and HYV paddy by adopting better cultural practices. As a result, the area under HYV paddy went on the decline in Korea. In Andhra, because of the wide gap between the yield of TV and HYV paddy, most of the area under paddy is covered by widely publicised HYV only.

HYV paddy accounted for only 32 per cent of the total cropped area in Korean villages, as against 89 per cent in Andhra. The inverse relationship between size and area under HYV in Korea is not found in Andhra for the first crop (Kharif) and the second crop (Rabi).

Structure of Assets and Liabilities of Farm-Households

There are differences in relative preference for investments among farm-households of Korea and Andhra. The Andhra preference for

Table 6.2 : Structure of Assets and Liabilities Size-wise—Korea and Andhra : 1986

S.No.	*Size-Group*	*Land*	*Dwelling House*	*Farm Building*	*Farm Machinery*	*Live-stock*	*Consumer durables*	*Financial Assets*	*Total*	*Liabilities as a percentage of assets*
I.	Korea	67.13	18.39	1.12	3.79	2.45	1.99	5.13	100 (15474)	5.95
	Andhra	68.64	21.55	5.05	0.09	1.58	1.47	1.62	100 (7219)	0.85
II.	Korea	62.90	18.73	0.91	3.77	5.77	1.73	6.19	100 (20329)	4.88
	Andhra	85.54	7.77	2.54	0.34	1.71	0.93	1.17	100 (14709)	0.16
III.	Korea	67.68	15.19	1.03	4.50	3.62	1.32	6.66	100 (30051)	5.13
	Andhra	89.77	5.39	1.80	0.16	1.05	0.86	0.97	100 (20316)	0.94
IV.	Korea	68.92	13.52	0.83	4.97	3.89	1.17	6.70	100 (39309)	4.06
	Andhra	76.60	12.77	5.56	2.34	0.12	0.74	0.97	100 (34939)	2.84
V.	Korea	82.89	7.52	0.29	6.64	0.51	0.60	1.55	100 (77893)	1.59
	Andhra	85.19	6.12	5.29	0.38	1.00	0.50	1.52	100 (63263)	1.15
Total	Korea	75.90	11.27	0.57	5.64	2..07	0.98	3.57	100 (40550)	3.00
	Andhra	83.19	8.40	4.60	0.66	1.12	0.70	1.33	100 (27673)	1.98

Note : Figures in brackets indicate value of assets in U.S. dollars.

gold and silver is not found in Korea, while Korean preference for consumer durables like VCP/VCR is absent in Andhra. Such items are excluded for reasons of comparability. The value of assets are shown in US dollars at 1986 exchange rates (Table 6.2).

The value of assets of Korean households are higher by around 46 per cent. Across size-groups there is parity among the higher strata while in the lower size groups, the disparities are pronounced indicating the better status of marginal and small farmers in Korea compared to Andhra.

With regard to structure of assets, land accounted for a lion's share in both though relatively higher in Andhra. Higher share of farm machinery and financial assets in Korea reflects on the labour scarce nature of farm economy and inflow of remittances. Investments in housing are higher in both. But in Korea it is out of necessity to withstand biting winter whereas in Andhra it is mostly for status considerations. Higher share of livestock in Korea, despite farm mechanisation, is on account of rearing of beef cattle, milch cattle, poultry and piggery. In Andhra, the low share of livestock is because of growing reliance on custom service for farm operations and absence of poultry and piggery.

Like assets, the liabilities are also higher in Korea. The positive association between size and liabilities, found in Korea is not present in Andhra (*see* Table 6.2). The higher proportion of liabilities to assets in Korea is indicative of higher investments in farming machinery and growing concern for achieving parity of living standards with urbanites.

Input-Use

As HYV paddy alone is grown in Andhra, comparison of inputs in physical units had to be limited to HYV paddy only. The inputs taken into consideration are use of NPK per hectare, bullock or machine labour and human labour days.

Use of NPK

The use of NPK in physical units and nutrient ratios in terms of K are presented in Table 6.3.

Table 6.3: NPK (Nutrients) used per hectare of HYV paddy siz-wise : Korea and Andhra—1986

Size-Group	Korea			Andhra		
	N	P_2O_5	K_2O	*N*	P_2O_5	*K O*
I.	157 (2.09)	64 (0.85)	75 (1.00)	120 (6.00)	50 (2.50)	20 (1.00)
II.	137 (2.01)	86 (1.26)	68 (1.00)	120 (4.80)	50 (2.00)	25 (1.00)
III.	142 (2.03)	67 (0.96)	70 (1.00)	115 (4.60)	55 (2.20)	25 (1.00)
IV.	138 (2.03)	63 (0.93)	68 (1.00)	130 (6.50)	60 (3.00)	20 (1.00)
V.	147 (1.99)	76 (1.03)	74 (1.00)	135 (5.40)	65 (2.60)	25 (1.00)
Total	143 (2.01)	74 (1.04)	71 (1.00)	130 (5.20)	60 (2.40)	25 (1.00)

Note: Figures in brackets are nutrient ratios in terms of K.

The use of fertilizers is generally higher in Korea. Korean farmers have been using chemical fertilizers much earlier than Andhra farmers. By late thirties an average of 22 kg. of fertilizers was used per hectare in Korea. The consumption of fertilizers per hectare of cropped area almost doubled during 1963-70 from 97 to 172 kg. Its use has further increased from 162 kg in 1970 to 289 kg. in 1978 but declined to 263 kg. in 1983 (Mohan Rao, 1986 p. 10). In Andhra, the use of chemical fertilizers began only in the post-Independence period and per hectare application of fertilizers in terms of N was only 31 kg in 1970-71, which increased to 74 kg. by 1976-89 (Parthasarathy, 1986; Appendix-III; Sarma, 1983, p.111).

The use of NPK per hectare of HYV also shows that it is higher in Korea across all size-groups. The relatively higher use of K in Korea is mostly to compensate for the deficiency of K in Korean soils. K is not so essential for the growth of paddy in Andhra The ratio of quantity of NPK in terms of K shows that Andhra farmers are using N and P in higher proportions.

Bullock/Machine Lobour

The use of bullock labour was relatively less in Korea even during sixties. It was 14 days per hectare in 1966 and declined to 12 days by 1970. The decline has been faster since mid-seventies. It declined from 10 days in 1976 to mere 5 days by 1981 and to 4 days by 1985 per hectare of land (NACF, 1968, p.114; MAF, 1972, p. 312; 1986, p. 323). It was much less per hectare of paddy. It declined from less than 4 days in 1981 to 2.5 days in 1985. This decline is seen more in the plains, compared to semi-plain and hilly regions.

In Andhra also, bullock labour use has been declining fast. The bullock labour days per hectare of irrigated paddy in West Godavari declined from around 25 days during 1957-60 to 1.72 days by 1980-81 (Sarveswara Rao, 1960, p. 191; Ramana and Sarma 1984, p. 158), as there has been an acceleration in the pace of mechanisation, with four-fold increase in the number of tractors (per 1000 hectares of cropped area) from 0.79 in 1966 to 3.67 in 1977.

None of the sample farm-households in Korea used bullock labour. In Andhra also, its use is rather low at 2.48 days on an average. Broadly, there is an inverse relationship between size of farm and use of bullock labour in Andhra, as there has been a growing dispensation of bullocks on considerations of cost of maintenance, shortage of permanent farm labour and developed market for custom hire-service in tractor-use.

The absence of use of bullock labour, acute shortage of farm labour and the consequent practice of frequent and manifold use of machines for various farm operations account for a nine-fold use of machine labour hours in Korea. While there is a positive relationship between size and use of machine hours in Korea, it is almost constant in Andhra except in the first group, which is attributable to the practice of depending on custom hire-service of tractor for preparatory and ploughing operations.

Human Labour

As Korea has experienced a significant structural transformation and Andhra presently continues to be similar to Korea of 1950 with a high proportion of work-force in agriculture, a reference to the broad trends in cultivated area per agricultural workers and labour-use becomes relevant before examining the labour input use on sample farms.

There is a gradual increase in the cultivated area per worker in Korea. In Andhra, there is no trend as such because of shift in cultivated area and in the number of workers. But, while it is four times higher in sixties it is twice that of Korea in 1981 (Annexure 6.1).

Historically, Korean farmers depend more on family labour, as most of them do not employ hired labour. In Korea, with the outflow of labour since mid-sixties and consequent rise in farm wages, there is decline in the total number of man-days employed per hectare of paddy and the proportion of hired labour (*see* Kim S. H., 1972, p.313; Kim, D.H., 1976, pp.38-40; Lee, J.H., 1972, p.194; Park, 1972, pp.5-6). More so since mid-seventies, for instance, the total number of human labour hours/day employed per hectare of paddy declined from 114 in 1976 to 103 and 95 in 1980 and 1985 respectively. Similarly, the proportion of hired human labour hours/day declined from 40.1 per cent in 1976 to 20.04 per cent by 1980. But, it increased to 26.5 per cent by 1985 (MAF, 1986, p. 323).

In Andhra, both the share, and the absolute numbers engaged in agriculture are on the rise. Its share formed 53, 61, 69 and 71 per cent in 1951, 1961, 1971 and 1981 respectively. Unlike in Korea, family labour is far less in Andhra. There is decline in use of hired human labour in Andhra, despite rising share of work-force in agriculture. For instance, in West Godavari district, the hired labour days per hectare of irrigated paddy increased from 127.36 during 1957-60 to 161 for Kharif and 198 for Rabi in 1968-69. But, by 1980, there is a marked decline towards pre-HYV level (Sarveswara Rao, 1960, p. 189; Ramana and Sarma, 1984, p.147). This decline is attributable to use of tractor for ploughing after dispensing with bullocks. There is also an atmosphere of decline in patron-client relationships with emerging trends of confrontation between labour and landed groups over wages and decline in the access to use of waste lands and similar public utilities enjoyed exclusively by the landed sections in the past.

Table 6.4 : Utilization of Human Labour (in-8 Hour Man-days) per hectare of HYV Paddy, Korea—1986

Size Group	*Nursery & Preparatory*	*Irrigation*	*Transplantation*	*Fertilizer application*	*Pesticides application*	*Weeding & interculture*	*Harvesting*	*Total Man-days*
I.	12 (10.35)	10 (8.62)	17 (14.66)	10 (8.62)	10 (8.62)	21 (18.10)	36 (31.03)	116 (100.00)
II.	11 (9.65)	9 (7.89)	19 (16.67)	9 (7.89)	7 (6.11)	23 (20.18)	36 (31.58)	114 (100.00)
III.	17 (15.05)	9 (7.96)	18 (15.93)	9 (7.96)	6 (5.31)	19 (16.81)	35 (30.98)	113 (100.00)
IV.	16 (15.09)	8 (7.55)	14 (13.21)	7 (6.60)	8 (7.55)	18 (16.98)	35 (33.02)	106 (100.00)
V.	15 (15.62)	5 (5.21)	16 (16.67)	7 (7.29)	7 (7.29)	15 (15.63)	31 (32.29)	96 (100.00)
Total	15 (14.42)	7 (6.73)	16 (15.38)	8 (7.69)	7 (6.73)	18 (17.30)	33 (31.75)	104 (100.00)

The share of family labour in total human labour days formed 70 to 75 per cent in Korea but in Andhra, it varied from around 1/3rd in the first to about 1/10th in the upper strata. The number of human labour days used per hectare of HYV paddy is 30 per cent higher in Andhra. In Korea the relatively less number of human days used per hectare is the result of frequent use of machine labour for various operations, which accounts for higher number of machine hours and consequent reduction in human labour days. The inverse relationship between size and use of human labour days in Korea reflects upon greater degree of mechanisation with increase in size of holding while no such pattern is discernible in Andhra.

Use of Human Labour

Operation-wise, use of human labour days per hectare of HYV paddy (Table 6.4 and 6.4.1) show that harvesting, weeding and inter-culture operations claimed higher shares in both, though relatively higher in Andhra. In Korea greater use of water pumps for lifting water, weeders and weedicides for weeding out and harvestors for harvesting, resulted in reduction of human labour days in these operations. In Andhra, the absence of use of machines for these operations resulted in higher share of human labour use for irrigation, weeding and inter-culture. Harvesting is done mostly on contract basis. As such, deflation of contract bill of harvesting, using the average wage rate of the season may lead to an over-estimation of man-days There are no significant differences in the use of labour for nursery, transplantation and fertilizer application in both. In Korea the higher proportion of man-days used for application of pesticides, despite use of high powered sprayers, is consequential to higher use of pesticides right from the nursery stage.

Yield Levels of HYV Paddy

Despite the relatively unfavourable cold climate, yields of paddy per hectare (for single crop) are much higher right from mid-fifties in Korea (Annexure 6.2). Historical traditions of introduction of non-conventional inputs like fertilizers and HYV paddy along with

Table 6.4.1 : Utilization of Human Labour (in 8 Hour Mandays) Per Hectare of HYV Paddy, Andhra–1986

Size-Group	*Nursery & Preparatory* operations	*Irrigation*	*Transplan-tation*	*Fertilizer application*	*Pesticides Application*	*Weeding & interculture*	*Harvesting*	*Total*
I.	22	23	20	10	4	28	43	157
	(14.67)	(15.33)	(13.33)	(6.67)	(2.66)	(18.67)	(28.67)	(100)
II.	20	18	20	7	1	24	40	130
	(15.38)	(13.85)	(15.38)	(5.38)	(0.77)	(18.46)	(30.78)	(100)
III.	18	19	20	7	2	30	42	138
	(13.04)	(13.77)	(14.49)	(5.07)	(1.45)	(21.74)	(30.44)	(100)
IV.	20	17	20	7	2	30	44	140
	(14.28)	(12.14)	(14.28)	(5.00)	(1.43)	(21.43)	(31.44)	(100)
V.	16	16	20	7	2	30	47	138
	(11.59)	(11.59)	(14.49)	(5.07)	(1.45)	(21.74)	(34.07)	(100)
Total	18	17	20	7	2	30	45	139
	(12.95)	(12.23)	(14.39)	(5.04)	(1.44)	(21.58)	(32.37)	(100)

several cultural practices by the Japanese at a much earlier stage than in Andhra and personal care of family labour account for higher yields in Korea. Andhra, inspite of a relatively favourable climate, did not have traditions of cropping practices similar to Korea, as the pre-Independence British colonial power promoted production of commercial crops than food crops. The use of fertilizers and pesticides was also low particularly prior to mid-sixties. The low use of family labour and diverse agro-climatic conditions also resulted in low average yields in Andhra.

The yield levels per hectare of HYV paddy is 20 per cent higher in Korea and there is a positive relationship between size and yield level (Table 6.5). The lower yield levels in the lower size-groups in Korea may be because of less significance attached to farming by marginal farm-households represented mostly by the aged. In higher size-groups, farming is looked at as a business proposition for attaining living standards, comparable to those living in towns.

Table 6.5: Yield Levels of HYV Paddy per Hectare in Korea and Andhra

(in kgs.)

Size-Group	*Korea*	*Andhra*
I.	4497	4177
II.	5457	4631
III.	5463	4435
IV.	5720	5354
V.	6055	4743
Total	5728	4759

In Andhra, there is no relationship between size of farm and yield levels. Further, yields on small farms are lower compared to the large farms. Moreover, farm as a source of living for the marginal household is inadequate within limited access to institutional support and the outward looking tendency of the big farm.

Yield Gaps

To estimate the gap between potential yield at the experimental station level and the actual yield obtained on the sample farms two popular varieties of paddy *viz.*, Milyang in Korea and Swarna in

Andhra are considered. The potential yield of Milyang is estimated at 6,500 kg. per hectare at the national level. The yield potential of Swarna, estimated by the local Maruteru Rice Research Centre, was 6,500 kg. per hectare.

The yield gap estimated here refers to the gap between the yield potential at the experimental station level and the yield obtained at the sample farms level for the two varieties—Milyang in Korea and Swarna in Andhra. The gap between the potential and actual yield of the two select varieties are shown in Table 6.6.

Table 6.6: Yield Gap between Potential Yields at the Experimental Station Level and Actual Yields on Sample Farms : Korea and Andhra (in percentages) 1985

Size-Group	*Korea*	*Andhra*
I.	6.69	28.62
II.	1.77	21.92
III.	1.84*	15.54
IV.	3.08	3.62
V.	4.31*	24.00
Total	2.92*	15.00

* Indicates yield level higher than the potential.

In Korea, the average yield exceeded the potential by around 3 per cent. In Andhra, the yield gap is around 15 per cent on an average.

Thus, when comparable regions are taken into account, the yield differences between Korea and Andhra are not very significant, though at the macro level, the variations are rather high. Even the yield gaps are not very significant, when viewed in relation to the equitable and efficient institutional services available to the Korean farmers as against limited and differential access to institutional services available to the Andhra farmers.

Physical Input-Output Relationship

To even out the price differences and exchange rates across the countries physical input-output relationships for two major inputs *i.e.*, fertilizer and human labour are considered (Table 6.7).

Table 6.7: Input-Output Ratios of N, NPK and Human Labour In Korea and Andhra in 1986

(In kgs. of paddy)

Size Group	*Korea*			*Andhra*		
	N	*N+P+K*	*Human Labour*	*N*	*N+P+K*	*Human Labour*
I.	28.64	15.19	38.76	34.81	21.98	26.61
II.	39.83	17.55	47.87	38.59	23.75	35.62
III.	38.47	19.58	48.35	38.57	22.74	32.14
IV.	41.45	21.26	53.96	41.18	25.50	38.24
V.	41.19	20.39	63.07	35.13	21.08	34.37
Total	40.06	19.89	55.08	36.61	22.13	34.24

There is an inverse relationship between input-use and output levels across size-groups for N, NPK and human labour in Korea except in the case of fertilizer use. However, no relationship could be seen in Andhra. Overall relationships show that Korean farmers are able to obtain higher output per unit of N and human labour compared to Andhra. Partly this is because of the relatively higher ratio of family labour and greater use of machinery per worker. However, the relative deficiency of the Korean soils in phosphorus account for the relatively lower output levels per unit of NPK.

Cost of Cultivation per hectare of HYV Paddy

The cost of cultivation. (on the basis of Cost A_2) per hectare of HYV paddy expressed in U.S. dollars and in terms of kg. of paddy is shown in Table 6.8.

As conversion of Won and rupee into dollars at 1986 exchange rates does not overcome the difference in the purchasing power parities, the analysis is limited to costs per hectare of HYV paddy in terms of paddy in kgs. The results show that there is no relationship between size and cost of cultivation of HYV paddy in Korea and Andhra. The data also reveal that the cost of production per hectare of HYV paddy is higher in Andhra by about 68 per cent at the aggregate level. They are also higher in all size-groups, though varied across size-groups from 32 per cent in the fourth size-group to 122 per cent in the second size group. With yield levels lower by 5 to 20 per cent and costs exceeding by 32 to 122 per cent, the Andhra farmers are worse-off, compared to their Korean counterparts, though one has to look at the purchasing power of paddy in terms of prices paid by farmers in both the countries.

Table 6.8: Cost of Cultivation (Cost A_2) per hectare of HYV Paddy : Korea and Andhra—1986

Size-Group	*Korea*		*Andhra*	
	In US dollars	*In kg. of Paddy*	*In US dollars*	*In kg. of Paddy*
I.	1020.38	1672	293.32	2444
II.	968.32	1587	423.28	3527
III.	1442.19	2364	450.40	3753
IV.	1225.38	2009	356.99	2975
V.	1522.88	2497	485.69	4047
Total	1326.24	2174	438.66	3656

Note : Price of paddy per kg at 1986 market prices in US dollars. Korea = 61 cents and Andhra = 12 cents.
(Cost A_2 includes all costs incurred on seed, farm yard manure and fertilizers, pesticides, animal and machine labour, hired human labour, irrigation, land revenue and taxes, depreciation, interest on working capital and rent paid).

Inputs that account for the differential cost structure and expenditure incurred on various items of paid-out costs expressed in terms of paddy are shown in Table 6.9. Details of expenditure in US dollars are presented in Annexure 6.3.

A comparison of costs incurred on various inputs in items of paddy (in kgs.) shows that in respect of six out of the ten items of cost, the Andhra farmers incurred more costs than their Korean counterparts. Size-wise also this is true except in few cases. These costs include seed, farm yard manure and chemical fertilizers, animal and machine labour, hired human charges, interest on working capital and rents paid.

The above differences largely pertain to variations in the price structure rather than differences in physical units. Unit prices of select farm and non-farm items having a bearing on the cost structure show that the favourable terms of trade for most of the

Table 6.9 : Cost of Cultivation (in kg of Paddy) per hectare of HYV Paddy : Korea and Andhra—1986

Size-Group	Seed		FYM and Chemical Fertilizers		Pesticides		Animal and Machine Labour		Hired Labour Charges		Irrigation Charges	
	Korea	Andhra	Korea	Andhra	Korea	Andhra	Korea	Andhra	Korea	Andhra	Korea	Andhra
I.	112	130	362	744	221	80	80	418	274	520	139	82
II.	98	132	571	844	249	188	61	526	270	301	34	79
III.	81	127	701	792	189	128	184	545	280	621	183	79
IV.	58	145	418	786	180	120	160	529	636	749	89	79
V.	71	136	693	825	217	185	173	499	567	1419	142	79
Total	77	135	602	811	213	160	146	507	474	1014	117	79
	(3.54)	(3.69)	(27.69)	(22.18)	(9.80)	(4.38)	(6.7)	(13.87)	(21.60)	(27.73)	(5.38)	(2.16)

(*Contd.*)

TABLE 6.9. *(Contd.)*

Size Group	Land Revenue and Taxes		Depreciation		Interest on working capital		Rent Paid		Total cost A_2	
	Korea	*Andhra*	*Korea*	*Andhra*	*Korea*	*Andhra*	*Korea*	*Andhra*	*Korea*	*Andhra*
I.	40	—	184	10	186	91	74	134	1672	2444
II.	33	—	114	99	101	198	56	1160	1587	3527
III.	37	7	111	100	190	237	408	1117	2364	3753
IV.	60	7	71	113	53	197	284	250	2009	2975
V.	71	7	287	212	168	291	108	394	2497	4047
Total	56	6	188	155	137	250	164	539	2174	3656
	(2.57)	(0.16)	(8.65)	(4.23)	(6.30)	(6.83)	(7.54)	(6.83)	(100)	(100)

Note : Figures in brackets indicate percentage to the total.

production inputs the Korean farmer enjoys *vis-a-vis* the Andhra farmer, accounts for the differential cost structure observed (Table 6.10). The predominance of family labour, also, accounts for the lower cost of cultivation. The higher interest charges in Andhra are partly due to relatively greater reliance on non-institutional sources. The existence of a large class of landless labour along with an equally significant number of marginal and small farmers on the one hand, and the reluctance of rentier classes to lease-out land out of scare of tenancy legislation on the other, accounts for the phenomenally higher rental charges in Andhra. In Korea, with a relatively large non-resident rentier class and without a significant class of labour dependent on agriculture for their survival the rental market for land is not exploitative compared to Andhra. Further, land is leased-in in Korea mostly to derive economies of scale in the use of machines and for attaining comparative living standards with urbanites, while in Andhra it is mostly to eke out a living except in the case of a few big farmers.

Table 6.10 : Prices paid by Farm Households for select items in terms of Paddy—1986

S. No.	Item	*Korea* Price in Won	*Korea* Price in kg of paddy	*Andhra* Price in Rupees	*Andhra* Price in kg of paddy
1.	N fertilizers (kg)	542	0.99	5.36	3.65
2.	Rental charges for power tiller/tractor per day	9800	17.98	12.00	8.16
3.	Farm wage per day	7000	12.84	12.00	8.16
4.	Tractor	529700	972.00	95000.00	64626.00
5.	Diesel oil (litre)	277	0.51	3.56	2.44

Source : Korea : MAF, 1986.
Andhra: Village Census Data, 1986.

The higher irrigation costs in Korea is because of the Government's insistence on cost effectiveness of the management of irrigation source managed by the farmers themselves through Farm Land Irrigation Associations (FLIA) and expenditure on the use of irrigation pumps by the farmers to lift water wherever necessary. In Andhra, no such principle is followed in collecting irrigation charges. The differences in the land revenue are rather wide, with Korean farmer paying 56 kg of paddy as against 6 kg.

by Andhra farmer. In Andhra, while marginal and small farmers are exempted from payment of land revenue, there is progression in land charges for higher size-groups.

Thus, the low cost structure of Korean farming is consequent upon high level of subsidy of industrial inputs and the higher price paid to paddy. The subsidy for bag of 75 kg of polished rice increased from 328 Won in 1970 to 11,900 Won in 1981. This has resulted in mounting deficit in the Grain Management Fund (Braverman *et al.*, 1983, p. 88). These policies are pursued in the larger goals of national self-sufficiency in food, to maintain social stability and to bring about parity in the urban-rural living standards. Korea could pursue this policy largely because of its industrial growth and fast declining rural population.

Gross Value of Production, Cost of Cultivation and Income per hectare of Cropped Area

Details on gross value of product, cost of production and farm business income per hectare of TV paddy in Korea, HYV paddy (second crop) in Andhra and for other crops in both cases in terms of paddy in kgs. are given in Annexures 6.4 and 6.4.1. The details of gross value of production, cost A_2 and farm business income per hectare of cropped area, expressed in kgs. of paddy are shown in Table 6.11 and these details expressed in US dollars are presented in Annexure 6.5.

The figures show that while the differences in the GVP are not very significant between Korea and Andhra, the paid-out costs in Andhra are more than double at the aggregate level. In three out of the five size-groups, the higher costs account for the low proportion of farm business incomes in Andhra. The very low share of farm business income in the gross value of product in many size-groups is attributable to the losses/low returns for other crops and unremunerative prices for cotton in the year under study.

Incomes of Farm-Households in Korea and Andhra

The incomes of farm-households in Andhra form just 1/3rd of that of Korean households (Table 6.11). Size-wise also, except in the first size-group, the incomes are far lower in Andhra. While there

Table 6.11 : Gross Value of Product, Cost A_2 and Farm Business Incomes of Farm-Households for HYV Paddy in Korea and Andhra—1986

(Units in kg. of paddy)

Size Group	*Gross Value of product*			*Cost A_2*			*Farm Business Income*			*Farm Business Income as a percent of GVP*	
	Korea K	*Andhra* A	*A/K*	*Korea* K	*Andhra* A	*A/K*	*Korea* K	*Andhra* A	*A/K*	*Korea*	*Andhra*
I.	4905	4200	0.86	1934	2741	1.42	2971	1459	0.49	60.57	34.74
II.	5725	4983	0.87	1567	4083	2.61	4158	900	0.22	72.62	18.06
III.	5113	4683	0.92	1549	3975	2.57	3564	708	0.20	69.70	16.15
IV.	5125	5200	1.01	1773	2933	1.65	3352	2267	0.67	65.40	43.60
V.	5879	4875	0.83	1634	4025	2.46	4245	850	0.20	72.20	17.43
Total	5672	4867	0.86	1641	3958	2.41	4031	909	0.23	71.06	18.67

is a positive association between size and farm household income in Korea, there is no such pattern in Andhra. The relatively low level of farm-household incomes coupled with higher size of farm-households in Andhra account for their poor living standards.

To sharply account for these differences details on farm and non-farm incomes are considered. In Korea, livestock incomes are mostly from sale of beef cattle, poultry, and also milk in few cases. The average cost of rearing beef-cattle, as reported by the Ri-Chiefs, and income received as reported by the households, are taken into account. Incomes from non-farm enterprises in Korea relate to earnings of family members who daily commute to their place of work in the nearby towns. The Income from livestock in Andhra refers to sale of milk only. To arrive at the net income from sale of milk, the average cost of production of milk as estimated by the local milk supply society is considered.

The ratios of Farm and Non-Farm Incomes to total wage and interest incomes are higher in Andhra. Incomes from farm wages, rentals and interest are higher by 4.36, 1.52 and 1.46 times respectively in Andhra. In all other respects, the ratios are far lower. The ratio of total farm incomes, salaries, remittances and non-farm incomes are 0.23, 0.55 and 0.59 respectively. Thus, in relative terms, the average farm-household of Andhra is much poorer, because of high cost structure of farm economy, negative incomes from livestock and comparatively low level of remittances.

However, if one looks at the relative share of various sources of income in the total incomes, the picture will be slightly different (see Annexures 6.6 and 6.6.1). While the share of income from agriculture continues to be low in Andhra *i.e.*, 56.36 per cent as against 76.38 per cent in Korea, the share of wage incomes is around 25 per cent as against less than two per cent in Korea. The relatively higher share of non-farm incomes in Andhra (43.64), as against 23.62 in Korea, is partly owing to selection of Andhra villages with relatively higher rural work-force in non-agricultural pursuits, with the belief that rural non-farm incomes are higher in Korea. Within non-farm, the share of income from non-farm enterprises and interest incomes are higher in Andhra.

Purchasing Power of Paddy and Living Standards

To examine the relative terms of trade of paddy growers in Korea and Andhra, the prices paid by farm-households for select items of consumption in kg. paddy during 1985-86 are considered. In working out these ratios, the data on prices paid by farm households in Korea as estimated by the Ministry of Agriculture are used. For Andhra, the prices paid by the rural households in the sample villages are considered.

A perusal of relative prices of manufactured and consumption goods paid by farmers in terms of paddy shows that, in most of the items considered, Andhra farm-households pay higher prices compared to Korean farm-households (Table 6.12).

Table 6.12 : Prices paid by Farm-Households for Select Items of Consumption in Korea and Andhra-1986

(in kg of paddy)

S. No.	*Item*	*Korea*		*Andhra*	
		Price in Won	*Price in kg. of paddy*	*Price in Rupees*	*Price in kg. of paddy*
1.	Rice	884	1.62	3.25	2.21
2.	Red Bean/Redgram dal	1072	1.97	6.50	4.42
3.	Chicken (kg.)	1036	1.90	12.00	8.16
4.	Eggs (10)	508	0.93	5.50	3.74
5.	Red Pepper/Dry Chillies (kg.)	3085	5.66	12.00	8.16
6.	Potato (kg.)	876	1.61	2.50	1.70
7.	Cucumber (kg.)	193	0.35	1.00	0.68
8.	Onion (kg.)	176	0.32	1.50	1.02
9.	Tomato (kg.)	247	0.45	2.00	1.36
10.	Egg plant/Brinjal	189	0.34	1.00	0.68
11.	Milk (litre)	313	0.57	3.50	2.38
12.	Sugar (kg.)	632	1.15	2.70	1.84
13.	Country liquor (100 ml)	94	0.17	5.00	3.40
14.	Cotton Cloth Medium Quality (yard)	558	1.02	10.00	6.80
15.	Toilet soap (140 gms)	207	0.38	5.50	3.74
16.	Laundry soap (140 gms)	190	0.35	4.00	2.72
17.	Umbrella Cotton (14 sticks)	3639	6.67	50.00	34.01
18.	Bicycle (26 inches)	58396	107.15	700.00	476.19
19.	Newspaper (per month)	2700	4.95	24.00	16.33
20.	Kerosene (litre)	291	0.53	1.60	1.09
21.	Cement (50 kg.)	2873	5.27	50.00	34.01
22.	Bus fare (10 km.)	176	0.32	0.48	0.33

Note : Korea 1 kg. of paddy = 545 Won (1985).
Andhra : 1 kg. of paddy= 1.47 Rupees (1985).

The differences in the prices paid by the Korean and Andhra farm-households during 1986 are attributable to the high rates of growth of industrial production in Korea and the significantly low percentage of agricultural work-force (22 per cent in 1985). The Government policies in Korea since seventies are also geared up to make agriculture more remunerative to ensure agricultural stability and also to promote parity in the living standards between the urban and rural households. This tantamounts to saying that Korea would gain very much by importing paddy rather than producing it. But, the Korean Government has opted for the survival of a peasant class for non-economic reasons like social stability.

Conclusion

The analysis of small farm rice economies of Korea and Coastal Andhra brings to a pertinent question. What accounts for Korean rural household's prosperity? Smaller proportion of landless and marginal farmers among cultivators is only a part of the answer. Higher yields per cropped area, higher average farm-size and efficiency of labour use as reflected in higher productivity for labour day are also a part of the answer. As factors which facilitated quick transition to an industrial State, agricultural progress and equity within agriculture made possible by structural reforms in agriculture and participatory nature of rural institutions are important. The major clue for this is provided by two factors (1) higher remittances and (2) favourable terms of trade. For instance in absolute terms the remittances of Korean farm-households are around one and half times the incomes of Andhra households. Further, a kg. of paddy in Korea gets 6 times the cloth it gets in India. Thus, it is the performance of the non-agricultural progress resulting in reduced costs that contributed to rural prosperity.

The elusive enigma remains: Can Andhra, the Rice Bowl of India, emulate Korea, by drawing relevant lessons from the structural transformation brought by institutional dynamics?

ANNEXURE 6.1

CULTIVATED AREA PER AGRICULTURAL WORKER—KOREA AND ANDHRA

(Area in hectares)

Korea		*Andhra*	
Year	*Area per Agricultural Worker*	*Year*	*Area per Agricultural Worker*
1953	0.256	1951	—
1960	0.254	1961	0.94
1970	0.320	1971	1.09
1980	0.409	1981	0.86
1985	0.460	—	—

Source : Korea : For 1953-70, (Ban *et al.*, 1980, p. 77)
1980-85, (MAF, 1986, p. 70)
Andhra : Government of India, 1981, p. 43.

ANNEXURE 6.2

THE YIELD LEVELS OF RICE—KOREA AND ANDHRA—1955-85

Year	*Korea*	*Andhra*	*Col. 2/Col. 3*
1955	2712	1323	0.49
1960	2712	1327	0.49
1965	2853	1296	0.45
1970	3277	1368	0.42
1975	3860	1641	0.442
1981	3750	2084	0.56
1985	4550	2480	0.54

Note : For 1981-85, the paddy yields in Korea are converted into rice at the conversion rate of 100 : 72.

Source : Korea : For 1955-75, (MAF, 1977, p. 82) (Yields given per Tanbo are converted) 1981-85, (MAFb, 1986, p. 139)

Andhra : For 1955-65 Planning and Cooperation Department, 1974, p. 123. For 1970-85, Bureau of Economics and Statistics, 1972, p. 164; 1977, p. 186; 1982, p. 204 and 1988, p. 102.

ANNEXURE 6.3

COST OF CULTIVATION (IN US. DOLLARS) PER HECTARE OF HYV PADDY : KOREA AND ANDHRA—1985-86

Size-Group	Seed		FYM and Chemical Fertilizers.		Pesticides		Animal and Machine Labour		Hired Human Labour Charges	
	Korea	*Andhra*	*Korea*	*Andhra*	*Korea*	*Andhra*	*Korea*	*Andhra*	*Korea*	*Andhra*
I.	68.61	15.62	220.91	89.29	135.11	9.59	48.59	50.19	167.27	62.41
	(6.72)	(5.32)	(21.65)	(30.44)	(13.24)	(3.27)	(4.76)	(17.11)	(16.39)	(21.28)
II.	59.97	15.86	348.08	101.26	151.63	22.52	37.45	63.12	164.67	36.08
	(6.19)	(3.75)	(35.94)	(23.93)	(15.66)	(5.32)	(3.87)	(14.91)	(17.01)	(8.52)
III.	49.28	15.22	427.39	95.08	115.02	15.30	112.26	65.42	171.10	74.46
	(3.42)	(3.38)	(29.64)	(21.11)	(7.98)	(3.40)	(7.78)	(14.52)	(11.86)	(16.53)
IV.	35.06	17.37	255.06	94.28	109.92	14.35	97.57	63.44	388.00	89.92
	(2.86)	(4.86)	(20.81)	(26.41)	(8.97)	(4.02)	(7.96)	(17.77)	(31.66)	(25.19)
V.	43.28	16.26	422.49	99.04	132.19	22.20	105.60	59.87	345.73	170.33
	(2.84)	(3.35)	(27.74)	(20.39)	(8.68)	(4.57)	(6.93)	(12.33)	(22.70)	(35.07)
Total	46.89	16.18	367.30	97.29	129.86	19.19	88.98	60.82	289.20	121.72
	(3.53)	(3.69)	(27.69)	(22.18)	(9.79)	(4.37)	(6.71)	(13.86)	(21.80)	(27.75)

ANNEXURE 6.3 (Contd..)

Size-Group	Irrigation Charges		Land Revenue and Taxes		Depreciation		Interest on Working Capital		Rent paid		Total Cost A_2	
	Korea	Andhra	Korea	Andhra	Korea	Andhra	Korea	Andhra	Korea	Andhra	Korea	Andhra
I.	84.89	9.83	24.35	0	112.04	2.46	113.29	21.73	45.32	32.20	1020.38	293.32
	(8.32)	(3.35)	(2.39)	(0)	(10.98)	(0.84)	(11.10)	(7.41)	(4.45)	(10.98)	(100)	(100)
II.	21.19	9.52	20.37	0	69.56	11.89	61.42	23.79	33.98	139.24	968.32	423.28
	(2.19)	(2.25)	(2.10)	(0)	(7.18)	(2.81)	(6.34)	(5.61)	(3.52)	(32.90)	(100)	(100)
III.	111.52	9.52	22.46	0.89	68.04	12.05	115.93	28.39	249.19	134.09	1442.19	450.40
	(7.73)	(2.11)	(1.56)	(0.19)	(4.72)	(2.69)	(8.04)	(6.30)	(17.27)	(29.77)	(100)	(100)
IV.	54.24	9.52	36.60	0.87	43.46	13.56	32.15	23.63	173.32	30.05	1225.38	356.99
	(4.43)	(2.67)	(2.99)	(0.24)	(3.55)	(93.80)	(2.62)	(6.62)	(14.14)	(8.42)	(100)	(100)
V.	86.96	9.52	43.16	0.87	174.90	25.37	102.84	34.97	65.73	47.26	1522.88	485.69
	(5.71)	(1.96)	(2.83)	(0.18)	(11.49)	(5.22)	(6.75)	(7.20)	(4.33)	(9.73)	(100)	(100)
Total	71.20	9.52	34.18	0.71	114.54	18.63	83.93	29.97	100.36	64.63	1326.44	438.66
	(5.37)	(2.18)	(2.58)	(0.16)	(8.63)	(4.24)	(6.33)	(6.83)	(7.57)	(14.74)	(100)	(100)

Note : Figures in brackets indicate percentage to the total.

ANNEXURE 6.4

PER HECTARE GROSS VALUE OF PRODUCT, COST A_2 AND FARM BUSINESS INCOME OF FARM—HOUSEHOLDS FOR SELECT CROPS IN KOREA—1985-86

(in terms of paddy in kgs.)

Size Group	TV Paddy			Other Crops		
	Gross value of product	Cost A_2	Farm Business income	Gross value of product	Cost A_2	Farm Business income
I.	5980	1565	4415	1094	46	1048
II.	6774	1648	5126	1995	868	1127
III.	6447	1361	5116	1169	626	543
IV.	5446	1653	3793	1415	664	751
V.	6424	1486	4938	1593	622	971
Total	6402	1494	4908	1506	637	869

ANNEXURE 6.4.1

PER HECTARE GROSS VALUE OF PRODUCT, COST A_2 AND FARM BUSINESS INCOME OF FARM-HOUSEHOLDS FOR SELECT CROPS IN ANDHRA—1985-1986

(in terms of paddy in kgs.)

Size Group	HYV Paddy (Rabi)			Other Crops		
	Gross value of product	Cost A_2	Farm Business income	Gross value of product	Cost A_2	Farm Business income
I.	4514	3152	1362	3218	4676	—1458
II.	4632	4702	—70	12548	7869	4679
III.	4205	3528	677	6698	5839	859
IV.	5205	2722	2483	5792	5191	601
V.	4514	3592	922	5852	5123	729
Total	4609	3540	1069	6333	5413	920

Annexure 6.5

GROSS VALUE OF PRODUCT, COST OF CULTIVATION AND FARM BUSINESS INCOME OF ALL CROPS FOR KOREA AND ANDHRA—1985-86

(Figures in US. dollars per hectare)

Size Group	Korea: Gross value of product of all crops	Korea: Cost A_2 of all crops	Korea: Farm business income	Andhra: Gross value of product of all crops	Andhra: Cost A_2 of all crops	Andhra: Farm business income
I.	2,992	1,180	1,812	504	329	175
			(60.56)			(34.72)
II.	3,492	956	2,536	598	490	108
			(72.62)			(18.06)
III.	3,119	945	2,174	562	477	85
			(69.70)			(15.12)
IV.	3,126	1,082	2,044	624	352	272
			(65.39)			(43.59)
V.	3,586	997	2,589	585	483	102
			(72.20)			(17.44)
Total	3,460	1,001	2,459	584	475	109
			(71.07)			(18.66)

Note : Figures in brackets indicate percentage of farm business income in the gross value of product.

ANNEXURE 6.6

FARM BUSINESS INCOME AND OTHER OFF-FARM AND NON-FARM INCOMES OF SAMPLE HOUSEHOLDS : KOREA—1985-86

(Figures in US Dollars/households)

Size Group	Farm Income					Non-Farm Income					Gross Total
	Agriculture	Livestock	Farm wages	Rentals from Agri. Machinery	Total farm income	Salaries	Non-farm enterprises	Remittances	Interest received	Total Non-farm income	
I.	384	0	297	147	828	989	0	348	90	1427	2255
	(17.03)		(13.17)	(6.52)	(36.72)	(43.86)		(15.43)	(3.99)	(63.28)	(100)
II.	2011	416	175	76	2678	1054	355	523	150	2082	4760
	(42.25)	(8.74)	(3.68)	(1.60)	(56.27)	(22.14)	(7.46)	(10.98)	(3.15)	(43.73)	(100)
III.	2739	1045	150	65	3999	890	0	602	200	1692	5691
	(48.13)	(18.36)	(2.64)	(1.14)	(70.27)	(15.64)		(10.58)	(3.51)	(29.73)	(100)
IV.	3678	398	83	43	4202	1309	0	1440	145	2894	7096
	(51.83)	(5.61)	(1.17)	(0.61)	(59.22)	(18.45)		(20.29)	(2.04)	(40.78)	(100)
V.	10963	284	0	34	11281	170	117	534	175	996	12277
	(89.30)	(2.31)		(0.28)	(91.89)	(1.38)	(0.95)	(4.35)	(1.43)	(8.11)	(100)
Total	4753	442	127	70	5392	774	130	606	157	1667	7059
	(67.33)	(6.26)	(1.80)	(0.99)	(76.38)	(10.98)	(1.84)	(8.58)	(2.22)	(23.62)	(100)

ANNEXURE 6.6.1.

FARM BUSINESS INCOME AND OTHER OFF-FARM AND NON-FARM INCOMES OF SAMPLE HOUSEHOLDS : ANDHRA, 1985-86

(Figures in US. Dollar per household)

Size-Group	Farm					Non-Farm					
	Agri-culture	Live-stock	Farm wages	Rentals from Ag. machinery/ livestock	Total farm income	Sala-ries.	Non-farm enter-prises	Remit-tances	Interest received	Total Non-farm income	Gross total
I.	64	-49	176	0	191	93	0	89	14	196	387
	(165.54)	(-12.66)	(45.48)		(49.36)	(24.03)		(23.00)	(3.61)	(50.64)	(100)
II.	95	-64	144	0	175	14	30	0	17	61	236
	(40.25)	(-27.12)	(61.02)		(74.15)	(5.93)	(12.71)		(7.21)	(25.85)	(100)
III.	106	-53	74	44	171	162	60	6	25	253	424
	(25.00)	(-12.50)	(17.45)	(10.38)	(40.33)	(38.21)	(14.15)	(1.41)	(5.90)	(59.67)	(100)
IV.	492	-193	128	74	501	0	60	19	40	119	620
	(79.35)	(-31.13)	(20.65)	(11.93)	(80.80)		(9.68)	(3.06)	(6.46)	(19.20)	(100)
V.	383	-126	19	17	293	129	0	48	120	297	590
	(64.91)	(21.36)	(3.22)	(2.88)	(49.65)	(21.86)		(8.15)	(20.34)	(50.35)	(100)
Total	209	-91	109	21	248	84	24	39	45	192	440
	(47.50)	(20.68)	(24.77)	(4.77)	(56.36)	(19.09)	(5.46)	(8.86)	(10.23)	(43.64)	(100)

7

MAJOR INFERENCES AND LESSONS DRAWN

Introduction

Korean success is labelled as 'enclave model of growth' (Todaro, 1981, p. 67) achieved by a 'strong-State' under unique circumstances; and as such it cannot be a model for Third World democratic States (Chandra, N.K., 1984, pp.74-5; Halliday, 1987, pp. 43-4). Pre-occupation with the inward *versus* outward looking strate-gies has led to a neglect of more fundamental aspects of Korean development process of relevance to Third World Countries.

It is true that Korea had unique features which cannot be duplicated even if one opts for them. But the fact that Korea, "a fairly Third World State can sustain growth by constantly upgrading its industrial structure breaking into world market for more advanced industrial products" (Halliday, 1987, p. 43) is in itself of great interest to countries struggling hard for a breakthrough, irrespective of the replica of Korean model.

The basic similarities in the initial conditions like colonial legacy, late entry into the development arena, common problems such as demographic pressure, non-viable small farm economy, shared concerns to bring about development to meet the revolution of rising expectations etc., between Korea and many Third World Countries like India provide a strong case for understanding Korean experience *vis-a-vis* India.

Major Inferences

The comparative outlook of Korean and Indian experience in rural transformation at the macro and micro levels brings out in bold relief some pertinent issues of interest to India in particular and South Asian countries in general.

Growth with Differential Transformation

With comparable initial conditions, Korea, a war-ravaged country without notable resource endowments, has emerged as an 'economic miracle' attracting world-wide attention. She achieved high rates of industrial growth *i.e.*, 18.6 per cent during 1962-72 that facilitated rural transformation through agrarian transition. Korea witnessed absolute decline in the agrarian population by 1971 and the percentage of agricultural population also sharply declined from 63.67 to 43.80 during 1951-72. The nature of transformation Korea has experienced paved for a reduction of poverty and for an improvement in the general standards of living. The percentage of those below poverty line declined from 40.9 to 6.8 during 1965-85, while per capita GDP in constant terms witnessed manifold increase *i.e.*, from US $ 60 in 1950 to US $ 647 by 1984. In contrast, the limited growth of Indian economy *i.e.*, 3.82 per cent instead of 8.2 per cent in Korea during 1962-82 did not help in overcoming the structural stagnation. With a marginal decline in the share of agricultural population from 61.10 per cent to 60.83 per cent during 1971-81, and a marked increase in absolute numbers from 149 to 198 million during the period, India continues to be a predominantly agrarian economy. Consequently, there are no perceptible changes for the better in the pattern of income distribution, reduction of poverty and improvement in the living standards of her people. Even by 1983, 36.90 per cent were below poverty line, while per capita income in constant terms doubled from US $ 65 to 125 during 1950-85.

Determinants of Growth and Differential Transformation

The fact that Korea, a small country, without natural resources could excel India, a subcontinent with abundant and enviable natural resources on the development arena, cannot be lightly brushed aside attributing the success to the small size, the U.S. Aid, external debt, or military regime, as these are not unique to Korea alone nor is it attributable to Confucianism which Korea has been practising for centuries.

The differential growth and the transformation Korea and India experienced are mainly attributable to three aspects *viz.*, (i) differences in colonial legacies; (ii) differences in unique features; and (iii) differences in the institutional structure and the strength and resilience of the sub-sectors of society and economy.

Differences in Colonial Legacies

As colonies of imperial powers both Korea and India were subjected to exploitation. But differences in the nature and character of the colonial powers exerted differential impact on the two countries with implications for growth and transformation. As a food importing colonial power, Japan had greater stakes in promoting food surplus in the colony. Towards this end, Japan carried on several agrarian reforms.

The measures it initiated to promote agricultural extension, introduction of non-conventional inputs like fertilizer, improved varieties of rice and development of irrigation helped to achieve a high rate of growth of output of 2.92 per cent during 1930-39 and set the base of agrarian development in Korea. It is said that during 1940-45 agricultural technicians became rulers of Korean farmers in forcing them to produce more food.

The reforms introduced by the Japanese like abolition of class system for recruitment, educational reforms like conduct of examinations in scientific and technical subjects, started in 1876, helped spread of education to wider sections of society. The industrialisation process it started helped absorption of agricultural labour. Thus steps taken by the Japanese colonialism despite exploitation facilitated Korea to build up an agriculture sector which could respond to the growing needs of her dynamic industrial growth in the post-colonial period.

British colonial power that ruled India for more than two hundred years crippled her capacities for agricultural growth by deforming her agrarian structure, for revenue, and ruined Indian rural industrial base for merchandising British manufactured cloth. This resulted in emergence of a large class of landless labour in India. Neglect of education, and failure to provide facilities for technical and vocational education had their adverse imprints on the post-Independence industrial growth with shortage of skilled manpower. The scant attention paid to education gets reflected in meagre allocation of 0.2 per cent of national income towards education. Thus, post-colonial India inherited an unenviable colonial legacy of high illiteracy, large class of landless labour and deformed agrarian structure unable to feed her millions.

Differences in Unique Features

Korea had the advantage of gaining access to liberal aid and credit to build up the economy and markets for her goods. Her unique geo-political situation helped her obtain generous US aid to gear up the war-ravaged economy to the take off stage. She had the unique advantage of receiving liberal aid of US $ 8,871 million or US $ 600 per capita during 1946-75, considered to be 3½ times and 8½ times higher than the aid for the whole of Latin America and whole of Africa respectively. It also had favourable access to credit from international funding agencies in building up the economy. Her foreign debt of about US $ 47 billion in mid-1986 was the largest in Asia and the fourth biggest in the world after the Latin America's "big three". In contrast to Korea, India's reliance on external assistance is minimal *i.e.*, US $ 52 per capita from 1947 to the end of March 1986.

Korea also had the unique advantage of being relieved in the initial stages several hurdles that confront many developing countries even today. She had an equitable social structure without a class of landless labour, had the advantage of having a human resource base which is largely literate with exposure to vocational skills. For instance, by 1960, about 72 per cent of the population were literate, while around 40 per cent of students were enrolled in vocational courses. These are the outcomes of the changes over time starting from the pre-colonial era, the Japanese colonial rule, the social turmoil during the Korean War and the compulsions for reforms in the wake of Communist threat from the North.

India on the other hand, had to usher in development in an unenviable socio-economic environment. Her unique and inequitious social structure, high degree of illiteracy (83.4 per cent in 1951), large class of landless poor and the formidable task of integrating the nation of the size of a subcontinent with diverse ethnic, religious, linguistic and cultural backgrounds crippled her growth effort.

Yet another feature not unique to Korea is her small size and homogeneous population. This conferred on her a distinct advantage to be relatively free from regional, religious and linguistic squabbles which often threaten national integrity and strife development efforts, a common phenomenon seen in India and in most of the developing countries.

Differences in Institutional Structures

Korea had the advantage of a strong State which can relentlessly pursue her development goals undeterred by other considerations. Her efforts are noteworthy in developing human resource base, in successfully implementing agrarian reforms, in evolving appropriate institutional structures for agricultural development and in building up a strong industrial structure to achieve a high growth and miraculous transformation.

Korea's human resource-base is her greatest pride. This has become possible as the leadership spared no efforts to enrich human capital through imparting skills. Korea successfully exploited the positive features of Confucianism, *viz.*, work ethic and diligence in inculcating upright values, conducive to keep up the tempo of rapid growth. Comparative studies on work efficiency proved that Koreans excel many others with a higher work ethic *i.e.*, effort propensity, social efficiency capital and rationality. Towards this end, Korea successfully tackled the problem of illiteracy with emphasis on primary and vocational education. This could be seen from near 96 per cent enrolment at primary level and 40 per cent of student enrolment in vocational courses at school level. General school education was also oriented to impart vocational skills, devotion to duty and proper values relating to environmental upkeep, the missing elements in many developing nations of Asia. Private industries were also compelled to impart skills to the talented youths.

Korea has also successfully implemented agrarian reforms in the initial period of independence. Success on this front with lower ceiling limits on ownership and abolition of tenancy helped transforming her agrarian structure into one dominated by landlord class to one of peasant proprietorship. This helped Korea to ensure a two-fold increase in the share of those owning 0.50 ha. and below and a decline in the share of landlord class from 26.4 per cent to one per cent in a short span of just one decade of 1945-55. Similarly noteworthy are her achievements in the area of tenancy. To illustrate, the percentage of area under tenancy declined from 66.7 to 13.5 and tenants among farm households from 86.2 to 26.4 during 1945-60. Such achievements are a rarity in the Third World Countries.

To complement land reforms she initiated agrarian reforms *viz.*, an efficient agricultural extension system and a sound rural delivery system through reorganizing cooperative structure. Korean agricultural extension system which had a relatively longer history of integration of research and extension was further geared up. It was also entrusted with the responsibility of training farmers, rural youths, students and teachers in agricultural high schools. Fostering farmers' organisations at the village level to support extension activities and demarcation of a limited area for every extension worker enhanced the effectiveness of the agricultural extension system.

Korea has reorganised cooperative institution with a strong national federation with branches at the county/district level to effectively guide, help and monitor the primaries. Primaries were also reorganised to render diversified and efficient services to the farmers. Further, she extended aid and made these institutions as the agents to supply farm inputs and mobilize marketable surplus, without crippling the autonomy at local level. These positive measures enabled Korean cooperatives to handle diversified services and build up creditable market standing in input supplies and marketing of cash crops. To illustrate, in early1970 cooperatives handled around 60 per cent of farm input supply and 73.9 per cent of cash crops.

The above steps initiated by the Korean State enabled her to achieve a lasting and self-sustaining growth of agricultural economy which has favourably responded to the growing needs of a fast expanding economy. The appropriate strategies to suit the stage of development made Korean agriculture to play a dutiful role by having borne the pangs of growth, despite adverse terms of trade for nearly two decades till seventies. Moreover, it has not only released its labour force to meet the manpower requirements of a high growth economy but also diversified itself to meet the changing demands for food and helped contain imports of rice.

The successful transition of an agricultural economy into a non-agricultural economy was made possible in Korea, apart from external factors, for her internal resilience. The trained manpower with commendable work ethic, labour intensive techniques of production in all major sub-sectors of the economy, and effective utilisation of the capital stock also contributed to her success in achieving higher rates of growth of more than 18 per cent in the manufacturing sector. This has gone a long way not only in improving per capita incomes but also in promoting rural living standards through favourable terms of trade to agriculture since mid-seventies.

Further, Korea had integrated her administrative structures connected with rural development under a single Ministry to co-ordinate and monitor the entire network. She has evolved a strategy of administration by identification, *i.e.*, fixing responsibilities for given tasks and linking promotion to performance. In early stages of transition, organised and judiciously nursed village level people's organisations to support the formal administrative channels. The egalitarian social and administrative structures and high levels of literacy made this task easier. These facilitated administrative coordination and enlisting people's participation in rural reconstruction through Saemaul Undong.

In contrast, in India, despite enviable resource endowments, the democratic 'soft State' which has to counter and reconcile with a host of conflicting group interests, has opted for a gradualistic approach to transformation resulting in limited growth. Its limitations in overcoming institutional obstacles also slowed down its growth potential and distorted percolation of benefits of growth among different strata of society.

India could not succeed in building up her human resources. Not only literacy levels continued to be low but the reforms on the educational front are not oriented to imbibe a sense of discipline, dignity of labour or to promote vocational skills or upright values conducive for development. The bias towards higher education for a long period also contributed to mass illiteracy. For instance, the literacy rate of India in eighties is comparable to that of Korea in 1950s or even earlier. The percentage of science students at University level is just around 1/5th in 1985-86. These had adversely affected institutional structures created and promoted by State to further development process.

Efforts at reforming agrarian structure and land tenures have met with limited success if any. Despite periodical legislation towards this end since post-Independence days, agrarian structure continued to be skewed and tenancy continues to be exploitative for want of political will for effective implementation of these reforms. During 1961-82, while the percentage share of marginal holdings increased from 60 to 66, their share in land increased from 7.59 to 12.22. Tenancy reforms resulted in resumption of land for personal cultivation by the absentee landlords without perceptible benefits in lowering rents.

In agricultural development, while its rate of growth stands at 2.5 per cent since sixties, at par with that of Korea, but agricultural productivity per worker and per hectare of cropped area continue to be lower than Korea. The contribution of agricultural extension and cooperatives to agricultural development leaves much to be desired. Extension was never an objective of the National Agricultural Research Institutes in India. Lack of integration between research and extension, failure to foster farmers' organisations at the village level, and widespread rural illiteracy limited the impact of agricultural extension.

Indian cooperative structures continue to suffer despite State partnership, multiplicity of national federations, and schemes of reorganisation and revitalisation of primary agricultural cooperatives. State aid and State partnership crippled the autonomy of cooperative at all levels. Absence of single agency above the primary level to coordinate various types of functional cooperatives, the weakness of the federal structures and competition with primaries for their own survival, without guiding and assisting the primaries, has not helped to improve their capacities as an effective rural delivery system. Primary agricultural cooperatives in India continue to be the weakest link in cooperative chain without any standing in the life of the rural households in India. Their poor market shares in early eighties *i.e.*, 29 per cent in credit, 52 per cent in fertilizer, 8 per cent in marketing are pointers to the relative poverty of cooperatives in India compared to Korea.

Indian industrial strategy helped in building up a strong industrial base in the basic and heavy industries. The fruits of which may be realised in future. But, Indian industrial sector continued to be sluggish. The high capital-output ratios, neglect of labour-intensive strategies in early stages of industrialisation, ineffective utilisation of capital stock with increase in idle capacity, neither contributed to growth nor helped the transition process.

Rural development and administration in India, with multiple structures and their multiplication over time has become unweildy resulting in problems of coordination. The Federal nature of the Indian State also added to the problem. In the given socio- economic milieu characterised by inequalities, her efforts at promoting voluntary groups at village level have not yielded dividends. These resulted in lopsided implementation of the development programmes in rural India.

The relative differences in the institutional structures and capacities of the State in altering them to subserve development goals get reflected in the field surveys conducted in Korea and Andhra.

Economy and Life in Korea and Andhra : Results of the Field Survey

The macro-level picture of differential transformation between the two societies also gets reflected in the demographic features, land tenure market mechanisms, access to and use of institutional sources in the micro level investigation. These in turn are manifest in the status of rural households and their living standards.

Korean transformation and consequent improvement in living standards eased demographic pressure and improved the human resource base. Andhra presents a contrasting picture for obvious reasons. To illustrate, Korean villages had small households (3.38) higher proportion of workers (54.55) low level of illiteracy among heads of rural households (5.23) and a higher percentage with technical education (17.42). In contrast, Andhra villages exhibit higher size of family (4.89), low proportion of workers (52.76) and high degree of illiteracy (51.09).

Relative differences in structure of rural households bear testimony to the Korean success in land reforms and Indian lapses. With high proportion of peasant households (76 per cent) and just one per cent of agricultural labour households Korea is in sharp contrast to Andhra with only 56 per cent of cultivating households and 20 per cent of agricultural labour households.

Values of Gini coefficients 0.009 for Korea and 0.51 for Andhra for all rural households and with less exploitative tenurial conditions further confirm the differences. In respect of tenancy, while Korean transformation facilitated greater access to leased-in area to marginal groups, in Andhra the low preference to lease-out land to marginal holdings accelerated the pace of proletarianisation of the marginal holdings and marginalisation of the small holdings.

Differential transformation in the two societies can also be seen from the relative status of rural households in various markets. Land market in Korea is transformed from one of 'buyers' in the pre-Green Revolution era to one of 'sellers' in the post-Green Revolution period with greater gains in land by marginal and small farmers. In Andhra it continued to be a 'buyers' market with comparatively low gains to the marginal groups, particularly in the pre-Green Revolution era.

In the case of labour market, while Korean mechanisation has been in tune with her labour scarce economy, in Andhra mechanisation co-existed with surplus labour and a large class of landless labour with adverse effects on rural employment. Further, the low percentage of households hiring out labour in the marginal households in Korea in contrast (about 2/3rds) to Andhra reflects on their relative economic status. While there are no observable differences in the credit market with high proportion of borrowers in both, the high and equitable access to institutional credit in Korea reflects upon the successful functioning of credit institutions. For instance, while the borrowers from institutions formed only 37 per cent in Andhra, it is around 81 in Korea. Similar differences manifest in the input market with predominance of private agencies in Andhra. High degree of patronage of cooperatives by Korean farmers for seed (42 per cent), fertilizer (100 per cent) and pesticides (74 per cent), is in marked contrast to Andhra. A relatively high percentage (50) of marginal farmers in the 'self-sufficiency' category in Korea and only 13 in Andhra reflects upon their non-viable character in Andhra.

The transformation Korea witnessed during 1970-86 could also be seen from a higher percentage of rural households (42) including the poor improving their status, and a large percentage of children of the rural households (53) employed outside the village. Andhra presents a different picture with 38 per cent of rural households reporting improvement in their status during the period and a very low percentage (8) of rural households with their children employed outside the village. Among the poor, while 65 per cent of agricultural labour households of Korea improved their status there has been hardly any change in about 2/3rds of these households in Andhra.

Similar differences are noted in the well-being and living conditions like housing, access to electricity, drinking water and consumer durables. Both in terms of percentage of rural households owning a house and type of house, Korea presents a better picture. The Roof Improvement Project which Korea implemented in early phase of Saemaul Undong gave fillip to rural housing. As a result, there are hardly any huts (0.89 per cent) in Korea, while more than half (58 per cent) of Andhra households dwell in huts. While electric power dawned on the Andhra villages little earlier than Korean villages under study, light is yet to dawn on more than 2/3rds of the Andhra rural households, while more than 90 per cent of Korean households had domestic power supply by 1980. Andhra presents a picture of Korea of 1970, with only 28 per cent of houses being electrified. Most of Korean natural villages under study have public water supply schemes from seventies under Rural Saemaul Undong. In Andhra only one village has protected water supply. Korean prosperity and her consumerism also get reflected in the rural life with more than half of the households possessing consumer durables like TV, VCP/VCR, Refrigerators and Rice Warmers while only 40 per cent of Andhra rural households have Radio/Transistor and two per cent possessing TV. Further, 60 per cent of Korean households have telephone, while such a facility is completely absent in Andhra with not even a public telephone.

Thus, the micro picture confirms to the macro scenario in both the cases.

Small Farm Rice Economy : Results of the Field Survey

The Korean industrial growth and consequent absorption of rural people in the secondary and tertiary sectors of the economy resulted in significant increase in land per agricultural worker. In Andhra, because of high growth rates of rural population, the per capita land available per agricultural population and per agricultural worker came down to around one-half of that in Korea. Similar differences are also noticeable in the value of agricultural production per agricultural worker. The micro study also confirms this. For instance, the average size of Korean farm is higher (1.95 ha.) than in Andhra (1.60 ha.). Parity in the value of assets in the higher size-groups and pronounced disparities in the lower size-groups are indicative of equitable percolation of benefits of growth in Korea. Higher share of farm machinery and financial assets in Korea reflects on the labour scarce nature of farm economy and inflow of remittances.

Input-use pattern like higher use of NPK per hectare, absence of bullock labour, greater use of family and exchange labour are characteristic features of Korean rice farm economy. Physical input-output relationships show that Korean farmers obtain higher output per unit of N and human labour compared to Andhra.

Farm economy in the rice-growing areas of both countries shows no significant difference in the yield levels *per se*. But the relatively better living standards of Korean farm-households can be attributed to the higher yields per capita and per worker despite small size of the Korean farm-household. Further, resources are used more efficiently. Moreover, terms of trade of the farmers are more favourable. As a result, as compared to India, the farm business income per agricultural population and per agricultural worker in Korea is higher by five and six times respectively.

A significant factor accounting for the higher standards of Korean farm-households is the favourable terms of trade for farm products made possible by the export-led Korean industrial growth. For instance, a kg. of paddy in Korea can procure six times the cloth it gets in India; while a bicycle costs a quintal of paddy in Korea, it costs about 5 quintal in Andhra. Also, the growth of the economy and absorption of rural youth in the secondary and tertiary sectors in the major cities of Korea facilitated augmenting the income of Korean rural households through remittances from outside. To illustrate, the average remittances of a Korean farm-household (US $ 606) are 50 per cent more than the gross income of a Andhra farm-household.

Lessons Drawn

Comparative experience of rural transformation in Korea and India showed that Korean transformation is undoubtedly unique. It is the result of a rather rare combination of factors that cannot be replicated by any other country.

It is most unfortunate that undue pre-occupation with export-oriented strategies has tended to distract attention from major lessons of Korean development process. It is one of the contributions of this study that it has focused on the most relevant aspects of Korea's development for Third World Countries yet to attain transition.

The study also offers valuable lessons worth attention of all concerned *i.e.*, the State, bureaucracy and the public at large, in countries struggling hard for agrarian transition and rural transformation.

State

Korean experience clearly brings to the fore that political will to redefine the role of the State the great transformator to act in ways that ensures growth and equity is vital for achieving any meaningful transformation. This is more so in countries where shift in the balance of class relations are hard to come by. Indian experience proves beyond doubt that mere rhetoric, institutional proliferation, populist schemes and perpetual promotion of ethos of dependency on the State is no short-cut to concerted action for transformation.

The study highlights the significance of equipping human resources base for development. Wiping out illiteracy, promotion of work ethic, imparting skills through vocational training in industry and agriculture are some of the valuable lessons Third World Countries can easily emulate for the good. In this context, the Korean practice of imparting discipline, altruistic values, concern for upkeep of environment at the elementary stage and exposing all to the science and art of farming at the secondary school level and through vocational schools deserve attention.

The experiences of Korea and India show that the State must have some control over outcomes of development, if transformation is to take place. True many States, particularly democratic 'soft States' cannot be expected to play the role of the Korean State, but it must also be realised that they also cannot afford to seek refuge for inaction always as it is equally herculian to prevent the masses from taking radical action.

A related aspect is the need to improve the capacity of the State to insulate itself from conflicting clientelist demands. It is not easy for a democratic State to insulate itself from pulls and pressures, when even the Korean 'strong-State' is not free from these predicaments. But what Korean experience shows is when it yielded, it did so for a better return. Even democratic States should explore such avenues rather than meekly obliging merely to stay in office.

One of the important lessons of Korean experience is that land-reforms facilitated growth and development of participatory institutions and thus enabled agriculture to respond to the needs of the non-agricultural sector in the critical stages of development.

It has clearly come out from the study that small farm economy is no hindrance to growth, provided rural institutions are transformed to serve small farms, should evoke immense interest among the South Asian economies struggling to make small farms viable. In this context, Third World countries could emulate the role played by the State in transforming the cooperatives to subserve rural transformation unfettered by bureaucratic interference.

The terms of trade have a widely differing role depending upon the stage of development. In the early stages, what is much more important is a stable price regime and availability of inputs and technology rather than shift in terms of trade in favour of agriculture. Shifting terms of trade will be feasible with nonagricultural development and becomes decisive as an instrument for reducing the rural-urban gap of incomes while egalitarian land-base permits the diffusion widely.

Employment oriented high rate of growth of non-agriculture facilitates improvement of rural levels of living through remittances from migrants through improvement of man-land ratios and favourable terms of trade.

The study also points out in vivid terms that there can be more specialisation in agriculture rather than rural areas becoming centres of non-farm economy. This implies that the Third World agrarian economies looking for spread of rural non-farm opportunities have to realize that it does not automatically follow from high growth industrialisation, but calls for more concerted efforts on the agricultural sector also.

Bureaucracy

In the area of development administration also, Korean experience shows that development-oriented organisations, strategy of administration by identification, and linking promotion to performance pays rich dividends. It also signifies the importance of constant follow up and monitoring, but does not call for interference by the Government. It also shows that effective extension calls for integration between research and extension at all levels. The success story of Korean agricultural extension vividly points out this.

People

The Korean message for the Third World public is development and is neither automatic nor the concern of the State alone. It calls for concern for development, willingness to make sacrifices for achieving the goals, extending a helping hand to the Government in delivering goods and taking pride in self-reliance on the part of people.

These are important lessons which Korean development offers to most of the Third World Countries. What is more important is that Korean State has played a decisive role in achieving this.

To conclude, if India can learn from Korea that small is beautiful, Korea can discern India's utmost concern for fierce political independence and consequential slow down of economic progress as a willing sacrifice. In this manner, Indian freedom is a double-edged sword glistening as a hope for the entire Third World Countries.

BIBLIOGRAPHY

Adelman, Irma and Robinson, *Income Distribution Policy in Developing Countries : A Case Study of Korea,* Oxford, 1978.

Adiseshiah, Malcolm, S., 'Futility of Aggregative Approach', *Economic and Political Weekly,* Vol. 7, 2105-6, 1972.

Ahluwalia, M.S., 'Inequality, Poverty and Development', *Journal of Development Economies*, 17, 307-42, 1976.

Ahn, Choong-Yong, *Economic Development of Korea : Strategies and Issues (Mimeo)*, Chung-Ang University, Seoul, 1985.

Alam, M. Shahid, 'Some Notes on Work Ethos and Economic Development', *World Development*, 13, 251-54, 1985.

Alexander, P.C., *Industrial Estates in India*, Bombay, 1963.

Anderson, D., 'Small Industry in Developing Countries : A Discussion of Issues', *World Development*, 10, 913-48, 1982.

Anderson, D., and Mark W. Leiserson, 'Rural Non-Farm Employment in Developing Countries', *Economic Development and Cultural Change*, 28, 227-48, 1980.

Andhra Pradesh Agricultural University (APAU), *Sixty Years of Rice Research at Maruteru* (1925-85), Hyderabad, 1986.

Appu, P.S., 'Agrarian Structure and Rural Development', *Economic and Political Weekly*, 9, A 70-4, 1974.

Ardhanareswaran, K.N., 'Role of Cooperatives in Agricultural Development', *NCDC Bulletin*, 23, 2-9, 1989.

Asian Development Bank (ADB), *Asian Agricultural Survey* 1976, Manila, 1977.

Bagchi, Amiya Kumar, 'Export Led Growth and Import Substituting Industrialization', *Economic and Political Weekly*, 12, 219-24, 1977.

Bagchi, Amiya Kumar, *Public Intervention and Industrial Restructuring in China, India and Republic of Korea*, New Delhi, 1987.

Balaguru, T., and K.V. Raman, 'Agricultural Research System in India', in K.V. Raman *et al.,* (eds.); *Agricultural Systems*, 95-121, 1988.

Ban, Sung Hwan, 'The Growth of Agricultural Output and Productivity in Korea, 1918-78' in Hou Chi-Ming *et al.*, (eds.); *Agricultural Development...*, 171-94, 1982.

Ban, Sung Hwan *et al.*, (eds.), *Rural Development*, Harvard, 1980.

Bandopadhyay, D., 'An Evaluation of Policies and Programmes for the Alleviation of Rural Poverty in India', in Rizwanul Islam (ed.); *Strategies for...*, 99-151, 1985.

——, Land-Reforms in India : An Analysis', *Economic and Political Weekly*, 21, A50-6, 1986.

Bardhan, Pranab, *The Political Economy of Development in India*, New Delhi, 1986.

Bhalla, G.S., 'Some Issues in Agricultural Development in India', in Brahmananda and Panchamukhi, (ed.), 228-69, 1987.

Bhalla, Surjit, S., and Prem Vashishtha, 'Income Distribution in India–A Re-examination in T.N. Srinivasan and Pranab Bardhan, (ed.), *Rural Poverty...*, 38-68, 1988.

Bhambhri, C.P., *Politics in India* 1947-87, New Delhi, 1988.

Bhatawdekar, M.V., 'Economic Growth and Educational Development : Lessons from the Case of Japan', *Economic and Political Weekly*, 7, 1793-1801, 1972.

Bhattacharya, B.B., and Hanumantha Rao, 'Agriculture-Industry Interrelations : Issues of Relative Prices and Growth in the Context of Public Investment', in VIII *World Economic Congress of the International Economic Association*, New Delhi, 54-84, 1986.

Bhattacharya, K.R, 'Science, the Fettered Giant : Can We Free it?' *Economic and Political Weekly*, 7, 1837-42, 1972.

Bhattacharya, Sibnath, *Rural Industrialization in India*, New Delhi, 1980.

Bishop, Peter, 'The Nature of Religion', in Peter Bishop and Darton Michael (eds.); *The Encyclopaedia of...*, 6-13.

Bishop, Peter and Darton Michael (eds.); *The Encyclopaedia of World Faiths : An Illustrated Survey of the World Living Religions*, London, 1987.

Black, C.E., *The Dynamics of Modernization*, New York, 1966.

Blumental, Tuvia and Chung Lee, 'Development Strategies of Japan and South Korea : A Comparative Study', *The Developing Economies*, 23, 221-35, 1985.

Booth Anne and R.M. Sundrum, *Labour Absorption in Agriculture*, Delhi, 1984.

Brahmananda, P.R., and V.R. Panchamukhi, (eds.); *The Development Process of the Indian Economy*, Delhi, 1987.

Brandt, V., *A Korean Village Between Farm and Sea*, Cambridge, 1971.

Braverman *et al.*, *Alternative Agricultural Pricing Policies in the Republic of Korea–World Bank Staff Working Paper*, 621, Washington D.C., 1983.

Bureau of Economics and Statistics, Government of Andhra Pradesh, *Season and Crop Report—Andhra Pradesh,* Hyderabad 1972, 1977 and 1982.

——, Statistical Abstract of Andhra Pradesh 1986, Hyderabad, 1988.

Byun, Hyung-Yoon, 'Industrial Structure of Korea', *The Seoul National University Economic Review*, 1, 33-69, 1967.

Caiden, Gerald, E., and Jun Young Duck, 'The Political Economy of Korean Development under the Park Government', in Bun Woong Kim *et. al.*, (eds.); *Administrative Dynamics and...*, 20-31, 1985.

Central Statistical Organization (CSO), Government of India, *Statistical Abstract of the Indian Union*—1966, 1985, New Delhi, 1967 and 1985.

Central Statistical Organization (CSO), *National Accounts Statistics*, New Delhi, 1976, 1979, 1981 and 1984.

Chakravarthy, S., 'Policy Making in Mixed Economy : The Indian Case', in P.R. Brahmananda and V.R. Panchamukhi (eds.); *The Development Process of...*, 718-33, 1987.

Chandra, Nirmal Kumar, 'North and South Korea : A Study in Two Paradigms of Development', Paper presented at the ICSSR Seminar on Marx, Schumpeter and Keynes on Capitalism (Jan. 27-30), New Delhi, 1984.

Chauhan, K.K.S., 'Fertilizer Distribution and Production by Cooperatives', *NCDC Bulletin*, 18, 11-14, 1984.

Cho, Dong-Pil, 'Agricultural Problems in Korea Today', *Korean Quarterly* 1, 113-20, 1959.

Chodak, Szyman, *Societal Development*, New York, 1973.

Choe, Yong Boo and Young Mahn Lee, *Rural Cottage Industry : Its Situation and Problems in Korea (Mimeo)*, Korean Rural Economics Institute, Seoul, 1980.

Choe, Yong Boo and Tae-Myung Kim, *Rural Industrialization in Korea : A Critical Assessment (Mimeo)*, Korea Rural Economics Institute, Seoul, 1981.

Choo, Bong-Kyu, 'A Study on Implications of Rural-Urban Migrants in Korea', *The Seoul National University Economic Review,* 13, 38-50, 1979.

Choo, Hakchung, 'Some Sources of Relative Equity in Income Distribution : A Historical Perspective', in Chuk-Kyo Kim (ed.); *Industrial and Social...*, 303-30, 1977.

Chopra, P.N., (ed.), *The Gazetteer of India (Vol. 3) : Economic Structure and Activities*, New Delhi, 1975.

Chu, Bong-Kyu, 'Mechanization in Korean Farming : Present Status, Obstructing Factors and Remedial Measures', in Southworth (ed.); *Farm Mechanization...*, 61-74,1972.

Chung, Young Il, 'An Overview of Rural Industrialization in Korea', *The Seoul National University Economic Review*, 15, 37-49, 1981.

Dandekar, V.M., 'Indian Economy Since Independence', *Economic and Political Weekly*, 23, 41-50, 1988.

Dandekar, R.N., Address of the General President to the All India Oriental Conference (January 5-7), 34th Session, Andhra University, Visakhapatnam, 1989.

Dantwala, M.L., 'Future of Institutional Reform and Technological Change in Indian Agricultural Development', *Economic and Political Weekly*, 12, 1299-1306, 1978.

——, 'Agrarian Structure and Agrarian Relations in India', in M.L. Dantwala *et al.*, (ed.); *Indian Agricultural Development...*, 59-88, 1986.

——, 'Strategy of Agricultural Development Since Independence', in M.L. Dantwala *et. al.*, (eds.); *Indian Agricultural Development...*, 1-15. 1986.

——, 'Poverty Alleviation Programmes : Reconsideration', in Department of Rural Development, Government of India, *National Seminar on Poverty...*, 77-80, 1988.

Dantwala *et. al.*, *Indian Agricultural Development Since Independence*, New Delhi, 1986.

Department of Agriculture and Cooperation, Government of India, 'Report of the Committee on Structure and Role of National Cooperative Societies–Summary of Conclusions and Recommendations', *National Bank News Review*, 3, 30-7, 1987.

Department of Rural Development, Government of India, *Report of the Committee to Review the Existing Administrative Arrangements for Rural Development and Poverty Alleviation Programmes*, New Delhi, 1985.

——, *National Seminar on Poverty Alleviation Programme*, New Delhi, 1988.

Desai, A.R., *Rural Sociology in India, Bombay*, 1978.

Desai, Ashok, V., 'Factors Underlying the Slow Growth of Indian Industry', *Economic and Political Weekly*, 14, 381-92, 1981.

Desai, P.B., *Planning in India* : 1951-78, New Delhi, 1979.

Devadoss, T.S., *Hindu Family and Marriage*, Madras, 1979.

Dharmakumar, (ed.), *The Cambridge Economic History of India* (Vol. 2), New Delhi, 1982.

——, 'South India', in Dharmakumar, *Ibid.*, 352-75, 1982.

Dubashi, P.R., 'Cooperative Perestroika', *NCDC Bulletin*, 23, 4-10, 1989.

Dulfer, E., *Operational Efficiency of Agricultural Cooperatives in Developing Countries*, FAO, Rome, 1974.

D.N., 'Political Economy of the Nehru Era', *Economic and Political Weekly*, 23, 2459-62, 1988.

Economic Planning Board (EPB), Government of the Republic of Korea, *Major Statistics of Korean Economy*. Seoul, 1984 and 1988.

Editor, 'Jawaharlal Nehru : The High Priest of Secularism by S. Gopal', (Book Review), *The Economist*, 274-95, 1980.

EPB, *Economic Survey : Annual Report of the Korean Economy*, Seoul, 1985.

——, *White Paper on Korean Economy*, Seoul, 1986.

Faber, Mike and Dudley Seers (eds.), *The Crisis in Planning : The Indian Experience* (Vol. II), London, 1972.

FAO, *Provisional Indicative World Plan for Agricultural Development* (Vol. 2), Rome, 1970.

Fingarette, Herbert, *Confucius–The Secular as Sacred*, New York, 1972.

Foster, George, M., *Traditional Societies and Technological Change*, New Delhi 1973.

Ghai, Dharam *et al.*, *Agrarian Systems and Rural Development*, London, 1979.

Goldsmith, Arthur, 'Popular Participation and Rural Leadership in Saemaul Movement', in Man-Gap Lee (ed.), *Towards A New Community*, 427-58, 1981.

Government of Andhra Pradesh, Census of India, 1971, *Village Survey Monograph—Unagatla*, Hyderabad, 1979.

Government of India, *Pocket Book on Population Statistics*, New Delhi, 1972.

——, *Seventh Five Year Plan* 1985-90 (Vol. I), New Delhi, 1985.

Government of India, *Census of India* 1971-Part-II B (I), New Delhi, 1975 and 1978.

——, *Census of India* 1981-Series I, Paper 3 of 1981 : *Provisional Population Totals-Workers and Non-Workers*, New Delhi, 1983.

——, *Census of India* 1981-Part-III A (I) and (II), New Delhi, 1987.

——, *India 1987 : A Reference Annual*, New Delhi, 1988.

Griffin, Keith, 'Rural Poverty in Asia : Analysis and Policy Alternatives', in Rizwanul Islam (ed.); *Strategies for...*, 29-65, 1985.

Gupta, D.B., *et al., Development Planning and Policy, Essays in Honour of Professor V.K.R.V. Rao*, New Delhi, 1982.

Hahn, Bae-Ho, *Communication Policies in the Republic of Korea*, Paris, 1978.

Halliday, Jan, 'The Economics of North and South Korea' in J. Sullivan, and R. Foss (eds.); *Two Koreas*, 19-55, 1987.

Han, Woo-Keun, *The History of Korea* (two Vols.), Seoul, 1974.

Hanson, A.H., *Planning and the Politicians and Other Essays*, London, 1969.

Hasan, Parvez and D.C. Rao, *Korea, Policy Issues for Long-Term Development*, Baltimore, 1979.

Hayami, Yujiro and Vernon W. Ruttan, *Agricultural Development : An International Perspective*, Baltimore, 1985.

Hazari, R.K., 'Industry in India : A Review of Performance', in Brahmananda and Panchamukhi, (eds.); *The Development Process of the Indian Economy*, 273-98, 1987.

Hein, Strefkerk, 'Too Little to Live on, Too Much to Die on–Employment in Small Scale Industries in Rural South Gujarat', *Economic and Political Weekly*, 16, 659-68, 1981.

Henthorn, William, E., *A History of Korea*, New York, 1971.

Herdt, R.W., 'Mechanization of Rice Production in Developing Asian Countries : Perspective, Evidence and Issues', 'International Rice Research Institute, Manila, 1-13, 1983.

Herring, Ronald, J., 'Managing the Great Transformation : The Truly Backward Class in Development', Working Draft Prepared for the *International Workshop on Rural Transformation in Asia*, New Delhi, 1986.

Heston, A., 'National Income', in Dharmakumar, *The Cambridge Economic...*, 376-462, 1982.

Ho, Samuel, P.S., 'Small Scale Enterprises in Korea and Taiwan', *World Development*, 10, 973-90, 1982.

Hoffman, George, W., 'Rural Transformation in Eastern Europe Since World War II', in Ivan Volgyes *et. al.*, (eds.), *The Process of Rural...*, 21-41, 1980.

Hoselitz, Bert, F., 'Economic Growth and Development : Non-Economic Factors in Economic Development', *The American Economic Review*, 47, 28-41, 1957.

Hou, Chi-ming, *et. al.*, (eds.), *Agricultural Development in Japan, China and Korea*, Taipei, 1982.

Hunter, Guy, *Modernizing Peasant Societies : A Comparative Study of Asia and Africa*, London, 1969.

Indian Institute of Public Opinion (IIPO), *Quarterly Economic Report*, 30, 13, 1986.

International Cultural Foundation (ed.); *Korean Society*, Seoul, 1982.

Islam, Rizwanul (ed.), *Strategies for Alleviating Poverty in Rural Asia*, Bangkok, 1985.

Iyengar, N.S., and P.R. Brahmananda, 'Estimated Distribution Parameters and their Behaviour in India', in P.R. Brahmananda and V.R. Panchamukhi (eds.); *The Development Process of...*, 82-105, 1987.

Jain, L.C., 'Development of Decentralized Industries : A Review and Some Suggestions', *Economic and Political Weekly*, 15, 1747-54, 1980.

——, 'A Heritage to Keep : The Handicrafts Industry, 1955-85', *Economic and Political Weekly*, 21, 873-87, 1986.

Jain, L.C., *et al.*, *Grass Without Roots : Rural Development Under Government Auspices*, New Delhi, 1985.

Jakhade, V.M. and T.R. Sundaram, 'Role of Agriculture in the Indian Economy' in M.L. Dantwala *et al.*, (ed.); *Indian Agricultural Development...*, 16-58, 1986.

Jones, Leroy P., and Il Sakong, *Government, Business and Entrepreneurship in Economic Development : The Korean Case*, Harvard, 1980.

Joshi, P.C., Programme of Studies on the Theme of Comparative Perspectives of Asian Rural Transformation, Note Prepared for the ICSSR under the IDPAD, (Mimeo), New Delhi, 1-4, 1983.

Jun, Jong Sup, 'The Paradoxes of Development : Problems of Korea's Transformation', in Bun Woong Kim *et al.*, (eds.); *Administrative Dynamics and...*, 56-75, 1985.

Jung, Yong-duk, 'Distributive Justice and Redistributive Policy in Korea', *Korean Social Sciences Journal*, 11, 143-62, 1984.

Kado, Ryohei, 'Employment Creation in Rural Areas : The Achievement of Saemaul Undong and Further Development', in Man Gap Lee (ed.); *Towards a New Community...*, 245-72, 1981.

Kahlon, A.S., 'Agricultural Price Policy and Terms of Trade', in Dantwala *et al.*, (ed.), 358-72, 1986.

Kahlon, A.S., and D.S. Tyagi, 'Inter-Sectoral Terms of Trade', *Economic and Political Weekly*, 52, A–173–184, 1980.

Kanwarlal, *Jawaharlal Nehru : Promise and Performance*, Delhi, 1970.

Kapp, William K., *Hindu Culture, Economic Development and Economic Planning : A Collection of Essays*, Bombay, 1963.

Kaul, J.N., 'Development of Indian Higher Education', *Economic and Political Weekly*, 7, 1645-52, 1972.

Kaviraj, Sudipta, 'A Critique of the Passive Revolution', *Economic and Political Weekly*, 23, 2429-44, 1988.

Keon, Michael, *Korean Phoenix : A Nation from the Ashes*, New Delhi, 1978.

Kim, An-Jae, 'Korean Economic Development and External Linkages', *The Journal of East Asian Affairs*, 1, 228-54, 1981.

Kim, Bun Woong, 'A Psychological Approach to Korean Bureaucracy', *Korean Journal of Public Administration*, 14, 266-76, 1976.

Kim, Bun Woong *et al.*, (eds.). *Administrative Dynamics and Development : The Korean Experience*, Seoul, 1985.

Kim, Bun Woong and Wha Joon Rho (eds.); *Korean Public Bureaucracy*, Seoul, 1982.

Kim, Chuk-Kyo (ed.); *Industrial and Social Development Issues*, Seoul, 1977.

Kim, Dong Hi, 'The Farm Mechanization Process in Korea', in Southworth (ed.); *Farm Mechanization...*, 50-60, 1972.

——, '*Small Farm Economy and Integrated Rural Development*', National Agricultural Economics Research Institute (Ministry of Agriculture and Fisheries), Seoul, 1976.

Kim, Jongbin, 'The Korean Economic Growth : 1962-76', *Asian Economies*, June, 47-71, 1980.

Kim, Kwang-Suk and Joon-Kyung Park, *Sources of Economic Growth in Korea* 1963-82, Seoul, 1985.

Kim, Kyong-Dong, 'Social Change and Societal Development in Korea Since 1945 : Modernization with Uneven Development', *Korea and World Affairs* 9, 756-88, 1985.

Kim, Mahn-Kee, 'Administrative Culture of Korea : A Comparison with China and Japan' *Korea Social Science Journal*, 10, 116-33.

Kim, Sung-Ung, 'The Role of Social Values and Competitiveness in Economic Growth : With Special Reference to Korea' in Durganand Sinha and Henry S.R. Kao (eds.); *Social Values and...*, 76-92, 1988.

Kim, Sung-Ho, 'A Socio-Economic Analysis of Farm Mechanization in Asiatic Paddy-Farming Societies with Special Reference to Korean and Japanese Cases', in H. Southworth (ed.); *Farm Mechanization...*, 304-18, 1972.

Kim, Woon-Keun, 'An Economic Analysis of Farm Land Leasing Systems in Korea', *Journal of Rural Development*, 9, 15-49, 1986.

Kim, Young-Chul, 'A Study of Agricultural Cooperative Movement and Factors Affecting Its Progress in Korea', Paper Presented for the Workshop on Case Studies of Cooperative Institutions for Development of the Rural Poor, Bangkok, 1986.

King, Ursula, 'Hinduism', in Peter Bishop and Darton Michael (eds.); *The Encyclopaedia of...*, 186-207, 1987.

Kothari, Rajni, 'Political Economy of Garibi Hatao', *Economic and Political Weekly*, 7, 1541-52, 1972.

Kothari, Rajni (ed.), *State and Nation Building–A Third World Perspective*, Delhi, 1976.

——, 'Integration and Performance : Two Pivots of India's Model of Nation Building', in Rajni Kothari (ed.); *Ibid.*, 193-228, 1976.

——, 'Masses, Classes and the State', *Economic and Political Weekly*, 21, 210-16, 1986.

Kotwal, O.P., *Indian Economy in Soviet Perspective*, New Delhi, 1979.

Krishna, K.L., 'Industrial Growth and Productivity in India', in P.R. Brahmananda and V.R. Panchamukhi (ed); *The Development Process of...*, 348-87, 1987.

Krishnarao, Y.V., 'Growth of Capitalism in Agriculture : A Case Study of Andhra Pradesh', in Y.V. Krishnarao *et al.*, (eds.), *Peasant Farming and...*, 1-61, 1984.

Krishnarao, Y.V., *et. al.*, (eds.), *Peasant Farming and Growth of Capitalism in Indian Agriculture*, Vijayawada, 1984.

Kurien, C.T., 'Small Sector in New Industrial Policy', *Economic and Political Weekly*, 13, 455-61, 1978.

——, 'The Dynamics of Rural Transformation : A Case Study of Tamil Nadu', in D.B. Gupta *et al.*, (eds.); *Development Planning and...*, 57-95, 1982.

Kurien, John, 'Towards Universal Elementary Education : Promise and Performance', *Economic and Political Weekly*, 16, 1608-17, 1981.

Kwan, Tai-Hwan *et al.*, 'Towards a Social Reporting System : A Critical Assessment of Its Current Status', *Bulletin of the Population and Development Studies Centre*, 10, 1-39, 1981.

Lakshminarayana, Unnava, *Malapalli (Telugu)*, Vijayawada, 1958.

Landsberger, Henry, A., 'Continuity and Change in Latin America's Rural Structure', in Ivan Volgyes *et al.*, (eds.); *The Process of Rural...*, 269-88, 1980.

Lee, Eddy, 'Egalitarian Peasant Farming and Rural Development : The Case of South Korea', in Dharam Ghai, *et al.*, (eds.); *Agrarian Systems and..*, 24-71, 1979.

Lee, Ho-Chol, 'Historical Pre-conditions for the Formation of the Korean Agricultural Economy Under Japanese Colonialism' (Master's Thesis Abstract), *Journal of Agricultural Education*, 9, 143-6, 1977.

Lee, Jeong Han, 'Need for Farm Adjustment to a Growing Economy and

Conditions for Farm Mechanization', in H. Southworth (ed.); *Farm Mechanization...*, 191-217, 1972.

Lee, Man-gap (ed.); *Towards a New Community Life,* Seoul, 1981.

——, *Sociology and Social Change in Korea*, Seoul, 1984.

Lee, Woo Jae, 'Report on the Survey of the General Situation of Tenancy', *Korean Agricultural Policy Review*, 2, 61-7, 1974.

Leipziger, Danny and Peter A. Petri, 'Korean Incentive Policies towards Industry and Agriculture', in VIII World Economic Congress of the International Economic Association, Sector Proportions and Economic Development : Country Case Studies, 18-56, 1986.

Lerner, Daniel, *The Passing of Traditional Society : Modernizing the Middle East*, Blenco, 1958.

Lindert, P.H., and J.G. Williamsen, 'Essays in Exploration, Growth, Equality and History', *Explorations in Economic History*, 22, 341-77, 1985.

Lonsdale, Richard, E. and William P. Avery, 'Patterns in Rural Transformation : A Concluding Review', in Ivan Volgyes *et al.*, (ed.); *The Process of Rural...*, 325-38, 1980.

Mac Iver, R.M. and Charles, H. Page., *Society : An Introductory Analysis*, London, 1965.

MAF, Government of Korea, *Year Book of Agriculture and Forestry Statistics*, Seoul, 1963, 1966, 1971, 1972, 1976, 1977, 1981, 1985, and 1986.

——, *Statistical Year Book of Agriculture, Forestry and Fisheries*, Seoul, 1986.

——, *Report on the Results of Farm Household Economic Survey*, Seoul, 1986.

Mahajan, O.P., 'Indian Economic Planning in Retrospect and Prospect', in P.R. Brahmananda and V.R. Panchamukhi (eds.); *The Development Process of...*, 734-51, 1987.

Mason, Edward, S., *et al.*, *The Economic and Social Modernization of the Republic of Korea*, Cambridge (U.S.A.), 1980.

Meier, Gerald, M., *Leading Issues in Economic Development*, New York, 1984.

Minhas, B.S., 'Objectives and Policy Frame of the Fourth Indian Plan', in Faber, Mike and Dudley Seers (eds.); *The Crisis in Planning :...*, 21-54, 1972.

Mitra, Ashok, *Terms of Trade and Class Relations*, London, 1977.

Mohan Rao, R.M., *The Problems of Administrative Coordination in a Panchayat Samithi in Guntur District in Andhra Pradesh (Mimeo)*,

Department of Rural Studies and Cooperation, Andhra University, Waltair, 1963.

——, Commercialization and Agricultural Growth in Asia : A Comparative Study of South Korea and Coastal Andhra', Paper presented at the *International Workshop on Rural Transfor-mation in Asia*, New Delhi, 1986.

——, 'Making Cooperatives Economically Viable–The Indian Scenario and Lessons from East Asian Experience', *Sahakarita Samsodhana*, 3, 1-12, 1988.

Mohan Rao, R.M. and D.S. Prasad, *Transformation of Primary Agricultural Credit Societies into Multipurpose Cooperatives (Mimeo)*, Department of Cooperation and Applied Economics, Andhra University, Waltair, 1985.

Mohanty, Manoranjan, 'Can We Attempt a Conceptual Breakthrough?' *Note on the Studies on Comparative Rural Transformation (Mimeo)*, Prepared for ICSSR under IDPAD, 1-2, 1983.

Moon, Pal Yong, 'The Evolution of Rice Policy in Korea' in Kim, Chuk Kyo (ed.); *Industrial and Social*........... 3-36, 1977.

——, 'Selected Issues in the Impact of Industrialization on Agriculture in Korea', *Journal of Rural Development*, 2, 159-70, 1979.

Moon, Seung Gyu *et al.*, 'Local Participation in Rural Development Planning in Korea–Its Functions and Dysfunctions' *The Korean Journal of Sociology*, 4, 105-19, 1968.

Morris, Morris D. and Henry, R. Luce, 'The Growth of Large Scale Industry to 1947', in Dharma Kumar (ed.); *The Cambridge Economic...*, 553-676, 1982.

Mosher, Arthur, T., *Thinking About Rural Development*, New York, 1976.

Moskowitz, Karl, 'Korean Development and Korean Studies–A Review Article', *Journal of Asian Studies*, 13, 63-90, 1982.

Murthy, K.S., *The Indian Spirit*, Waltair, 1965.

Myrdal, Gunnar, *Asian Drama : An Inquiry into the Poverty of Nations* (3 Vols.) New Delhi, 1982.

NACF, *Agricultural Year Book* 1968, Seoul, 1968.

——, *Agricultural Cooperatives in Korea*, Seoul, 1978 and 1989.

——, *Agricultural Cooperative Year Book* 1984, Seoul, 1984.

Nair, Kusum, *Blossoms in the Dust*, New York, 1962.

Nasir, Tyabji, 'Capitalism in India and the Small Industries Policy', *Economic and Political Weekly*, 15, 1721-32, 1980.

National Sample Survey (NSS) Government of India, *Report on Land Holdings (Some Aspects of Ownership Holdings), Eighth Round*, No. 36, July 1954–April 1955, Delhi, 1961.

——, *Some Aspects of Operational Holdings, (State and All India Estimates Based on Major Crop Season of the Agricultural Year) 1981-1982, 37th Round, No. 331,* New Delhi, 1986.

——, 'A Note on Some Aspects of Ownership Holdings : NSS, 36th Round', *Sarvekshana*, 11, 1987.

——, 'A Note on Some Aspects of Operational Holding : NSS, 37th Round', *Sarvekshana*, 12, 24-52, 1988.

Naya, Seiji, 'Asian and Pacific Developing Countries : Performance and Issues', *Asian Development Review*, 1, 1-40, 1983.

Nayyar, Deepak, 'Industrial Development in India : Some Reflections on Growth and Stagnation', *Economic and Political Weekly,* 13, 1265-78, 1978.

Nijhawan, Inder P., 'Socio-Political Institutions, Cultural Values and Attitudes : Their Impact on Indian Economic Development', in Uppal, J.S., (ed.); *India's Economic Problem...*, 23-42, 1975.

Paik, Wan Ki, 'Psychocultural Approach to the Study of Korean Bureaucracy', in Bun Woong Kim and Wha Joon Rho (eds.); *Korean Public Bureaucracy*, 64-89, 1982.

Pak, Ki-Hyuk, 'Farmland Tenure in the Republic of Korea', *Extension Bulletin of Food and Fertilizer Technology Centre*, (No. 183), Taipei City, 1983.

Papola, T.S., and V.N. Misra, 'Some Aspects of Rural Industrialization', *Economic and Political Weekly*, 15, 1733-46, 1980.

Paranjape, H.K., 'Political and Administrative Problems of Implementing the Indian Plan', in Kamta Prasad (ed.); *Planning and Its...*, 106-44, 1984.

——, 'Indian Liberalisation : Perestroika or Salaami Tactics?' *Economic and Political Weekly*, 23, 2343-58, 1988.

Park, Chong Kee (ed.), *Macro Economic and Industrial Development in Korea,* Seoul, 1980.

Park, Jin Hwan, 'Facts and Problems of Farm Mechanization : The Case of Korea', in H. Southworth (ed.); *Farm Mechanization...*, 1-26, 1972.

——, *Development of Primary Agricultural Cooperatives in Korea (Mimeo)*, Agricultural Cooperative Junior College, Seoul, 1981.

——, 'Role of Agricultural Cooperatives in Integrated Development', Paper presented at the International Forum on *Industrialization and Urban-Rural Linkages*, (October 16-25), Seoul, 1984.

Park, Tai Sik and Ki Yong Hong, 'A Historical Review on Agricultural Extension Work with Emphasis on Japanese Regime in Korea' (Summary), *Journal of Korean Agricultural Education*, 4, 39-41, 1972.

Parthasarathy, G., *Changes in Rice Farming and Their Social and Economic Impact (Mimeo)*, Andhra University, Waltair, 1973.

——, *Green Revolution and the Weaker Section,* Bombay, 1976.

——, 'Integrated Rural Development Concepts, Theoretical Base and Contradiction', in D.B. Gupta *et. al.*, (eds.); *Development Planning and...*, 96-108, 1982.

——, 'Agrarian Class Formation : A Study of Andhra Pradesh', Paper Presented at the *International Workshop on Rural Transformation in Asia*, New Delhi, 1986.

——, 'Poverty Allevation Programmes : Lessons of the Past and Issues for the Future', in Department of Rural Development, Government of India, *National Seminar on...*, 84-90, 1988.

——, *Agricultural Growth, Rural Development and Poverty*, Calcutta, 1989.

Parthasarathy, G. and B. Prasada Rao, *Implementation of Land Reforms in Andhra Pradesh*, Calcutta, 1969.

Pavaskar, Madhoo, 'Public Intervention in Agricultural Marketing', in Dantwala *et al.*, (eds.); *Indian Agricultural...*, 329-57, 1986.

Perlin, Frank, 'Comparative History or Gropping Around on all Fours', Paper presented at *International Workshop on Rural Transformation in Asia* (October 2-4), New Delhi, 1986.

Petrov, Victor, *India : Spotlight on Population*, Moscow, 1985.

Planning and Cooperation Department, Government of Andhra Pradesh, *Perspective Plan for Coastal Andhra : Resource Inventory* (Vol. 1), Hyderabad, 1974.

Planning Commision, Government of India, *Fourth Five Year Plan 1969-74*, New Delhi, 1969.

——, *Seventh Five Year Plan* 1985-90, New Delhi, 1985.

Prasad, Kamta (ed.), *Planning and Its Implementation*, New Delhi, 1984.

Prasada Rao, B. and L.K. Mohan Rao, *Studies in the Economics of Farm Management in the Command Area of Nagarjuna Sagar Project, Andhra Pradesh*, New Delhi, 1988.

Progress Publishers, *Marx Engels–Selected Works,* Moscow, 1986.

Rice, Jeffrey, 'The Institutional Constraints on Technology Transfer to Small Farmers', *Economic Bulletin for Asia and Pacific*, 41-61, 1976.

Rajkrishna, 'Small Farmer Development', *Economic and Political Weekly*, 14, 913-18, 1979.

Ram Gopal, *India under Indira*, New Delhi, 1986.

Ramakrishna, V., *Social Reform in Andhra* (1848-1919), New Delhi, 1983.

Raman, K.V., *et al.*, (eds.); *Agricultural Research Systems and Management in the 21st Century*, Hyderabad, 1988.

Ramana, K.V., and P.V. Sarma, *Socio-Economic and Agro-Economic Survey of Godavari Delta Region*, Andhra University, Visakhapatnam, 1984.

Ramana Rao, A.V., *Economic Development of Andhra Pradesh (1766-1957)*, Bombay, 1958.

Ramaswamy, A.S., 'Rural Industrialization : A Theoretical and Prospective Approach', in Society of Social Economists (ed.); *Readings in Integrated...*, 387-99, 1987.

Rami Reddy, S., and C.S. Murthy, *Savings and Investment Behaviour of Rural Households (A Study of Coastal Districts of Andhra Pradesh—Mimeo)*, Centre for Development and Planning Studies, Andhra University, Vishakhapatnam, 1987.

Randhava, M.S., *A History of the Indian Council of Agricultural Research*, New Delhi, 1979.

Randhawa, N.S, *Growth, Equity and Poverty in Far East–Performance of Countries (Draft)*, FAO, Rome, 1-31, 1986.

Rao, G.N., 'Canal Irrigation and Agrarian Change in Colonial Andhra : A Study of Godavari District 1850-90', *The Indian Economic and Social History Review*, 25, 25-60, 1988.

Rao, V.K.R.V., 'Savings, Capital Formation and National Income', *Economic and Political Weekly*, 15, 965-77, 1980.

——, *India's National Income, 1950-80 : An Analysis of Economic Growth and Change*, New Delhi, 1983.

Rao, V.M., 'Barriers in Rural Development', *Economic and Political Weekly*, 18, 117-90, 1983.

Rao, V.M., and S. Erappa, 'IRDP and Rural Diversification : A Study of Karnataka', *Economic and Political Weekly*, 21, 151-60, 1986.

Rath, N., 'Prices, Costs of Production and Terms of Trade in Indian Agriculture', *Indian Journal of Agricultural Economics*, 4, 451-81, 1985.

Reddy, M.P.R., *Peasant and State in Modern Andhra History*, Kavali, 1986.

Reddy, V.M. and P. Raghunatha Rao, *Andhra Under British Rule*, Hyderabad, 1975.

Reserve Bank of India (RBI), *Report of the Committee to Review Arrangements for Institutional Credit for Agriculture and Rural Development (CRAFICARD)*, Bombay, 1981.

——, 'All India Debt and Investment Survey 1981-82 : Assets and Liabilities of Households as on 30th June 1981; Salient Aspects', *Reserve Bank of India Bulletin*, 40, 437-53, 1986.

Rudra, Ashok, 'Class Relations in Indian Agriculture', *Economic and Political Weekly*, 13, 998-1004, 1978.

Rostow, W.W., *Stages of Economic Growth*, Cambridge, 1960.

Rural Development Administration (RDA), Republic of Korea, *Agricultural Extension Services in Korea*, Seoul, 1986.

Sakong, Il, 'Macro Economic Aspects of the Public Enterprise Sector, in Chong Kee Park (ed.); *Macro Economic and...*, 99-128, 1980.

Sanyal, S.K., 'A Review of the Conceptual Framework of Land Holding Surveys', *Indian Journal of Agricultural Economics*, 31:3, 1-10, 1976.

Sarma, P.V., *Demand for Fertilizers in Andhra Pradesh*, Andhra University, Waltair, 1983.

Sarveswara Rao, B., *Studies in the Economics of Farm Management in West Godavari District*, Delhi, 1960.

——, *The Economic and Social Effects of Zamindari Abolition in Andhra*, Delhi, 1963.

Schotter, Andrew, *The Economic Theory of Social Institutions*, Cambridge, 1981.

Shetty, S.L.,'Structural Retrogression in the Indian Economy Since the Mid-Sixties', *Economic and Political Weekly*, 13, 185-244, 1978.

Shetty, S.L., and K.A. Menon, 'Saving and Investment Without Growth, *Economic and Political Weekly*, 15, 927-36, 1980.

Shin, Yong-Ha, 'Kwajon Land Reform and the Establishment of Private Landlordism in the Early Yi Dynasty of Korea 1391-1470', *The Seoul National University Economic Review*, 4, 1-55, 1970.

——, 'Land Tenure System in Korea 1910-45', *The Seoul National University Economic Review*, 5, 1-28, 1971.

Shivamaggi, H.B., 'Credit for Agriculture and Rural Development', in Dantwala *et al.*, (eds.); *Indian Agricultural...*, 270-307, 1986.

Snong, Soong N., 'South Korean Model for Industrialization : Theory and Reality', *Asian Profile*, 17, 513-22, 1989.

Sidhu, D.S. and A.J. Singh, 'Domestic Terms of Trade and Economic Development in India', *Indian Journal of Agricultural Economics*, 34(4) 104-13, 1979.

Sidhu, D.S. and A.J. Singh, 'Technological Change in Indian Agriculture', in M.L. Dantwala *et. al.*, (eds.), *Indian Agricultural...*, 140-61, 1986.

Sigurdson, Jan and Young Chul Kim, 'Relationship Between Farm Mechanization, Rural Industrialization and Saemaul Movement in Korea', in Man Gap-Lee (ed.), *Towards a New Community*, 203-44, 1981.

Singer, Milton, *When A Great Tradition Modernizes*, New York, 1972.

Singh, Randhir, 'Vision for the Future, One View', *Economic and Political Weekly*, 24, 723-5, 1989.

Sinha, Durganand, 'Basic Indian Values and Behaviour Dispositions in the context of National Development : An Appraisal', in Durganand Sinha and Henry S.R. Kao, (eds.); *Social Values and...*, 31-55, 1988.

Sinha, Durganand and Henry S.R. Kao, (eds.), *Social Values and Development : Asian Perspectives*, New Delhi, 1988.

Slater, Gilbert (ed.), *Some South Indian Villages* (Vol. I), Madras, 1918.

Smith, Harold E., 'Toward A Clarification of the Concept of Social Institution', *Sociology and Social Research*, 48, 197-206, 1964.

Smith, Havard, 'Confucianism', in Peter Bishop and Michael Darton, (eds.); *The Encyclopaedia of...*, 273-8, 1987.

Society of Social Economists, Tamil Nadu (ed.), Readings in Integrated Rural Development, New Delhi, 1987.

Song, Byung-Nak, 'Economic Development and Rural-Urban Transformation', in Chong Kee Park (ed.); *Macro Economic and...*, 339-402, 1980.

Song, Hae Kyun, 'Impact and Development of Agricultural Education', *Journal of Korean Agricultural Education*, 11, 10-17, 1979.

Southworth, H., *Farm Mechanization in East Asia,* Singapore, 1972.

Srinivas, M.N., *Social Change in Modern India*, New Delhi, 1972.

Srinivasan, T.N., and Pranab Bardhan (eds.), *Rural Poverty in Asia*, Delhi, 1988.

Steinberg, David I., 'Socio-Political Factors and Korea's Future Economic Policies', *World Development*, 16, 19-34, 1988.

Subba Rao, K., 'Farm Prices : A Survey of Debate', in Dantwala *et al.*, (ed.), 373-84, 1986.

Sullivan, J. and R. Foss, (eds.), *Two Koreas—One Future*? Madisan, 1987.

Taylor, Donald, C., 'Farm Management : Its Role in Alleviating Institutional Constraints Facing Asian Small Farms', *ADC Teaching and Research Forum's Reprint*, New York, 1980.

Tendulkar, S.D., 'Economic Inequalities and Poverty in India : An Interpretative Overview', in P.R. Brahmananda and V.R. Panchamukhi (eds.); *The Development Process of...*, 106-43, 1987.

Thamarajakshi, 'Inter-Sectoral Terms of Trade and the Marketed Surplus of Agricultural Produce : 1951-52 to 1965-66', *Economic and Political Weekly* 4, 1969.

Thiesenhusen, William, C., 'Current Development Patterns and Agrarian Policy in Latin America', in Ivan Volgyes *et. al.*, (eds.); *The Process of Rural...*, 128-39, 1980.

Todaro, Michael, P., *Economic Development in Third World*, New York, 1981.

Tripathi, R.C., 'Aligning Development to Values in India', in Durganand Sinha and Henry S.R. Kao, (eds.), *Social Values and...*, 315-33, 1988.

United Nations, Department of Economic Affairs, *Land Reform : Defects in Agrarian Structure as Obstacles to Economic Development*, New York, 1951.

Uppal, J.S., (ed.); *India's Economic Problems—An Analytical Approach*, New Delhi, 1975.

Vaidyanathan, A., 'Constraints on Growth and Policy Options', *Economic and Political Weekly*, 12, 1643-50, 1977.

——, 'Labour Use in Rural India : A Study of Spatial and Temporal Variations', *Economic and Political Weekly*, 21, A130-46, 1986.

Veit, Lawrence A., *India's Second Revolution : The Dimensions of Development*, New York, 1976.

Vepa, Ram K., 'Small Industry Development Restructuring Institutional Finance', *Economic and Political Weekly*, 22, 78-82, 1987.

Volgyes, Ivan, 'Rural Transformation : A Field for Comparative Study', in Ivan Volgyes, *et al.*, (eds.); *The Process of Rural...*, 3-18, 1980.

——, 'Economic Aspects of Rural Transformation in Europe', in Ivan Volgyes, *et al.*, (eds.), *Ibid.*, 89-127, 1980.

Volgyes, Ivan *et. al.*, (eds.), *The Process of Rural Transformation : Eastern Europe, Latin America and Australia*, New York, 1980.

Vyas, V.S., 'Structural Change in Agriculture and the Small Farm Sector', *Economic and Political Weekly*, 11, 24-32, 1978.

——, 'Asian Agriculture : Achievements and Challenges', *Asian Development Review*, 1, 27-44, 1983.

Vyas, V.S., and George Mathai, 'Farm and Non-Farm Employment in Rural Areas', *Economic and Political Weekly*, 13, 333-48, 1978.

Wade, Robert, 'The Market for Public Office : Why the Indian State is not Better at Development?, *World Development*, 13, 467-97, 1985.

Whang, In-joung, 'Government Commitment to Rural Development', *Journal of Rural Development*, 3, 173-92, 1980.

Wolf, Jr. Charles, 'Institutions and Economic Development', *American Economic Review*, 45, 867-83, 1955.

Woo, Ki-Do, 'Labour Force, Wage Level and Economic Growth in Korea', *Asian Economies*, 2, 12-51, 1972.

World Bank, *Rural Non-Farm Enterprises*, Washington D.C., 1978.

——, *World Development Report*, Washington D.C. 1978, 1981, 1987, 1988 and 1989.

——, *Thailand : Rural Growth and Employment*, Washington D.C. 1983.

Woronoff, Jan., *Korea's Economy : Man-Made Miracle*, Seoul, 1983.

Yang, Duck Jung and Dilbert Siegel, 'Testing Perceptions of Distributive Justice in Korea', in Bun Woong Kim, *et. al.*, (eds.), *Administrative Dynamics and...*, 380-404, 1985.

Yi, Hae Yong and Woo-Keun Han, 'Discussion : Korean Society', in International Cultural Foundation (ed.), *Korean Society...*, 163-78, 1982.

Yong, Key, P. and Gregory Henderson, 'An Outline of the Korean Confucianism', *Journal of Asian Studies*, 18, 81-101, 1959.

——, *Ibid.*, 18, 259-76, 1959.

Yoo, Jong-Hae and Larry L. Wade, 'A Study on Current Korean Political Culture : An Interpretative Perspective', *The Journal of East Asian Affairs*, 1, 118-77, 1981.

INDEX